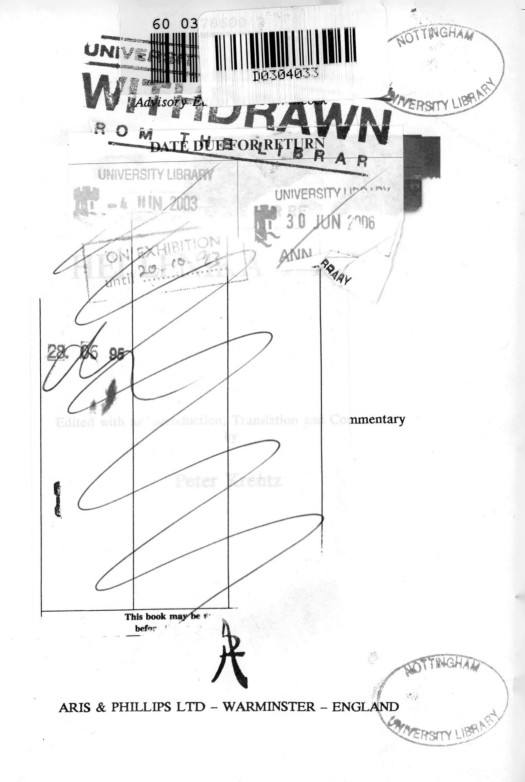

Advisory E...

Edited with an Introduction, Translation and Commentary
by
Peter Krentz

ARIS & PHILLIPS LTD – WARMINSTER – ENGLAND

ISSN Classical Texts 0953–7961
ISBNS   cloth   0 85668 463 5
              limp   0 85668 464 3

Printed and published in England by Aris & Phillips Ltd, Teddington House, Warminster, Wiltshire BA12 8PQ

CONTENTS

PREFACE

Xenophon's *Hellenika* I-II.3.10 is the only fully extant narrative of the end of the Peloponnesian War written by a contemporary. Its reputation has suffered by comparison with Thucydides, whose unfinished work covers the earlier years of the war. Yet in antiquity Xenophon was held in high regard: The literary critic Dionysios of Halikarnassos, for example, ranked him with Herodotos, Thucydides, Philistos and Theopompos as the historians worth imitating (*Letter to Pompey* 3). In part divergent assessments of Xenophon stem from the application of different standards. Scholars in the past generation (notably Breitenbach, Henry and now Gray) have stressed that Xenophon's *Hellenika* must be understood as a literary work on its own terms before modern historians can assess its quality.

Since the publication of Underhill's commentary in 1906 one other development has made his work outdated. The publication and study of the papyrus fragments known as the *Hellenika Oxyrhynchia* have given us parts of an alternative narrative written in the fourth century, and have made it respectable to take the later history of Diodoros seriously, since Diodoros' ultimate source appears to be this anonymous author (probably either Kratippos or Theopompos).

A fellowship from the National Endowment for the Humanities enabled me to begin this project during a year at the American School of Classical Studies at Athens, and summer travel grants from Davidson College have helped me since my return. I thank M. M. Willcock, Barry Strauss, Glenn Bugh and Jeri Fischer for commenting on an earlier draft; Lee Norris for helping me prepare the maps; M. M. Willcock and Michael Toumazou for proofreading the Greek text.

I dedicate this book to Tyler, whose arrival made the final revisions a challenging task for his happy but distracted father, and to Jeri, who has given me Tyler and much more.

All three-figure dates are BC.

iv

INTRODUCTION

1. Xenophon's Life and Works

"Xenophon was the son of Gryllos, an Athenian, from Erchia. He was modest and very handsome." With these words Diogenes Laertios, writing in the third century after Christ, began the sketch (2.48-59) that is our most important source for Xenophon's life apart from Xenophon's own writings. It leaves many questions unresolved, including the dates of Xenophon's birth and exile. Diogenes says Xenophon flourished in the fourth year of the ninety-fourth Olympiad, or 401/0, implying a birthdate of 441/0 (2.55; compare *FGrHist* 244 F 343). Some scholars take this tradition seriously (M. Falappone, "Note di biografia senofontea," *Quaderni di storia antiqua* 5 [1979] 283-91), noting that it fits Xenophon's presence at *Symp.* 1.1 (dramatic date 422) and the story that Sokrates saved his life at the battle of Delion in 424 (Str. IX.2.7; Diog. Laert. 2.22). But at *Anab.* III.1.25 Xenophon represents himself arguing in 401 that he is not too young to replace Proxenos as general, which ought to make him younger than Proxenos, who was "about thirty" years old when he died (*Anab.* II.6.20; on Xenophon's comparative youth see also III.1.14). Therefore Xenophon was probably born between 430 and 425.

About Xenophon's youth we can say that his family was wealthy, for he took his own horses with him to Asia Minor in 401 (*Anab.* III.3.19), and that he studied with Sokrates. More doubtful are the late stories that he also learned from Isokrates (Phot. *Bibl.* 486 b 36) and, while a prisoner at Thebes, from Prodikos (Philostr. *Vit. Soph.* 1.12). Some scholars have asserted that the details in the *Hellenika* show that Xenophon witnessed Thrasyllos' Ionian campaign in 410, the battle of Arginousai in 406, and the arrival of the news from Aigospotamoi in 405. But such arguments are inconclusive, and we cannot even be certain that Xenophon served in the cavalry under the oligarchy of the Thirty in 404/3, though it seems likely.

In his *Anabasis* Xenophon tells how he became one of Kyros' "Ten Thousand" Greek mercenaries in 401, when Kyros revolted against his older brother, the Persian king; how, after Kyros' death, he became a general, replacing his friend Proxenos; how he helped lead the Greeks on their long march to the Black Sea; how he became their sole commander for a campaign with Seuthes in Thrace; and how he eventually brought the remnants of the mercenary force to the Spartan commander Thibron in 399.

He probably remained in Asia Minor, campaigning under Thibron and Derkylidas. The "leader of the Kyreians" in *Hell*. III.2.7, who blames Thibron for the mercenaries' misbehavior, is probably Xenophon himself. He also probably married his wife, Philesia, during this period. Philesia gave birth to two sons, perhaps twins, Gryllos and Diodoros (Diog. Laert. 2.52).

Xenophon joined Agesilaos in Asia Minor and returned to Greece with the Spartan king in 394 (*Anab*. V.3.6). He must therefore have been present at the battle of Koroneia, but it is uncertain whether he fought against Athens, as Plut. *Ages*. 18.2 says, for this is only Plutarch's interpretation of *Anab*. V.3.6. Xenophon implies that he was present out of friendship for Agesilaos rather than hostility for Athens, and twice states that Herippidas (not he himself) commanded the Kyreian unit (*Hell*. IV.2.4, 3.15-18; *Ages*. 2.10-11). Still, Plutarch need not be wrong.

After the battle Xenophon accompanied Agesilaos to Sparta (Diog. Laert. 2.51-52; Plut. *Ages*. 20). The Athenians had exiled Xenophon between 399 and 394, most likely after the outbreak of the Korinthian War in 395 made Xenophon's pro-Spartan and anti-Persian activities contrary to current Athenian interests (C. J. Tuplin, "Xenophon's Exile Again," *Homo Viator* [Bristol 1987] 59-68). The Lakedaimonians rewarded him with an estate at Skillous, part of the territory Sparta had recently taken from Elis (*Hell*. III.2.21-31). Agesilaos also arranged for Xenophon's sons to be educated at Sparta (Plut. *Ages*. 20.2, *Mor*. 212B; Diog. Laert. 2.54 on the authority of Diokles), an honor that also provided the Lakedaimonians with hostages to guarantee Xenophon's loyalty.

At *Anab*. V.3.7-13, Xenophon describes with evident fondness a portion of his Skillous estate that he purchased with money promised to Artemis of Ephesos (V.3.4):

> Xenophon purchased a site for Artemis where the god [Apollo] had instructed. A river Selinous happened to run through the land; in Ephesos a river Selinous also runs past the temple of Artemis. Both rivers contain fish and shellfish. The land at Skillous also has hunting for all kinds of game. Xenophon built an altar and a temple from the sacred money and thereafter he used the tenth part of the land's produce for a sacrifice to Artemis. All the citizens and neighboring men and women participated in the festival. Artemis supplied those who stayed in tents with barley, bread, wine and desserts as well as a share of the animals sacrificed from the sacred herd and the animals killed in hunting. For Xenophon's and other citizens' sons,

and any men who wished, went hunting for the festival. They caught boars, roes and stags both on the sacred ground and on Mount Pholoe. As one proceeds along the road from Sparta to Olympia the site is about twenty *stadia* [3.6 km.] from the temple of Zeus at Olympia. The sacred ground contains a meadow and wooded mountains, adequate for pigs and goats and oxen and horses, so that the animals of those who came to the festival had plenty to eat. Around the temple itself a grove of fruit trees was planted to produce whatever fruit was in season. The temple is a smaller version of the great temple in Ephesos, and the image resembles the one in Ephesos as much as a cypress statue can resemble one of gold. Next to the temple stands a pillar inscribed as follows:

> THIS LAND IS SACRED TO ARTEMIS. WHOEVER OWNS IT AND HARVESTS ITS PRODUCE IS TO SACRIFICE THE TENTH PART EVERY YEAR AND TO CARE FOR THE TEMPLE FROM THE REMAINDER. IF SOMEONE DOES NOT FULFILL THESE OBLIGATIONS ARTEMIS WILL TAKE NOTICE.

In this idyllic setting Xenophon began a productive literary career that continued until the 350s. Besides the *Hellenika*, he wrote:

- *Anabasis*, a third-person account of the Ten Thousand in which Xenophon himself figures prominently;
- *Kyroupaideia*, a historical novel that explores leadership by telling of the Persian king Kyros the Great;
- *Agesilaos*, an encomium in honor of the Spartan king who befriended Xenophon;
- *Lakedaimonion Politeia*, on the institutions that made Sparta great;
- *Poroi*, a discussion of how Athens could improve its financial situation;
- several technical treatises (*Hipparchikos*, or *The Cavalry Commander*; *Peri Hippikes*, or *On Horsemanship*; and *Kynegetikos*, or *On Hunting*);
- a number of Sokratic works. *Apologia* and *Memorabilia* defend Sokrates' conduct at his trial and his way of life. In *Oikonomikos* Sokrates and Ischomachos discuss household management, with parallels to city government. The *Symposion* begins with the claim that good men's less serious moments are worth recording, and the dinner party provides occasions for Sokrates to comment on such varied topics as gender, dancing as exercise

and drinking. The *Hieron*, a dialogue between Hieron the tyrant of Syracuse and Simonides the wise poet on the subject of a tyrant's happiness, also counts as a Sokratic writing, though Sokrates does not appear.

Ancient critics saw Xenophon as a philosopher who also wrote history (Diog. Laert. 2.48). His philosophical interests, ethical rather than metaphysical or epistemological, are most obvious in his Sokratic works. But they resonate throughout all his writings, even those that seem most technical. One example: *Kynegetikos* is a primer on how to hunt, including such details as the number of threads to use for various nets and forty-seven appropriate names for hunting dogs. Yet it begins with a list of famous heroes who learned hunting from Cheiron, and ends with a discussion of the virtues to be gained from hunting. First among these benefits is physical conditioning, but Xenophon also claims that hunters are hard workers, pious, good to their parents and friends and useful to the whole city. He says that he wishes the treatise to *be* rather than to *seem* useful, so that it will stand unrefuted for all time (13.7). Readers can see a similar goal behind his other writings. Though Xenophon tried different literary forms, all of his works are in some measure didactic.

The Spartan defeat at Leuktra in 371 meant Xenophon had to leave Skillous (Diog. Laert. 2.53). Though the Athenians rescinded his exile (Diog. Laert. 2.59 = Istros, *FGrHist* 334 F 32), there is no evidence that he returned to Athens, and Diogenes says that he settled at Korinth (2.53). He did, however, send his sons to join the Athenian cavalry. Gryllos died fighting at Mantineia in 362 (Diog. Laert. 2.54 = Ephoros, *FGrHist* 70 F 85; Paus. VIII.11.6; at *Hell.* VII.5.17 Xenophon says that "good men died," without naming his son). Countless encomiums written in Gryllos' honor, "in part to please his father" (Diog. Laert. 2.55 = Aristotle F 68 Rose), as well as Gryllos' presence on a painting of the battle in the Stoa Poikile (Paus. I.3.4), attest the rehabilitation of Xenophon's reputation at Athens.

Xenophon himself died sometime after 355, the last datable reference in his works (*Poroi* 5.9), either at Korinth (Diog. Laert. 2.56, citing Demetrios Magnes and giving the erroneous date 360/59 on the authority of Stesikleides of Athens) or at Skillous (Paus.V.6.6, on the dubious authority of Eleians who claimed that their ancestors had pardoned Xenophon and allowed him to keep his estate, on which they were able to point out Xenophon's tomb).

The discovery in 1940 of a portrait identified as "Xenophon" by an inscription has enabled the identification of a number of other portraits, all copied from a bronze original dated 335-30 (E. Minakaran-Hiesgen, "Untersuchungen zu den Porträts des Xenophon und des Isokrates," *Jahrbuch des Deutschen Archäologischen Instituts* 85 [1970] 112-41).

2. *Hellenika* I-II.3.10

The *Hellenika* spans almost half a century, from autumn 411 to summer 362. Xenophon wrote the latest datable passage (VI.4.37) during Tisiphonos' rule in Thessaly, which began in 358 or 357 (Diod. XV.61, XVI.14.1) and ended in 353 (Diod. XVI.35). When did Xenophon compose other parts? "Analysts" have identified two or three or four or five distinct sections, composed in chronological order or not (Henry reviews these efforts caustically). Insofar as a consensus emerged, it was that Xenophon wrote the "continuation" (I-II.3.10, the section that completes Thucydides' history of the Peloponnesian War) significantly earlier than the rest of the *Hellenika*. This first section makes some attempt to follow Thucydides' chronological system of war-years divided into summers and winters; it contains no references to sacrifices before battles, unlike the later books; it lists figures (especially numbers of ships and days) more frequently and more precisely than the later books do; and it has a distinctive vocabulary, especially in the use of particles (M. MacLaren, "On the Composition of Xenophon's *Hellenica*," *American Journal of Philology* 55 [1934] 121-39, 249-62).

In some respects, however, the contrast has been exaggerated (see Dover's lucid discussion in *HCT* 5.442-43). Indications of time are irregular in the continuation (Xenophon misses the beginning of one spring and mentions the beginning of winter only twice) and, though less common, do appear in the remainder of the *Hellenika* (see I.1.37 n.). Similarly the continuation contains some approximate figures and the rest some precise ones. Moreover we must compare comparable items: The ship numbers in the continuation ought to be compared with ship numbers (or lack thereof) in passages narrating events at sea, not with the rounded troop figures and estimated distances that are the majority of figures after II.3.10. The description of naval operations in V.1.1-28, for example, contains nine specific figures.

Nevertheless the "unitarians" who believe Xenophon wrote the *Hellenika* as a continuous whole in his old age (notably H. Baden, "Untersuchungen zur Einheit der *Hellenika* Xenophons" [diss. Hamburg 1966], and Gray) have not invalidated the statistical evidence about Xenophon's vocabulary. Xenophon drafted the continuation some time before the rest. But this conclusion has limits. We do not know whether Xenophon wrote the first draft before he left Athens in 401, during his years in exile at Skillous in the 380s and 370s (as seems most probable to me) or after he moved to Korinth in the 360s. Nor do we know how much he revised the continuation when he finished the book later.

Xenophon's sources--about which he says nothing--hold mysteries as well. Henry (54-88) and Dover (*HCT* 5.437-44) ought to have squelched the surprisingly tenacious theory that Xenophon used Thucydides' notes. The foundations of this theory, Diog. Laert. 2.57 ("and it is said that although he was in a position to claim as his own the books of Thucydides, since no one knew oι them, he made them famous of his own accord") and the mediaeval manuscripts titled "the missing portions (*paraleipomena*) of Thucydides," cannot bear its weight.

Most likely Xenophon relied exclusively on his eyes and ears. The single reference in the *Hellenika* to "all the historians" (*syngrapheis*, VII.2.1) does not show that he used other writers as sources. Breitenbach (1674-80) argues that the details in I-II.3.10 show that Xenophon used an Athenian literary source or sources, but every good storyteller knows the value of details, and Xenophon could have heard many of them without going to a written source. For instance, he knew the Theban Koiratadas (*Anab.* VII.1.33-41), who might have described Athens' recapture of Byzantion and his own escape (I.3.14-22). He might have learned about the battles of Arginousai and Aigospotamoi from the Megarian Hermon, Kallikratidas' pilot at the former (I.6.32) and Lysandros'·at the latter (Demos. 23.212; Paus. X.9.7), particularly if Hermon was the anonymous Megarian cited at *Oik.* 4.20 as the source for a story told by Lysandros. We can never be certain, of course, about any source's identity, and reasonable persons can disagree even about a passage's viewpoint: While most scholars believe Xenophon relied on a Spartan for his account of the battle of Notion, Breitenbach credits it to an Athenian ("Die Seeschlacht bei Notion (407/06)," *Historia* 20 [1971] 168-71). Multiple sources are also possible, and Xenophon surely heard a great deal, in one way or another, before he put pen to papyrus.

Nor can we know--though again we can speculate--what Xenophon witnessed himself. An exception is the battle of Koroneia (IV.3.15-20), at which Xenophon was certainly present. He was equally certainly absent from the battle of the Nemea River (IV.2.16-23)--but could a reader unaware of Xenophon's biography tell the difference? Such is the difficulty of identifying events which Xenophon saw himself. Another example: It has been suggested that Xenophon was present when the news about the disaster at Leuktra arrived at Sparta during the *gymnopaidiai* festival (VI.4.16; Cawkwell 13). Yet Xenophon had probably attended this festival on previous occasions, as other foreigners had (note *Mem.* I.2.61), and he had probably seen (or heard of) Spartan reactions to bad news at other times (note IV.5.10). How confident can we be that he witnessed the scene in 371?

Xenophon did not search out witnesses systematically, interrogate them carefully and compare their stories rigorously to determine the truth. He was much less concerned than Thucydides with chronology, as his failure to mark the beginning of one campaigning season shows. His military and political narrative falls far short of completeness. Omissions in the continuation include important information about Ionia (see I.4.8 n.), the Thraceward region (I.4.9 n.), the west (I.4.10, I.5.21 nn.), the mainland (I.2.18 n.) and even Attika (Diod. XIII.72.3-73.2), as well as about internal matters such as the return to full democracy at Athens and the accession of king Pausanias at Sparta (Diod. XIII.75.1). His silence leaves us to debate. Did the fleet operate in the Hellespont independently of the government at Athens (I.2.1 n.)? Did the Spartans institute a new law limiting the term of their admirals (I.5.1 n.)?

Xenophon had his own distinctive approach to history, more influenced by Herodotos than Thucydides, and better illumined by reading Xenophon's other writings than by studying his predecessors. Since H. R. Breitenbach's germinal study, "Historiographische Anschauungsformen Xenophons" (diss. Basel 1950), scholars have increasingly recognized that the *Hellenika* shows many typical Xenophontic concerns: justice, piety, power, tyranny, loyalty, the mutability of human affairs, the qualities of good commanders, and so on. In a revealing comment at V.1.4, after describing the goodwill Teleutias' men felt for their departing commander, Xenophon says:

> I know that I am not describing here any expenditure or danger
> or stratagem worth reporting; but, by Zeus, this seems to me
> worth consideration, what Teleutias did that made the men he
> commanded feel this way. For this is a human achievement
> more worth reporting than great wealth or dangers.

Xenophon wrote history to instruct. This instruction aimed at contemporaries, as stressed by C. J. Tuplin, who calls *Hell.* III-VII "political propaganda" for a 350s audience ("Xenophon: A Didactic Historian?" *Proceedings of the Classical Association, London* 74 [1977] 26-27). But it is not only propaganda. Like the *Kynegetikos*, the *Hellenika* reveals timeless lessons ranging from the practical to the moral and ethical, and Xenophon selected his material accordingly. Sometimes he spells out a story's point. The fall of Mantinea, he says, taught men not to put a river through city walls (V.2.5). Most stories, however, do not end with an explicitly stated lesson, though it is there for the observant. This is true on the broadest level as well. At least two great themes run throughout the work, uniting it to some degree, though it is not tightly knit. The first is that injustice leads to failure (I.1.27, 7.1 n.); the second, that it is good to forgive and forget (I.1.20, 2.13-14, 3.19, 5.19, II.1.31-32, 2.20). Unmentioned in the continuation but still important, even dominant in Xenophon's interpretation of events is the role of the divine. At the end of the *Hellenika* Xenophon says that the god determined the outcome of the battle of Mantineia (VII.5.26). Divine agency appears elsewhere as well (IV.4.12, VII.5.13), most strikingly at Leuktra (VI.4.3), where the god seemed to lead the Spartans toward their disastrous defeat because they broke a vow when they seized the Theban acropolis (V.4.1). The reader familiar with the theme of piety in Xenophon's other works will realize that these comments apply to Athens' fall in the continuation too.

Xenophon's interest in teaching raises the question of reliability, for he may have been tempted to "improve" a story to make a point. Unlike Thucydides, Xenophon makes no claim about his accuracy in the *Hellenika*--and even if he had we would still have to assess the claim's validity. For instance, despite its specific historical setting the *Symposion* ought not be taken as an accurate narrative of a particular dinner party, though Xenophon begins by saying he was present (I.1); and the work in which he makes his most explicit claim to have researched his topic, the *Kyroupaideia* (I.1.6), is a literary fiction.

To judge the *Hellenika*'s reliability we must not only assess it on its own (is it credible? does it follow storytellers' patterns that suggest unreliability? does it reveal bias?), but also compare it to other sources. This task is difficult and controversial, since the two most important writers, Diodoros of Sicily and Plutarch, both lived centuries later. In the first century BC Diodoros wrote the only other surviving narrative of the Ionian War. Diodoros has significantly different versions of all the major battles between 411 and 404 (Abydos, Kyzikos, Notion, Mytilene, Arginousai, Aigospotamoi) as well as of crucial events that took place in Athens itself, such as Alkibiades' homecoming and the Arginousai trial. Diodoros was not an original researcher, and did not even trouble to compare available accounts. For mainland and Aegean affairs in the fifth century he followed the fourth century historian Ephoros. For 411-404 Ephoros took an occasional detail from Xenophon (see I.5.14 n.), but depended primarily on a detailed contemporary narrative now preserved only on papyrus fragments (see McKechnie and Kern). The surviving portions of this work, known as the *Hellenika Oxyrhynchia*, concern mainly the years 396-95, but also deal with Thrasyllos' Ionian expedition in 410 and the battle of Notion in 406, and it seems certain that the original dealt with the entire period 411-394 or 387. (It may have begun with midsummer 411, supplementing or correcting Thucydides.)

Diodoros' stock has therefore risen considerably. He can never be dismissed--at least, not with any confidence--on the grounds that his information does not go back to a contemporary source. But neither can we be certain that his abbreviated third-hand narrative reproduces the original fairly. His accounts of the battles of Notion (XIII.71.2-4) and Sardis (XIV.80), which can be compared to extant portions of the *Hellenika Oxyrhynchia*, show the kind of mistakes Ephoros-Diodoros can make. Dates are particularly untrustworthy, for Ephoros organized his material by subject (κατὰ γένος) and Diodoros had difficulty putting it into his own annalistic form.

In the second century after Christ, Plutarch composed his parallel *Lives* of famous Greeks and Romans. His *Alkibiades* and *Lysandros* contain a great deal of information about the end of the Peloponnesian War, but they are biographies, not history, and biographies of a peculiar sort. Plutarch was interested in showing character. As he explains in the first section of his *Alexander*, little anecdotes or jokes often reveal more about a person's character than battles or sieges. His *Lives* therefore draw on Plutarch's wide reading in numerous authors of various sorts and varying reliability.   In *Alkibiades* and *Lysandros* he refers to nineteen writers ranging from tragic and comic poets to politicians and philosophers. Of the fourth-century historians he cites Theopompos and Ephoros in addition to Xenophon. But though we can name many of the authors he read, we often cannot identify the source for a particular story. Another difficult problem for the modern historian is Plutarch's disinterest in strict chronology, though the *Lives* proceed chronologically for the most part.

Current scholars disagree on Xenophon's trustworthiness. Anderson sees Xenophon as an honest reporter of what he knew, sometimes ill-informed but partial only due to circumstances that did not allow him to collect information freely. For Cawkwell, on the other hand, Xenophon was an unreliable, forgetful old man when he wrote the second part of the *Hellenika*, and (though younger) no more reliable when he wrote the continuation. Gray finds him a storyteller who may fudge facts for the sake of story and moral point. These opinions are not as contradictory as they first appear. Xenophon might have been honest in the sense that he thought he was telling the truth, even as he subconsciously altered the facts.

3.   The Peloponnesian War

The Peloponnesian War broke out in the spring of 431, more than twenty years before Xenophon's narrative begins. According to Thucydides, the growth of Athenian power made the Spartans afraid and compelled them to fight. The Athenians had built an empire in the Aegean by taking the lead in the war against the Persians after the Greeks repulsed the Persian invasion of 480. The new alliance of 478/7, sworn at the sacred island of Delos, began as a confederation of independent island and coastal states which agreed to provide either money or ships to continue the fighting. Athens provided both treasurers and generals in addition to the largest naval contingent. The league became an empire as Athens compelled states to remain loyal; rebels lost their fleets and had to pay tribute. By mid-century active fighting against the Persians had stopped, but no relaxation of Athenian demands followed.

Sparta's attitude toward Athens' actions had been suspicious from the start and occasionally hostile, but in 446/5 Sparta recognized Athens' naval empire in return for Athens' surrender of its possessions on the mainland. Subsequent Athenian activity at Thourii in southern Italy and Amphipolis in Thrace kept Sparta apprehensive, and Athens' alliance with previously-neutral Kerkyra after Kerkyra went to war with Sparta's ally Korinth began the disputes that led to Sparta's declaration of war.

Sparta's professed war aim was to liberate the Greeks. As the Spartan king Archidamos had foreseen, however, it was not easy for a land power to defeat a naval power. Early Peloponnesian hopes for effective naval operations proved fruitless, and without the prospect of help against Athens' fleet its subjects were unwilling to revolt. Sparta was reduced to invading Attika annually. These invasions were indecisive, for the Athenians stayed behind their walls rather than accept the challenge to battle. Brief invasions--the longest lasted forty days--could do only limited damage to Athenian farms, and the Athenians could import whatever they needed by sea, since they had connected the city to the port, Peiraieus, by long walls. The most harmful consequence of the Peloponnesian invasions--and it was only partly their doing--was the plague that killed perhaps a third of the Athenian population between 430 and 426. Athens, on the other hand, found equal difficulty trying to harm vital Peloponnesian interests. Biannual invasions of the Megarid hurt Megara but no more, and large naval expeditions around the Peloponnese produced insufficient results to justify their expense.

After several years both sides launched bold attempts to break the stalemate: Athens by building a permanent fort at Pylos (425), where Kleon captured 120 Spartiates and established a refuge for runaway Spartan slaves; Sparta by sending Brasidas by land to the coast of northeastern Greece (424), the one part of Athens' empire Sparta could attack by land, where Brasidas climaxed a string of successes by taking Amphipolis. After Kleon and Brasidas both died fighting during Athens' attempt to recover Amphipolis, the two sides reached an agreement, known as the Peace of Nikias, in 421. The treaty was unpopular with Sparta's allies, and only partly implemented. In 420 Athens made an alliance with some disaffected Spartan allies and with Sparta's old enemy Argos, whose thirty-year peace with Sparta had recently expired, but the Spartans defeated this combination at the battle of Mantinea in 418, ending Athenian hopes of a victory on land.

In 415 Athens accepted an offer to intervene in Sicily. Peloponnesian colonies in the west meant the possibility of naval aid to the Spartans; this aid had not materialized so far, but it might in the future. The Athenians all but captured the most powerful city in Sicily, Korinth's colony Syracuse, but the campaign ended in disaster in 413 when Athens failed to get its defeated force out in time. The Peloponnesians had sent a limited (though crucial) amount of aid to Syracuse, and had also finally dared to fortify Dekeleia in Attika as a base from which to harass the

Athenians without pause.

The final phase of the war is therefore called the Dekeleian War, or sometimes the Ionian War because the scene of the fighting shifted eastward. The news of Athens' losses in Sicily prompted numerous Athenian allies to revolt, even including Chios, the one remaining ally to have its own fleet. The Persians also expressed a willingness to join Sparta, in part because about 414 Athens had supported a rebel named Amorges against the King. Two Persians, in fact: Tissaphernes, satrap of Sardis, offered financial support for Ionian campaigns, and Pharnabazos, satrap of Daskyleion, wanted the Peloponnesians to attack further north. The Spartans chose initially to side with Chios and Tissaphernes. Athens negotiated with Tissaphernes too, and even changed the democracy to an oligarchy for a few months in 411, but they could not match the Spartan offer, which conceded the King's right to rule the Greeks in Asia Minor. In the summer of 411 the Spartan admiral Mindaros, in disgust at Tissaphernes' failure to bring the Phoenician fleet he had promised and over repeated difficulties in getting adequate pay for the troops, took the fleet north to join Pharnabazos. The Athenians won a minor but heartening victory at Kynossema, and Tissaphernes planned to go to the Hellespont in order to restore good relations with the Spartans. Here Thucydides breaks off, and here, roughly, Xenophon begins.

4. The Chronology of the Ionian War (411-404)

The problem is simply stated. In a narrative of events from autumn 411 to the end of summer 404--that is, seven war-years--Xenophon marks the start of a new campaigning season six times, as follows:

I.2.1	"in the next year . . . at the beginning of the summer"
I.3.1	"during the next year . . . when the winter ended . . . at the beginning of the spring"
I.4.1-2	"the winter . . . at the beginning of the spring"
I.6.1	"in the next year"
II.1.10	"in the next year"
II.3.1	"in the next year"

Therefore he failed to note the beginning of one year. Which one? We can narrow the period of uncertainty, for I.6.1 refers to 406: The lunar eclipse mentioned there happened on 15 April 406, and the battle of Arginousai (I.6.26-35) took place in 406/5 during the archonship of Kallias (Aristot. *Ath. Pol.* 34.1, Athen. 5.218 a). We can also date the battle of Kyzikos (I.1.11-23) to early 410: Diodoros begins his account with "when the winter ended" (XIII.49.2), and the peace discussions after the battle took place in 411/10 during the archonship of Theopompos (Philochoros, *FGrHist* 328 F 138).

Three solutions have been proposed. (I ignore the possibility that an entire year elapsed between the last event recorded by Thucydides and the first mentioned by Xenophon; Busolt [3.2.1521 n. 1] refutes this suggestion.) The oldest, suggested by Dodwell in 1702, suggests that a new campaign begins at I.1.9. Thus the battle of Rhoiteion/Abydos occurred at the beginning of winter 411/10 and the battle of Kyzikos in spring 410; I.2.1 marks the campaign of 409, I.3.1 of 408, I.4.2 of 407. This chronology agrees with Dionysios of Halikarnassos (hyp. Lys. 32), who dates Thrasyllos' departure for Ionia to the archonship of Glaukippos, 410/9. It also finds some support in schol. Aristoph. *Frogs* 1422, which puts Alkibiades' return to Athens in the archonship of Antigenes (407/6), for on this chronology Alkibiades at least stayed in Athens for part of this archon year. On the other hand, it contradicts Diod. XIII.64.7, which says the Lakedaimonians recaptured Pylos after fifteen years of Athenian occupation, and it makes both Alkibiades and Thrasyllos idle for more than a year.

The second solution, first proposed by Haacke in 1822, starts a new season at I.5.11 rather than I.1.9. Thus the battle of Kyzikos belongs to the early spring 410; I.2.1 notes the summer of 410; I.3.1 marks the campaign of 409 and I.4.2 of 408. This chronology agrees with Diod. XIII.64.7 (discussed above), but it conflicts with schol. Aristoph. *Frogs* 1422 and Diony. Halik. hyp. Lys. 32. It also makes the year following the battle of Notion in spring 407 strangely quiet, and the generals elected after Notion (I.5.16) are still in command at Arginousai in autumn 406 (I.6.16, 29-30).

N. Robertson offers a third interpretation, beginning a new campaigning season at I.4.11 ("The Sequence of Events in the Aegean in 408 and 407 B.C.," *Historia* 29 [1980] 282-301). Thus I.2.1 notes the summer of 410; I.3.1 marks the campaign of 409 and I.4.2 of 408, yet Notion is early in 406. In Robertson's view Alkibiades spent an entire campaigning season in Karia, and Kyros took more than a year to reach Sardis after his father named him *karanon*.

The following chart compares the three chronologies.

	Haacke	Robertson	Dodwell
winter 411/10	battle of Abydos	battle of Abydos	battle of Abydos

410	battle of Kyzikos Thrasyllos in Ionia	battle of Kyzikos Thrasyllos in Ionia	battle of Kyzikos
winter 410/9	Thrasyllos and Alkibiades in the Hellespont Pylos recaptured	Thrasyllos and Alkibiades in the Hellespont Pylos recaptured	
409	capture of Byzantion	capture of Byzantion	Thrasyllos in Ionia
winter 409/8			Thrasyllos and Alkibiades in the Hellespont Pylos recaptured
408	Boiotios' return Kyros arrives as *karanon* Alkibiades in Karia Alkibiades' homecoming	Boiotios' return Alkibiades in Karia	capture of Byzantion
407	battle of Notion		Boiotios' return

		Kyros arrives as *karanon*	Kyros arrives as *karanon*
			Alkibiades in Karia
		Alkibiades' homecoming	Alkibiades' homecoming
406		battle of Notion	battle of Notion
	battle of Arginousai	battle of Arginousai	battle of Arginousai

While none of these chronologies can be ruled out, a choice must be made. Each has a period of relative inactivity. In my judgment, Robertson has a good case that raising one hundred talents in Karia might have filled a campaigning season (see I.4.9 n.) and that Kyros might have taken a year to move from somewhere east of Gordion to Sardis, given the slow pace of events in the Persian empire. Notice, for what it is worth, that Diodoros does not mention Kyros' arrival (XIII.70.3) until after Alkibiades' homecoming. Therefore I accept Robertson's chronology, with one modification noted at I.4.10.

5. The Text

The manuscripts are the following:

B	Parisinus 1738	early 14C
P	Vaticanus Palatinus 140	14C
M	Ambrosianus A4 inf.	1344
L	Parisinus Coislinianus 317	late 14 or early 15C
V	Marcianus 368	late 14 or early 15C
D	Parisinus 1642	early 15C
T	Matritensis 4561	1427
u	Urbinas 117	14-15C
n	Neapolitanus 22.1	15C
c	Parisinus 2080	mid-15C
h	British Museum add. ms. 5110	mid-15C

g	Marcianus 365	1436
m	Laurentianus 69.15	1455
f	Leidensis Perizonianus F 6	1456
b	Marcianus 364	1469
e	Parisinus 1739	third quarter of 15C
a	Parisinus 1793	about 1535

The text in this edition is based on the readings reported by Marchant, Hude and Hatzfeld. I have relied on D. F. Jackson's demonstration that the most important manuscripts are B and P ("The Papyri of Xenophon's *Hellenica*," *Bulletin of the American Society of Papyrologists* 6 [1969] 45-52 and "The *TLDV* Manuscripts of Xenophon's *Hellenica* and Their Descendants," *Transactions of the American Philological Association* 105 [1975] 175-87). M descends from the same hyparchetype as P, as do (via a lost intermediary) L, V, D and T (for T see F. Gomez del Rio, "Manoscritos de Jenofonte en bibliotecas espāñolas," *Emerita* 26 [1958] 319-54). All the other manuscripts descend from T, except h, which is a copy of L.

Thus the text should be based on B, P and M, while T (the best of the *TLDV* group, and the oldest manuscript to contain a complete text for book V) should be used to supplement lacunae in *BPM*. Π (*P. Rainer* 6 p. 97, third century), containing I.2.2-5.8, is generally close to the manuscripts; where it differs, I agree with Hatzfeld that the manuscript reading is generally preferable. I cite other manuscripts only where they may have a useful correction. I have not indicated all variations in spelling and accentuation.

BIBLIOGRAPHY AND ABBREVIATIONS

In the introduction and commentary I cite all of the following by author's name. I give publication information for most articles where they are cited.

Greek Text

Delebecque, É., ed. and comm., *Xénophon, Helléniques, Livre I*. Paris 1964.

Hatzfeld, J., ed., *Xénophon, Helléniques* (Budé) 2 vols. Paris 1936-39.

Hude, C., ed., *Xenophon, Hellenica* (Bibliotheca Teubneriana) Leipzig 1930.

Marchant, E. C., ed., *Xenophon, Historia Graeca* (Oxford Classical Texts) Oxford 1900.

Works Cited and Abbreviations

Anderson, J. K. *Xenophon*. London 1974.

Amit, M. *Athens and the Sea*. Brussels 1965.

Beloch, K. J. *Griechische Geschichte*^{2}, 4 vols. in 8. Strassburg and Berlin 1912-27.

Best, J. G. P. *Thracian Peltasts and Their Influence on Greek Warfare*. Groningen 1969.

Bicknell, P. J. *Studies in Athenian Politics and Genealogy*. Wiesbaden 1972.

Bommelaer, J. F. *Lysandre de Sparte*. Paris 1981.

Bradeen, D. W. *The Athenian Agora* vol. 17 *Inscriptions: the Funerary Monuments*. Princeton 1974.

Breitenbach, H. R. "Xenophon von Athen," *Real-Encyclopädie der classischen Altertumswissenschaft* 18A (1967) 1570-2052.

Brumfield, A. C. *The Attic Festivals of Demeter and Their Relation to the Agricultural Year*. New York 1981.

Buchanan, J. J. *Theorika*. New York 1962.

Bugh, G. R. *The Horsemen of Athens*. Princeton 1988.

Burkert, W. *Greek Religion*. Cambridge, MA 1985.

Busolt, G. *Griechische Geschichte*, 3 vols. in 4. Gotha 1893-1904.

Cartledge, P. *Sparta and Lakonia*. London 1979.

Casson, L. *Ships and Seamanship in the Ancient World*. Princeton 1971.

Cawkwell, G. Introduction and Notes to Xenophon, *A History of My Times*, tr. R.

Warner. Harmondsworth 1979.

Cook, J. M. *The Persian Empire*. New York 1983.

Davies, J. K. *Athenian Propertied Families 600-300 B.C.* Oxford 1971.

De Ste. Croix, G. E. M. *The Origins of the Peloponnesian War*. Ithaca 1972.

Dittenberger, W., ed. *Sylloge Inscriptionum Graecarum³*. Leipzig 1915-24.

FGrHist = Jacoby, F., ed. and comm., *Die Fragmente der griechischen Historiker*. Berlin 1923-30; Leiden 1940-.

Fuks, A. *The Ancestral Constitution*. London 1953.

Gray, V. *The Character of Xenophon's* Hellenica. Baltimore 1989.

Hamilton, C. D. *Sparta's Bitter Victories*. Ithaca 1979.

Hansen, M. H. *Eisangelia*. Odense 1975.

----------. *The Sovereignty of the People's Court in Athens in the Fourth Century B.C. and the Public Action against Unconstitutional Proposals*. Odense 1974.

Harrison, A. R. W. *The Law of Athens*, vol. 1. Oxford 1971.

Hatzfeld, J. *Alcibiade*. Paris 1940.

HCT = A. W. Gomme, A. Andrewes and K. J. Dover, *A Historical Commentary on Thucydides*, 5 vols. Oxford 1944-81.

Henry, W. P. *Greek Historical Writing*. Chicago 1966.

Higgins, W. E. *Xenophon the Athenian*. Albany 1977.

Hignett, C. *A History of the Athenian Constitution*. Oxford 1952.

Hirsch, S. W. *The Friendship of the Barbarians*. Hanover 1985.

Hornblower, S. *Mausolus*. Oxford 1982.

IG = *Inscriptiones Graecae*.

Jordan, B. *The Athenian Navy in the Classical Period*. Berkeley 1975.

Kagan, D. *The Fall of the Athenian Empire*. Ithaca 1987.

Krentz, P. *The Thirty at Athens*. Ithaca 1982.

Leaf, W. *Strabo on the Troad*. Cambridge 1923.

Lewis, D. M. *Sparta and Persia*. Leiden 1977.

Lotze, D. *Lysander und der Peloponnesische Krieg*. Berlin 1964.

Lynch, J. P. *Aristotle's School*. Berkeley 1972.

MacDowell, D. M. *The Law in Classical Athens*. Ithaca 1978.

McKechnie, P. R. and S. J. Kern. *Hellenica Oxyrhynchia*. Warminster 1988.

Meiggs, R. *The Athenian Empire*. Oxford 1972.

Meiggs, R. and D. M. Lewis, eds. *A Selection of Greek Historical Inscriptions to the End of the Fifth Century B.C.* Oxford 1969.

Mikalson, J. D. *The Sacred and Civil Calendar of the Athenian Year*. Princeton 1975.

Morrison, J. S. and J. F. Coates. *The Athenian Trireme*. Cambridge 1986.

Morrison, J. S. and R. T. Williams. *Greek Oared Ships 900-322 B.C.* Cambridge

1968.

Mosley, D. J. *Envoys and Diplomacy in Ancient Greece*. Wiesbaden 1973.

Ober, J. *Fortress Attica*. Leiden 1985.

Osborne, M. *Naturalization in Athens*, 4 vols. Brussels 1981-83.

Ostwald, M. *From Popular Sovereignty to the Sovereignty of Law*. Berkeley 1986.

Parker, R. A. and W. H. Dubberstein. *Babylonian Chronology 626 B.C. - A.D. 45*, 2nd ed. Chicago 1946.

Pouilloux, J. *Recherches sur l'historie et les cultes de Thasos*, vol. 1. Paris 1954.

Pritchett, W. K. *The Greek State at War*, vols. 1-4. Berkeley 1971-85.

Quinn, T. J. *Athens and Chios, Lesbos and Samos*. Oxford 1981.

Rhodes, P. J. *A Commentary on the Aristotelian 'Athenaion Politeia'*. Oxford 1981.

Roberts, J. T. *Accountability in Athenian Government*. Madison 1982.

Sealey, R. *The Athenian Republic*. University Park, PA 1987.

SEG = Supplementum Epigraphicum Graecum.

Shipley, G. *A History of Samos 800-188 BC*. Oxford 1987.

Simon, E. *Festivals of Attika*. Madison 1983.

Stillwell, R., ed. *The Princeton Encyclopedia of Classical Sites*. Princeton 1976.

Strauss, B. S. *Athens after the Peloponnesian War*. Ithaca 1987.

Tod, M. N. *A Selection of Greek Historical Inscriptions*, vol. 2. Oxford 1948.

Tuplin, C. J. "Military engagements in Xenophon's *Hellenica*," in I. S. Moxon, J. D. Smart and A. J. Woodman, eds., *Past Perspectives* (Cambridge 1986) 37-66.

Underhill, G. E. *A Commentary on the Hellenica of Xenophon*. Oxford 1906.

Walbank, F. W. *A Historical Commentary on Polybius*, vol. 1. Oxford 1957.

Walbank, M. B. *Athenian Proxenies of the Fifth Century B.C.* Toronto 1978.

Wycherley, R. E. *The Stones of Athens*. Princeton 1978.

XENOPHON,

HELLENIKA I-II.3.10

ΧΕΝΟΦΩΝΤΟΣ *ΕΛΛΗΝΙΚΑ*

I

1

1 Μετὰ δὲ ταῦτα οὐ πολλαῖς ἡμέραις ὕστερον ἦλθεν ἐξ Ἀθηνῶν Θυμοχάρης ἔχων ναῦς ὀλίγας· καὶ εὐθὺς ἐναυμάχησαν αὖθις Λακεδαιμόνιοι καὶ Ἀθηναῖοι, ἐνίκησαν δὲ Λακεδαιμόνιοι ἡγουμένου Ἀγησανδρίδου. 2 Μετ' ὀλίγον δὲ τούτων Δωριεὺς ὁ Διαγόρου ἐκ Ῥόδου εἰς Ἑλλήσποντον εἰσέπλει ἀρχομένου χειμῶνος τέτταρσι καὶ δέκα ναυσὶν ἅμα ἡμέρᾳ. κατιδὼν δὲ ὁ τῶν Ἀθηναίων ἡμεροσκόπος ἐσήμανε τοῖς στρατηγοῖς. οἱ δὲ ἀνηγάγοντο ἐπ' αὐτὸν εἴκοσι ναυσίν, ἃς ὁ Δωριεὺς φυγὼν πρὸς τὴν γῆν ἀνεβίβαζε τὰς αὑτοῦ τριήρεις, ὡς ἤνοιγε[1], περὶ τὸ Ῥοίτειον. 3 ἐγγὺς δὲ γενομένων τῶν Ἀθηναίων ἐμάχοντο ἀπό τε τῶν νεῶν καὶ τῆς γῆς μέχρι οἱ Ἀθηναῖοι ἀπέπλευσαν εἰς Μάδυτον πρὸς τὸ ἄλλο στρατόπεδον οὐδὲν πράξαντες. 4 Μίνδαρος δὲ κατιδὼν τὴν μάχην ἐν Ἰλίῳ θύων τῇ Ἀθηνᾷ, ἐβοήθει ἐπὶ τὴν θάλατταν, καὶ καθελκύσας τὰς ἑαυτοῦ τριήρεις ἀπέπλει, ὅπως ἀναλάβοι τὰς μετὰ Δωριέως. 5 οἱ δὲ Ἀθηναῖοι ἀνταναγαγόμενοι[2] ἐναυμάχησαν περὶ Ἄβυδον κατὰ τὴν ἠόνα, μέχρι δείλης ἐξ ἑωθινοῦ[3]. καὶ τὰ μὲν νικώντων, τὰ δὲ νικωμένων, Ἀλκιβιάδης ἐπεισπλεῖ δυοῖν δεούσαις εἴκοσι ναυσίν. 6 ἐντεῦθεν δὲ φυγὴ τῶν Πελοποννησίων ἐγένετο πρὸς τὴν Ἄβυδον· καὶ ὁ Φαρνάβαζος παρεβοήθει, καὶ ἐπεισβαίνων τῷ ἵππῳ εἰς τὴν θάλατταν μέχρι δυνατὸν ἦν ἐμάχετο, καὶ τοῖς ἄλλοις τοῖς αὑτοῦ ἱππεῦσι καὶ πεζοῖς παρεκελεύετο. 7 συμφράξαντες δὲ τὰς ναῦς οἱ Πελοποννήσιοι καὶ παραταξάμενοι πρὸς τῇ γῇ ἐμάχοντο. Ἀθηναῖοι δὲ ἀπέπλευσαν, τριάκοντα ναῦς τῶν πολεμίων λαβόντες κενὰς καὶ ἃς αὐτοὶ ἀπώλεσαν κομισάμενοι, εἰς Σηστόν. 8 Ἐντεῦθεν πλὴν τετταράκοντα νεῶν ἄλλαι ἄλλῃ ᾤχοντο ἐπ' ἀργυρολογίαν ἔξω τοῦ Ἑλλησπόντου· καὶ ὁ Θράσυλλος, εἷς ὢν τῶν στρατηγῶν, εἰς Ἀθήνας ἔπλευσε ταῦτα ἐξαγγελῶν καὶ στρατιὰν καὶ ναῦς

---

[1] ἤνοιγε: ἤνυε Underhill ἤνυτε Kondos
[2] ἀνταναγαγόμενοι Hertlein: ἀνταναγόμενοι codd.
[3] ἐξ ἑωθινοῦ del. Brückner

XENOPHON, *HELLENIKA*

I

1

1 Then, not many days later, Thymochares arrived from Athens with a few ships, and immediately the Lakedaimonians and Athenians fought another naval battle. Under the leadership of Agesandridas, the Lakedaimonians won.

2 A little after this, at the beginning of winter, Dorieus the son of Diagoras from Rhodes sailed into the Hellespont with fourteen ships at dawn. The Athenian lookout on duty for the day saw him and signalled to the generals. They put out against him with twenty ships, from which Dorieus fled toward the land. He tried to beach his triremes, as he got clear of the Athenians, round about Rhoiteion. **3** When the Athenians approached they fought from the ships and the land until the Athenians sailed off to Madytos to the rest of the fleet, without accomplishing anything.

4 Mindaros saw the fight while at Ilion sacrificing to Athena, and went to the sea to help. Launching his triremes, he set sail in order to pick up Dorieus' triremes. **5** The Athenians, putting out against him, fought round about Abydos along the shore from morning until late afternoon, winning in some places but losing in others. Then Alkibiades sailed up with eighteen ships, **6** and the Peloponnesians fled toward Abydos. Pharnabazos came to their aid and, riding his horse as far as possible into the sea, he fought and encouraged his horsemen and infantry. **7** The Peloponnesians fought by packing their ships closely together and drawing up in line along the shore. The Athenians sailed away to Sestos after capturing thirty enemy ships without their crews and recovering the ships they themselves had lost.

8 From there all except forty of the Athenian ships scattered to collect money outside the Hellespont, and Thrasyllos, one of the generals, sailed to Athens to report what had happened and to request troops and ships.

αἰτήσων.

9 Μετὰ δὲ ταῦτα Τισσαφέρνης ἦλθεν εἰς Ἑλλήσποντον· ἀφικόμενον δὲ παρ' αὐτὸν μιᾷ τριήρει Ἀλκιβιάδην ξένιά τε καὶ δῶρα ἄγοντα συλλαβὼν εἶρξεν ἐν Σάρδεσι, φάσκων κελεύειν βασιλέα πολεμεῖν Ἀθηναίοις. 10 ἡμέραις δὲ τριάκοντα ὕστερον Ἀλκιβιάδης ἐκ Σάρδεων μετὰ Μαντιθέου τοῦ ἁλόντος ἐν Καρίᾳ ἵππων εὐπορήσαντες νυκτὸς ἀπέδρασαν εἰς Κλαζομενάς.

11 Οἱ δ' ἐν Σηστῷ Ἀθηναῖοι, αἰσθόμενοι Μίνδαρον πλεῖν ἐπ' αὐτοὺς μέλλοντα ναυσὶν ἑξήκοντα, νυκτὸς ἀπέδρασαν εἰς Καρδίαν. ἐνταῦθα δὲ καὶ Ἀλκιβιάδης ἧκεν ἐκ τῶν Κλαζομενῶν σὺν πέντε τριήρεσι καὶ ἐπακτρίδι. πυθόμενος δὲ ὅτι αἱ τῶν Πελοποννησίων νῆες ἐξ Ἀβύδου ἀνηγμέναι εἶεν εἰς Κύζικον, αὐτὸς μὲν πεζῇ ἦλθεν εἰς Σηστόν, τὰς δὲ ναῦς περιπλεῖν ἐκεῖσε ἐκέλευσεν. 12 ἐπεὶ δ' ἦλθον, ἀνάγεσθαι ἤδη αὐτοῦ μέλλοντος ὡς ἐπὶ ναυμαχίαν ἐπεισπλεῖ Θηραμένης εἴκοσι ναυσὶν ἀπὸ Μακεδονίας, ἅμα δὲ καὶ Θρασύβουλος εἴκοσιν ἑτέραις ἐκ Θάσου, ἀμφότεροι ἠργυρολογηκότες. 13 Ἀλκιβιάδης δὲ εἰπὼν καὶ τούτοις διώκειν αὐτὸν ἐξελομένοις τὰ μεγάλα ἱστία αὐτὸς ἔπλευσεν εἰς Πάριον· ἀθρόαι δὲ γενόμεναι αἱ νῆες ἅπασαι ἐν Παρίῳ ἓξ καὶ ὀγδοήκοντα τῆς ἐπιούσης νυκτὸς ἀνηγάγοντο, καὶ τῇ ἄλλῃ ἡμέρᾳ περὶ ἀρίστου ὥραν ἧκον εἰς Προκόννησον. 14 ἐκεῖ δ' ἐπύθοντο ὅτι Μίνδαρος ἐν Κυζίκῳ εἴη καὶ Φαρνάβαζος μετὰ τοῦ πεζοῦ. ταύτην μὲν οὖν τὴν ἡμέραν αὐτοῦ ἔμειναν, τῇ δὲ ὑστεραίᾳ Ἀλκιβιάδης ἐκκλησίαν ποιήσας παρεκελεύετο αὐτοῖς ὅτι ἀνάγκη εἴη καὶ ναυμαχεῖν καὶ πεζομαχεῖν καὶ τειχομαχεῖν· Οὐ γὰρ ἔστιν, ἔφη, χρήματα ἡμῖν, τοῖς δὲ πολεμίοις ἄφθονα παρὰ βασιλέως. 15 τῇ δὲ προτεραίᾳ, ἐπειδὴ ὡρμίσαντο, τὰ πλοῖα πάντα καὶ τὰ μικρὰ συνήθροισε παρ' ἑαυτόν, ὅπως μηδεὶς ἐξαγγείλαι τοῖς πολεμίοις τὸ πλῆθος τῶν νεῶν, ἐπεκήρυξέ τε, ὃς ἂν ἁλίσκηται εἰς τὸ πέραν διαπλέων, θάνατον τὴν ζημίαν.

16 Μετὰ δὲ τὴν ἐκκλησίαν παρασκευασάμενος ὡς ἐπὶ ναυμαχίαν ἀνηγάγετο ἐπὶ τὴν Κύζικον ὕοντος πολλῷ. ἐπειδὴ δ' ἐγγὺς τῆς Κυζίκου ἦν, αἰθρίας γενομένης καὶ τοῦ ἡλίου ἐκλάμψαντος καθορᾷ τὰς τοῦ Μινδάρου ναῦς γυμναζομένας πόρρω ἀπὸ τοῦ λιμένος καὶ ἀπειλημμένας ὑπ' αὐτοῦ, ἑξήκοντα οὔσας. 17 οἱ δὲ Πελοποννήσιοι ἰδόντες τὰς τῶν Ἀθηναίων τριήρεις οὔσας πλείους τε πολλῷ ἢ πρότερον καὶ πρὸς τῷ λιμένι, ἔφυγον εἰς τὴν γῆν· καὶ συνορμίσαντες τὰς ναῦς ἐμάχοντο ἐπιπλέουσι τοῖς ἐναντίοις. 18 Ἀλκιβιάδης δὲ ταῖς εἴκοσι τῶν νεῶν περιπλεύσας ἀπέβη εἰς τὴν γῆν. ἰδὼν δὲ ὁ Μίνδαρος, καὶ αὐτὸς ἀποβὰς ἐν τῇ γῇ μαχόμενος ἀπέθανεν· οἱ δὲ μετ' αὐτοῦ ὄντες ἔφυγον. τὰς δὲ ναῦς οἱ Ἀθηναῖοι ᾤχοντο ἄγοντες ἁπάσας εἰς Προκόννησον πλὴν τῶν Συρακοσίων· ἐκείνας δὲ αὐτοὶ κατέκαυσαν οἱ Συρακόσιοι. ἐκεῖθεν δὲ τῇ ὑστεραίᾳ ἔπλεον οἱ Ἀθηναῖοι ἐπὶ Κύζικον.

19 Οἱ δὲ Κυζικηνοὶ τῶν Πελοποννησίων καὶ Φαρναβάζου ἐκλιπόντων

9 Then Tissaphernes came to the Hellespont; he arrested Alkibiades, who visited him in a single trireme bringing friendly gifts and other presents, and imprisoned Alkibiades in Sardis, saying that the King had instructed him to fight the Athenians. **10** After thirty days Alkibiades and Mantitheos (who had been captured in Karia) secured horses and escaped during the night from Sardis to Klazomenai.

11 The Athenians in Sestos, realizing that Mindaros was about to sail against them with sixty ships, escaped during the night to Kardia. Alkibiades came there from Klazomenai with five triremes and a skiff. When he learned that the Peloponnesian ships had put to sea from Abydos for Kyzikos, he himself went overland to Sestos and he instructed the ships to sail there. **12** After they arrived and as he was about to put to sea for a naval battle, Theramenes sailed in with twenty ships from Macedonia and Thrasyboulos with twenty others from Thasos. Both of them had been collecting money. **13** Telling them to remove their main sails and follow him, Alkibiades sailed to Parion. Altogether eighty-six ships gathered at Parion. They put to sea during the following night and arrived about breakfast-time the next day at Prokonnesos. **14** There they learned that Mindaros was in Kyzikos, along with Pharnabazos and the infantry. Therefore that day they remained at Prokonnesos, and on the following day Alkibiades called an assembly and told them they would have to fight at sea and on land and against the walls. "For we have no money," he said, "while the enemy has an unlimited amount from the King." **15** When they anchored on the previous day he had gathered all the merchant vessels and small boats, so that no one should report to the enemy how many ships they had, and he announced that anyone caught sailing across to the opposite shore would be executed.

16 After the assembly he prepared for a naval battle and put to sea, in heavy rain, for Kyzikos. When he was near Kyzikos the sky cleared and the sun shone, so that he could see Mindaros' sixty ships training far from the harbor and cut off by himself. **17** The Peloponnesians, seeing that the Athenian triremes were much more numerous than before and were close to the harbor, fled to the land. Anchoring their ships closely together, they fought against the attackers sailing against them. **18** Alkibiades sailed round with twenty ships and disembarked on land. Mindaros saw him and, disembarking himself, died fighting on land; those who were with him fled. The Athenians went to Prokonnesos, taking all the ships except those of the Syracusans, which the Syracusans burned themselves. **19** On the next day the Athenians sailed against Kyzikos. The Kyzikenes,

αὐτὴν ἐδέχοντο τοὺς Ἀθηναίους. **20** Ἀλκιβιάδης δὲ μείνας αὐτοῦ εἴκοσιν ἡμέρας καὶ χρήματα πολλὰ λαβὼν παρὰ τῶν Κυζικηνῶν, οὐδὲν ἄλλο κακὸν ἐργασάμενος ἐν τῇ πόλει ἀπέπλευσεν εἰς Προκόννησον. ἐκεῖθεν δ' ἔπλευσεν εἰς Πέρινθον καὶ Σηλυμβρίαν. **21** καὶ Περίνθιοι μὲν εἰσεδέξαντο εἰς τὸ ἄστυ τὸ στρατόπεδον· Σηλυμβριανοὶ δὲ ἐδέξαντο μὲν οὔ, χρήματα δὲ ἔδοσαν. **22** ἐντεῦθεν δ' ἀφικόμενοι τῆς Καλχηδονίας εἰς Χρυσόπολιν ἐτείχισαν αὐτήν, καὶ δεκατευτήριον κατεσκεύασαν ἐν αὐτῇ, καὶ τὴν δεκάτην ἐξέλεγον τῶν ἐκ τοῦ Πόντου πλοίων, καὶ φυλακὴν ἐγκαταλιπόντες ναῦς τριάκοντα καὶ στρατηγὼ δύο, Θηραμένην καὶ Εὔμαχον, τοῦ τε χωρίου ἐπιμελεῖσθαι καὶ τῶν ἐκπλεόντων πλοίων καὶ εἴ τι ἄλλο δύναιντο[1] βλάπτειν τοὺς πολεμίους. οἱ δ' ἄλλοι στρατηγοὶ εἰς τὸν Ἑλλήσποντον ᾤχοντο.

23 Παρὰ δὲ Ἱπποκράτους τοῦ Μινδάρου ἐπιστολέως εἰς Λακεδαίμονα γράμματα πεμφθέντα ἑάλωσαν εἰς Ἀθήνας λέγοντα τάδε· Ἔρρει τὰ κᾶλα.[2] Μίνδαρος δ' ἀπεσσύα[3]. πεινῶντι τὤνδρες. ἀπορίομες τί χρὴ δρᾶν. **24** Φαρνάβαζος δὲ παντὶ τῷ τῶν Πελοποννησίων στρατεύματι καὶ τοῖς συμμάχοις παρακελευσάμενος μὴ ἀθυμεῖν ἕνεκα ξύλων, ὡς ὄντων πολλῶν ἐν τῇ βασιλέως, ἕως ἂν τὰ σώματα σῶα ᾖ, ἱμάτιόν τ' ἔδωκεν ἑκάστῳ καὶ ἐφόδιον δυοῖν μηνοῖν, καὶ ὁπλίσας τοὺς ναύτας φύλακας κατέστησε τῆς ἑαυτοῦ παραθαλαττίας γῆς. **25** καὶ συγκαλέσας τούς τε ἀπὸ τῶν πόλεων στρατηγοὺς καὶ τριηράρχους ἐκέλευε ναυπηγεῖσθαι τριήρεις ἐν Ἀντάνδρῳ ὅσας ἕκαστοι ἀπώλεσαν, χρήματά τε διδοὺς καὶ ὕλην ἐκ τῆς Ἴδης κομίζεσθαι φράζων. **26** ναυπηγουμένων δὲ οἱ Συρακόσιοι ἅμα τοῖς Ἀντανδρίοις τοῦ τείχους τι ἐπετέλεσαν, καὶ ἐν τῇ φρουρᾷ ἤρεσαν πάντων μάλιστα. διὰ ταῦτα δὲ εὐεργεσία τε καὶ πολιτεία Συρακοσίοις ἐν Ἀντάνδρῳ ἐστί. Φαρνάβαζος μὲν οὖν ταῦτα διατάξας εὐθὺς εἰς Καλχηδόνα ἐβοήθει.

27 Ἐν δὲ τῷ χρόνῳ τούτῳ ἠγγέλθη τοῖς τῶν Συρακοσίων στρατηγοῖς οἴκοθεν ὅτι φεύγοιεν ὑπὸ τοῦ δήμου. συγκαλέσαντες οὖν τοὺς ἑαυτῶν στρατιώτας Ἑρμοκράτους προηγορ οῦντος[4] ἀπωλοφύροντο τὴν ἑαυτῶν συμφοράν, ὡς ἀδίκως φεύγοιεν ἅπαντες παρὰ τὸν νόμον· παρήνεσάν τε προθύμους εἶναι καὶ τὰ λοιπά, ὥσπερ τὰ πρότερα, καὶ ἄνδρας ἀγαθοὺς πρὸς τὰ ἀεὶ παραγγελλόμενα, ἑλέσθαι δὲ ἐκέλευον ἄρχοντας, μέχρι ἂν ἀφίκωνται οἱ ᾑρημένοι ἀντ' ἐκείνων. **28** οἱ δ' ἀναβοήσαντες ἐκέλευον

---

[1] δύναιντο Hempel: δύνατο B ἠδύνατο rell. del. Delebecque
[2] κᾶλα Bergk: καλά codd.
[3] ἀπεσσύα: ἀπέσσυα B Bekker Anecd. Gr. p. 422 ἀπέσσυται PM ἀπέσσουα Plut. Alk. 28, Eustath. ad Il. 117 ἀπεσσία Hesych. s.v. (Plut., Eustath. om. δ')
[4] προηγορ οῦντος V: προηγοῦντος rell.

since the Peloponnesians and Pharnabazos had abandoned the city, admitted the Athenians. **20** Alkibiades remained there for twenty days and took a great deal of money from the Kyzikenes, but sailed back to Prokonnesos without doing any other harm in the city. From Prokonnesos he sailed to Perinthos and Selymbria. **21** The Perinthians admitted the troops into the city, and the Selymbrians, though not admitting them, gave money. **22** From there they went to Chrysopolis in Kalchedonia and fortified it. They established a customs house and began to collect the ten per cent tax from merchant vessels coming from the Black Sea. They also left, as a guard, thirty ships and two generals, Theramenes and Eumachos, to look after the place and the outgoing merchant ships and to harm the enemy in any other way they could. The other generals went to the Hellespont.

23 A message from Hippokrates, Mindaros' vice-admiral, was intercepted on its way to Lakedaimon and taken to Athens. It said: "The ships are lost. Mindaros is dead. The men are hungry. We do not know what to do." **24** Pharnabazos urged the entire Peloponnesian army and the allies not to be discouraged in regard to timber --for there was a great deal of timber in the King's territory--so long as their bodies were safe, and he gave each man a cloak and money to buy food for two months, and he armed sailors and stationed them as guards of his coastal territory. **25** He also called together the generals and captains from the cities and told them to build triremes in Antandros, as many as each city had lost; he gave them money and instructed them to get wood from Mt. Ida. **26** While the construction was going on the Syracusans, together with the Antandrians, completed part of the wall, and the Syracusans made themselves most popular in guard-duty. For these reasons the Syracusans now have the privileges of benefactors and the rights of citizens in Antandros. Having made these arrangements, Pharnabazos immediately went to the aid of Kalchedon.

27 During this time the news came from home to the Syracusan generals that they had been exiled by the commons. They called their soldiers together and, with Hermokrates as their spokesperson, lamented their misfortune, that all of them were exiled unjustly and illegally. They encouraged the soldiers to be enthusiastic in the future, as they had been in the past, to respond like brave men to whatever orders they received and to choose commanders to serve until their replacements arrived. **28** The men, particularly the captains and the marines and the pilots, shouted that

κείνους ἄρχειν, καὶ μάλιστα οἱ τριήραρχοι καὶ οἱ ἐπιβάται καὶ οἱ κυβερνῆται. οἱ δ' οὐκ ἔφασαν δεῖν στασιάζειν πρὸς τὴν ἑαυτῶν πόλιν· εἰ δέ τις ἐπικαλοίη τι αὐτοῖς, λόγον ἔφασαν χρῆναι διδόναι, μεμνημένους "Οσας τε ναυμαχίας αὐτοὶ [τε]¹ καθ' αὑτοὺς νενικήκατε καὶ ναῦς εἰλήφατε, ὅσα τε μετὰ τῶν ἄλλων ἀήττητοι γεγόνατε ἡμῶν ἡγουμένων, τάξιν ἔχοντες τὴν κρατίστην διά τε τὴν ἡμετέραν ἀρετὴν καὶ διὰ τὴν ὑμετέραν προθυμίαν καὶ κατὰ γῆν καὶ κατὰ θάλατταν ὑπάρχουσαν². 29 οὐδενὸς δὲ οὐδὲν ἐπαιτιωμένου, δεομένων ἔμειναν ἕως ἀφίκοντο οἱ ἀντ' ἐκείνων στρατηγοί, Δήμαρχός τ' Ἐπικύδου³ καὶ Μύσκων Μενεκράτους καὶ Πόταμις Γνωσία. τῶν δὲ τριηράρχων ὁμόσαντες οἱ πλεῖστοι κατάξειν αὐτούς, ἐπὰν εἰς Συρακούσας ἀφίκωνται, ἀπεπέμψαντο ὅποι ἐβούλοντο πάντας ἐπαινοῦντες· 30 ἰδίᾳ δὲ πρὸς Ἑρμοκράτην προσομιλοῦντες μάλιστα ἐπόθησαν τήν τε ἐπιμέλειαν καὶ προθυμίαν καὶ κοινότητα· ὧν γὰρ ἐγίγνωσκε τοὺς ἐπιεικεστάτους καὶ τριηράρχων καὶ κυβερνητῶν καὶ ἐπιβατῶν, ἑκάστης ἡμέρας τὸ πρῷ καὶ πρὸς ἑσπέραν συναλίζων⁴ πρὸς τὴν σκηνὴν τὴν ἑαυτοῦ ἀνεκοινοῦτο ὅ τι ἔμελλεν ἢ λέγειν ἢ πράττειν, κἀκείνους ἐδίδασκε κελεύων λέγειν τὰ μὲν ἀπὸ τοῦ παραχρῆμα, τὰ δὲ βουλευσαμένους. 31 ἐκ τούτων Ἑρμοκράτης τὰ πολλὰ ἐν τῷ συνεδρίῳ ηὐδόξει, λέγειν τε δοκῶν καὶ βουλεύειν τὰ κράτιστα. κατηγορήσας δὲ Τισσαφέρνους ἐν Λακεδαίμονι Ἑρμοκράτης, μαρτυροῦντος καὶ Ἀστυόχου, καὶ δόξας τὰ ὄντα λέγειν, ἀφικόμενος παρὰ Φαρνάβαζον, πρὶν αἰτῆσαι χρήματα λαβών, παρεσκευάζετο πρὸς τὴν εἰς Συρακούσας κάθοδον ξένους τε καὶ τριήρεις. ἐν τούτῳ δὲ ἧκον οἱ διάδοχοι τῶν Συρακοσίων εἰς Μίλητον καὶ παρέλαβον τὰς ναῦς καὶ τὸ στράτευμα.

32 Ἐν Θάσῳ⁵ δὲ κατὰ τὸν καιρὸν τοῦτον στάσεως γενομένης ἐκπίπτουσιν οἱ λακωνισταὶ καὶ ὁ Λάκων ἁρμοστὴς Ἐτεόνικος. καταιτιαθεὶς δὲ ταῦτα πρᾶξαι σὺν Τισσαφέρνει Πασιππίδας ὁ Λάκων ἔφυγεν ἐκ Σπάρτης· ἐπὶ δὲ τὸ ναυτικόν, ὃ ἐκεῖνος ἠθροίκει ἀπὸ τῶν συμμάχων, ἐξεπέμφθη Κρατησιππίδας, καὶ παρέλαβεν ἐν Χίῳ.

33 Περὶ δὲ τούτους τοὺς χρόνους Θρασύλλου ἐν Ἀθήναις ὄντος Ἄγις ἐκ τῆς Δεκελείας προνομὴν ποιούμενος πρὸς αὐτὰ τὰ τείχη ἦλθε τῶν Ἀθηναίων· Θράσυλλος δὲ ἐξαγαγὼν Ἀθηναίους καὶ τοὺς ἄλλους τοὺς ἐν τῇ πόλει ὄντας ἅπαντας παρέταξε παρὰ τὸ Λύκειον γυμνάσιον, ὡς μαχούμενος, ἂν

---

¹ τε om. cu
² μεμνημένους . . . ὑπάρχουσαν Dindorf post παραγελλόμενα (§ 27), Schneider post ἀντ' ἐκείνων (§ 27) transposuit
³ τ' Ἐπικύδου Cobet: τε πιδόκου codd.
⁴ συναλίζων Morus: συναυλίζων codd.
⁵ Θάσῳ: Ἰασῳ Kahrstedt

the generals should remain in command. The generals, however, said that they could not revolt against their city; if anyone had something to say against them, the men must allow him to speak, remembering "how many naval battles you won and how many ships you captured, and how many times you with your allies were undefeated under our command, having the place of honor in the formation because of our excellence and your enthusiasm on land and sea." 29 When no one brought any charges against them, on request they remained until their replacements arrived, Demarchos the son of Epikydes and Myskon the son of Menekrates and Potamis the son of Gnosias. Most of the captains swore that, when they returned to Syracuse, they would have the generals recalled, and they sent the exiled generals wherever they wished to go, praising them all. 30 Privately they told Hermokrates they would particularly miss his care and enthusiasm and accessibility, for every morning and evening he used to gather at his tent the best of the captains and pilots and marines whom he knew, and he would discuss what he intended to say or do. He would explain his thinking to them, and ask them to respond, sometimes on the spot, and sometimes after thinking things over. 31 As a result, Hermokrates had an excellent reputation in the assembly, where he seemed to be the best speaker and adviser. After accusing Tissaphernes in Lakedaimon and, with Astyochos as his witness, convincing the Lakedaimonians that he spoke the truth, when he visited Pharnabazos he received money before he asked for it, and began to prepare mercenaries and triremes for his return to Syracuse. Meanwhile the new Syracusan generals reached Miletos and took over the ships and the army.

32 In Thasos, at about this time, during a civil disorder the Lakedaimonian sympathizers were driven out along with the Lakonian governor Eteonikos. Pasippidas the Lakonian, who was accused of being responsible, along with Tissaphernes, for what had happened, was exiled from Sparta. Kratesippidas was sent out to command the fleet that Pasippidas had gathered, and he took it over in Chios.

33 Also at about this time, while Thrasyllos was in Athens, Agis made a foraging expedition from Dekeleia up to the walls themselves of Athens. Thrasyllos led out the Athenians and all the others in the city and arranged them in formation near the Lykeion *gymnasion*, with the intention of fighting if the enemy advanced.

προσίωσιν. **34** ἰδὼν δὲ ταῦτα Ἆγις ἀπήγαγε ταχέως, καί τινες αὐτῶν ὀλίγοι τῶν ἐπὶ πᾶσιν ὑπὸ τῶν ψιλῶν ἀπέθανον. οἱ οὖν Ἀθηναῖοι τῷ Θρασύλλῳ διὰ ταῦτα ἔτι προθυμότεροι ἦσαν ἐφ᾿ ἃ ἧκε, καὶ ἐψηφίσαντο ὁπλίτας τε αὐτὸν καταλέξασθαι χιλίους, ἱππέας δὲ ἑκατόν, τριήρεις δὲ πεντήκοντα. **35** Ἆγις δὲ ἐκ τῆς Δεκελείας ἰδὼν πλοῖα πολλὰ σίτου εἰς Πειραιᾶ καταθέοντα, οὐδὲν ὄφελος ἔφη εἶναι τοὺς μετ᾿ αὐτοῦ πολὺν ἤδη χρόνον Ἀθηναίους εἴργειν τῆς γῆς, εἰ μή τις σχήσοι καὶ ὅθεν ὁ κατὰ θάλατταν σῖτος φοιτᾷ· κράτιστόν τε εἶναι καὶ Κλέαρχον τὸν Ῥαμφίου πρόξενον ὄντα Βυζαντίων πέμψαι εἰς Καλχηδόνα τε καὶ Βυζάντιον. **36** δόξαντος δὲ τούτου, πληρωθεισῶν νεῶν ἔκ τε Μεγάρων καὶ παρὰ τῶν ἄλλων συμμάχων πεντεκαίδεκα στρατιωτίδων μᾶλλον ἢ ταχειῶν ᾤχετο. καὶ αὐτοῦ τῶν νεῶν τρεῖς ἀπόλλυνται ἐν τῷ Ἑλλησπόντῳ ὑπὸ τῶν Ἀττικῶν ἐννέα νεῶν, αἳ ἀεὶ ἐνταῦθα τὰ πλοῖα διεφύλαττον, αἱ δ᾿ ἄλλαι ἔφυγον εἰς Σηστόν[1], ἐκεῖθεν δὲ εἰς Βυζάντιον ἐσώθησαν.

37 [Καὶ ὁ ἐνιαυτὸς ἔληγεν, ἐν ᾧ Καρχηδόνιοι Ἀννίβα ἡγουμένου στρατεύσαντες ἐπὶ Σικελίαν δέκα μυριάσι στρατιᾶς αἱροῦσιν ἐν τρισὶ μησὶ δύο πόλεις Ἑλληνίδας Σελινοῦντα καὶ Ἱμέραν.][2]

2

1 Τῷ δὲ ἄλλῳ ἔτει [ᾧ ἦν Ὀλυμπιὰς τρίτη καὶ ἐνενηκοστή, ᾗ προστεθεῖσα ξυνωρὶς ἐνίκα Εὐαγόρου Ἠλείου, τὸ δὲ στάδιον Εὐβώτας Κυρηναῖος, ἐπὶ ἐφόρου μὲν ὄντος ἐν Σπάρτῃ Εὐαρχίππου, ἄρχοντος δ᾿ ἐν Ἀθήναις Εὐκτήμονος,][3] Ἀθηναῖοι μὲν Θορικὸν ἐτείχισαν, Θράσυλλος δὲ τά τε ψηφισθέντα πλοῖα λαβὼν καὶ πεντακισχιλίοις τῶν ναυτῶν πέλτας ποιησάμενος ὡς ἅμα καὶ πελτασταῖς ἐσομένοις[4] ἐξέπλευσεν ἀρχομένου τοῦ θέρους εἰς Σάμον.

2 Ἐκεῖ δὲ μείνας τρεῖς ἡμέρας ἔπλευσεν εἰς Πύγελα· καὶ ἐνταῦθα τήν τε χώραν ἐδήου καὶ προσέβαλλε τῷ τείχει. ἐκ δὲ τῆς Μιλήτου βοηθήσαντές τινες τοῖς Πυγελεῦσι διεσπαρμένους ὄντας τῶν Ἀθηναίων τοὺς ψιλοὺς ἐδίωκον. **3** οἱ δὲ πελτασταὶ καὶ τῶν ὁπλιτῶν δύο λόχοι βοηθήσαντες πρὸς τοὺς αὑτῶν ψιλοὺς ἀπέκτειναν ἅπαντας τοὺς ἐκ Μιλήτου ἐκτὸς ὀλίγων, καὶ

---

[1] Σηστόν: Ἄβυδον coni. Breitenbach
[2] Καὶ . . . Ἱμέραν del. Sievers
[3] ᾧ ἦν . . . Εὐκτήμονος del. Marsham Dindorf
[4] πεντακισχιλίοις τ. ν. πέλτας ποιησάμενος ὡς ἅ. κ. πελτασταῖς ἐσομένοις Madvig: πεντακισχιλίους τ. ν. πελταστὰς π. ὡς ἅ. κ. πελτασταῖς ἐσ. codd. ὡς ἅμα . . . ἐσομένοις del. Schneider ὡς ἅμα . . . χρησόμενος Weiske ὡς ἅμα . . . ἐσομένους Riemann τοῖς ἅμα . . . ἐσομένοις Delebecque

34 When Agis saw this, however, he retreated hurriedly, and a few of those in the rear were killed by the light-armed. Therefore the Athenians were still more enthusiastic about the matters for which Thrasyllos had come, and they voted that he should enlist one thousand hoplites, one hundred cavalry, and fifty triremes.

35 From Dekeleia Agis saw many grain ships sailing into Peiraieus, and he said that it would do no good for his troops to cut off the Athenians from their land, which they had done for some time already, unless someone seized the source of the grain that was coming in by sea. The best idea would be to send Klearchos the son of Ramphias, who was the Byzantine *proxenos*, to Kalchedon and Byzantion. **36** This proposal was approved. Klearchos set out with fifteen ships, troop-carriers rather than fast ships, manned by the Megarians and other allies. Of his ships three were destroyed in the Hellespont by the nine Athenian ships that always guarded the merchant ships there, but the others fled to Sestos, and from there reached Byzantion safely.

37 [So ended the year in which the Carthaginians under the leadership of Hannibal invaded Sicily with 100,000 soldiers. In three months they took two Greek cities, Selinos and Himera.]

2

1 In the next year, [during which the ninety-third Olympiad took place, in which Euagoras of Elis won the two-horse chariot race--a new event--and Eubatas of Kyrene won the *stadion* race, Euarchippos being ephor at Sparta and Euktemon archon at Athens,] the Athenians fortified Thorikos and Thrasyllos, taking the ships that had been voted and making shields for five thousand of the sailors, so they could also serve as peltasts, sailed at the beginning of the summer to Samos.

2 After remaining there for three days he sailed to Pygela, where he ravaged the land and attacked the fortifications. Some men came from Miletos to help the people of Pygela, and they pursued the scattered Athenian light-armed. **3** But the peltasts and two divisions of hoplites came to the aid of their light-armed and killed all those from Miletos, except a few, and captured about two hundred hoplite shields,

ἀσπίδας ἔλαβον ὡς διακοσίας, καὶ τροπαῖον ἔστησαν.

4 Τῇ δὲ ὑστεραίᾳ ἔπλευσαν εἰς Νότιον, καὶ ἐντεῦθεν παρασκευασάμενοι ἐπορεύοντο εἰς Κολοφῶνα. Κολοφώνιοι δὲ προσεχώρησαν. καὶ τῆς ἐπιούσης νυκτὸς ἐνέβαλον εἰς τὴν Λυδίαν ἀκμάζοντος τοῦ σίτου, καὶ κώμας τε πολλὰς ἐνέπρησαν καὶ χρήματα ἔλαβον καὶ ἀνδράποδα καὶ ἄλλην λείαν πολλήν. **5** Στάγης δὲ ὁ Πέρσης περὶ ταῦτα τὰ χωρία ὤν, ἐπεὶ οἱ Ἀθηναῖοι ἐκ τοῦ στρατοπέδου διεσκεδασμένοι ἦσαν κατὰ τὰς ἰδίας λείας, βοηθησάντων τῶν ἱππέων ἕνα μὲν ζωὸν ἔλαβεν, ἑπτὰ δὲ ἀπέκτεινε. **6** Θράσυλλος δὲ μετὰ ταῦτα ἀπήγαγεν ἐπὶ θάλατταν τὴν στρατιάν, ὡς εἰς Ἔφεσον πλευσούμενος. Τισσαφέρνης δὲ αἰσθόμενος τοῦτο τὸ ἐπιχείρημα, στρατιάν τε συνέλεγε πολλὴν καὶ ἱππέας[1] ἀπέστελλε παραγγέλλων πᾶσιν [εἰς Ἔφεσον][2] βοηθεῖν τῇ Ἀρτέμιδι.

7 Θράσυλλος δὲ ἑβδόμῃ καὶ δεκάτῃ ἡμέρᾳ μετὰ τὴν εἰσβολὴν εἰς Ἔφεσον ἔπλευσε, καὶ τοὺς μὲν ὁπλίτας πρὸς τὸν Κορησσὸν ἀποβιβάσας, τοὺς δὲ ἱππέας καὶ πελταστὰς καὶ ἐπιβάτας καὶ τοὺς ἄλλους πάντας πρὸς τὸ ἕλος ἐπὶ τὰ ἕτερα τῆς πόλεως, ἅμα τῇ ἡμέρᾳ προσῆγε δύο στρατόπεδα. **8** οἱ δ' ἐκ τῆς πόλεως ἐβοήθησαν Ἐφέσιοι[3] οἵ τε σύμμαχοι οὓς Τισσαφέρνης ἤγαγε, καὶ Συρακόσιοι οἵ τ' ἀπὸ τῶν προτέρων εἴκοσι νεῶν καὶ ἀπὸ ἑτέρων πέντε, αἳ ἔτυχον τότε παραγενόμεναι, νεωστὶ ἥκουσαι μετὰ Εὐκλέους τε τοῦ Ἵππωνος καὶ Ἡρακλείδου τοῦ Ἀριστογένους στρατηγῶν, καὶ Σελινούσιαι δύο. **9** οὗτοι δὲ πάντες πρῶτον μὲν πρὸς τοὺς ὁπλίτας τοὺς ἐν Κορησσῷ ἐβοήθησαν· τούτους δὲ τρεψάμενοι καὶ ἀποκτείναντες ἐξ αὐτῶν ὡσεὶ ἑκατὸν καὶ εἰς τὴν θάλατταν καταδιώξαντες πρὸς τοὺς παρὰ τὸ ἕλος ἐτράποντο. ἔφυγον δὲ κἀκεῖ οἱ Ἀθηναῖοι, καὶ ἀπώλοντο αὐτῶν ὡς τριακόσιοι. **10** οἱ δὲ Ἐφέσιοι τροπαῖον ἐνταῦθα ἔστησαν καὶ ἕτερον πρὸς τῷ Κορησσῷ. τοῖς δὲ Συρακοσίοις καὶ Σελινουσίοις κρατίστοις γενομένοις ἀριστεῖα ἔδωκαν καὶ κοινῇ καὶ ἰδίᾳ πολλοῖς, καὶ οἰκεῖν ἀτελεῖ[4] ἔδοσαν τῷ βουλομένῳ ἀεί· Σελινουσίοις δέ, ἐπεὶ ἡ πόλις ἀπωλώλει, καὶ πολιτείαν ἔδοσαν.

11 Οἱ δ' Ἀθηναῖοι τοὺς νεκροὺς ὑποσπόνδους ἀπολαβόντες ἀπέπλευσαν εἰς Νότιον, κἀκεῖ θάψαντες αὐτοὺς ἔπλεον εὐθὺ[5] Λέσβου καὶ Ἑλλησπόντου. **12** ὁρμοῦντες δὲ ἐν Μηθύμνῃ τῆς Λέσβου εἶδον παραπλεούσας ἐξ Ἐφέσου τὰς Συρακοσίας ναῦς πέντε καὶ εἴκοσι· καὶ ἐπ' αὐτὰς ἀναχθέντες τέτταρας μὲν

---

[1] ἱππέας Π: ἱππεῖς codd. item I.7.2 et saepe
[2] εἰς Ἔφεσον del. Hartman
[3] Ἐφέσιοι Sauppe: σφίσιν codd. Ἐφεσίοις Kurz ⟨σὺν δὲ⟩ σφίσιν Simon ὄψιοι Delebecque συχνοί Delebecque
[4] ἀτελεῖ Madvig: ἀτέλειαν codd.
[5] εὐθὺ Π ἐπὶ codd.

and erected a trophy.

4 On the next day they sailed to Notion. From there, after making preparations, they proceeded to Kolophon, which came over peacefully. During the following night they invaded Lydia, at the time when the grain was ripening, and they burned many villages and captured money and slaves and a great deal of other booty. **5** Stages, the Persian, was in the area when the Athenians scattered from their camp in search of private booty. When the horsemen came up in support he captured one alive and killed seven others. **6** Then Thrasyllos led the army back to the sea, with the intention of sailing to Ephesos. But when Tissaphernes learned of this attack, he collected a large army and sent horsemen to tell everyone to aid Artemis.

7 On the seventeenth day after the raid Thrasyllos sailed to Ephesos. He disembarked the hoplites near Koressos, and the cavalry, peltasts, marines and all the others near the marsh on the opposite side of the city. At dawn he led the two divisions forward. **8** The Ephesians from the city came out to meet him, along with the allies whom Tissaphernes led and the Syracusans from the previous twenty ships and from five others that had recently arrived with the generals Eukles, the son of Hippon, and Herakleides, the son of Aristogenos, and the crews of two ships from Selinos. **9** These all moved first against the hoplites in Koressos. After routing them and killing about one hundred and pursuing the rest to the sea, they turned to the Athenians advancing from the marsh. These also fled, and about three hundred of them died. **10** The Ephesians erected one trophy there and another at Koressos. They awarded the prizes for valor to the men of Syracuse and Selinos, both collectively and to many individually, and they granted exemption from ᵗ ᵗtion to any who wished at any time to live at Ephesos; to the men of Selinos, since their city had been destroyed, they also granted citizenship.

11 After taking up their dead under a truce, the Athenians sailed back to Notion, and after burying the corpses there they set sail immediately for Lesbos and the Hellespont. **12** While they were anchored at Methymna on Lesbos they saw the twenty-five Syracusan ships sailing past from Ephesus. They put out against them,

ἔλαβον αὐτοῖς ἀνδράσι, τὰς δ' ἄλλας κατεδίωξαν εἰς Ἔφεσον. 13 καὶ τοὺς μὲν ἄλλους αἰχμαλώτους Θράσυλλος εἰς Ἀθήνας ἀπέπεμψε πάντας, Ἀλκιβιάδην δὲ Ἀθηναῖον, Ἀλκιβιάδου ὄντα ἀνεψιὸν καὶ συμφυγάδα, κατέλευσεν[1]. ἐντεῦθεν δὲ ἔπλευσεν εἰς τὴν Σηστὸν πρὸς τὸ ἄλλο στράτευμα· ἐκεῖθεν δὲ ἅπασα ἡ στρατιὰ διέβη εἰς Λάμψακον.

14 Καὶ χειμὼν ἐπῄει, ἐν ᾧ οἱ αἰχμάλωτοι Συρακόσιοι, εἰργμένοι τοῦ Πειραιῶς ἐν λιθοτομίαις, διορύξαντες τὴν πέτραν, ἀποδράντες νυκτὸς ᾤχοντο εἰς Δεκέλειαν, οἱ δ' εἰς Μέγαρα.

15 Ἐν δὲ τῇ Λαμψάκῳ συντάττοντος Ἀλκιβιάδου τὸ στράτευμα πᾶν οἱ πρότεροι στρατιῶται οὐκ ἐβούλοντο τοῖς μετὰ Θρασύλλου συντάττεσθαι, ὡς αὐτοὶ μὲν ὄντες ἀήττητοι, κεῖνοι δὲ ἡττημένοι ἥκοιεν. ἐνταῦθα δὴ ἐχείμαζον ἅπαντες Λάμψακον τειχίζοντες. 16 καὶ ἐστράτευσαν πρὸς Ἄβυδον· Φαρνάβαζος δ' ἐβοήθησεν ἵπποις πολλοῖς, καὶ μάχῃ ἡττηθεὶς ἔφυγεν. Ἀλκιβιάδης δὲ ἐδίωκεν ἔχων τούς τε ἱππέας καὶ τῶν ὁπλιτῶν εἴκοσι καὶ ἑκατόν, ὧν ἦρχε Μένανδρος, μέχρι σκότος ἀφείλετο. 17 ἐκ δὲ τῆς μάχης ταύτης συνέβησαν οἱ στρατιῶται αὐτοὶ αὑτοῖς καὶ ἠσπάζοντο τοὺς μετὰ Θρασύλλου. ἐξῆλθον δέ τινας καὶ ἄλλας ἐξόδους τοῦ χειμῶνος εἰς τὴν ἤπειρον καὶ ἐπόρθουν τὴν βασιλέως χώραν.

18 Τῷ δ' αὐτῷ χρόνῳ καὶ Λακεδαιμόνιοι τοὺς εἰς τὸ Κορυφάσιον τῶν Εἱλώτων ἀφεστῶτας ἐκ Μαλέας ὑποσπόνδους ἀφῆκαν. κατὰ δὲ τὸν αὐτὸν καιρὸν καὶ ἐν Ἡρακλείᾳ τῇ Τραχινίᾳ Ἀχαιοὶ τοὺς ἐποίκους, ἀντιτεταγμένων πάντων πρὸς Οἰταίους πολεμίους ὄντας, προέδοσαν, ὥστε ἀπολέσθαι αὐτῶν πρὸς ἑπτακοσίους σὺν τῷ ἐκ Λακεδαίμονος ἁρμοστῇ Λαβώτῃ.

19 [Καὶ ὁ ἐνιαυτὸς ἔληγεν οὗτος, ἐν ᾧ καὶ Μῆδοι ἀπὸ Δαρείου τοῦ Περσῶν βασιλέως ἀποστάντες πάλιν προσεχώρησαν αὐτῷ.][2]

3

1 Τοῦ δ' ἐπιόντος ἔτους ὁ ἐν Φωκαίᾳ νεὼς τῆς Ἀθηνᾶς ἐνεπρήσθη πρηστῆρος ἐμπεσόντος. ἐπεὶ δ' ὁ χειμὼν ἔληγε, [Παντακλέους μὲν ἐφορεύοντος, ἄρχοντος δ' Ἀντιγένους,] ἔαρος ἀρχομένου, [δυοῖν καὶ εἴκοσιν ἐτῶν[3] τῷ πολέμῳ παρεληλυθότων,][4] οἱ Ἀθηναῖοι ἔπλευσαν εἰς Προκόννησον παντὶ τῷ στρατοπέδῳ. 2 ἐκεῖθεν δ' ἐπὶ Καλχηδόνα καὶ Βυζάντιον

---

[1] κατέλευσεν: ἀπέλυσεν Wolf κατηλέησεν Feder κατελεήσας ἀπέλυσεν Breitenbach κατέλυσεν Delebecque
[2] Καὶ ὁ ... αὐτῷ del. Unger Dindorf
[3] ἐτῶν Dindorf: ἐτοῖν codd.
[4] Παντακλέους ... παρεληλυθότων del. Marsham

captured four with their crews, and chased the rest back to Ephesos. **13** Thrasyllos sent all the other captives to Athens, but he stoned to death Alkibiades the Athenian, the cousin and fellow exile of Alkibiades. Then he sailed to Sestos to join the other fleet, and from there the entire force crossed over to Lampsakos.

14 Winter now approached. During this winter the Syracusan prisoners, who were held in the stone quarries of Peiraieus, dug through the rock and escaped during the night. Most went to Dekeleia, a few to Megara.

15 In Lampsakos Alkibiades tried to organize the entire army into a single formation, but the old soldiers did not want to serve in the same ranks as those who arrived with Thrasyllos, on the grounds that they were unbeaten but those had come from a defeat. They all, however, spent the winter there fortifying Lampsakos. **16** They also made an expedition against Abydos. Pharnabazos, who brought a large cavalry force to its defense, was defeated in battle and fled. Alkibiades pursued him with the cavalry and 120 of the hoplites, whom Menandros led, until darkness prevented further pursuit. **17** As a result of this battle the soldiers came together of their own accord and welcomed Thrasyllos' men. During the winter they went out on some other campaigns into the interior and ravaged the King's land.

18 During this time the Lakedaimonians let go under a treaty the helots who had revolted and fled from Malea to Koryphasion. Also at about the same time the Achaians in Herakleia Trachinia betrayed the immigrants when they were all drawn up against their enemies the Oitaians, with the result that about 700 of them died, with the Lakedaimonian governor Labotas.

19 [So ended this year, in which the Medes who had revolted from Dareios the Persian King yielded to him again.]

3

1 During the next year the temple of Athena in Phokaia burned when it was struck by lightning. When the winter ended, [Pantakles being ephor and Antigenes archon,] at the beginning of the spring, [after twenty-two years of the war had elapsed,] the Athenians sailed to Prokonnesos with their entire force. **2** From there

ὁρμήσαντες ἐστρατοπεδεύσαντο πρὸς Καλχηδόνι. οἱ δὲ Καλχηδόνιοι προσιόντας αἰσθόμενοι τοὺς Ἀθηναίους, τὴν λείαν ἅπασαν κατέθεντο εἰς τοὺς Βιθυνοὺς Θρᾷκας, ἀστυγείτονας ὄντας. 3 Ἀλκιβιάδης δὲ λαβὼν τῶν τε ὁπλιτῶν ὀλίγους καὶ τοὺς ἱππέας, καὶ τὰς ναῦς παραπλεῖν κελεύσας, ἐλθὼν εἰς τοὺς Βιθυνοὺς ἀπῄτει τὰ τῶν Καλχηδονίων χρήματα· εἰ δὲ μή, πολεμήσειν ἔφη αὐτοῖς. οἱ δὲ ἀπέδοσαν. 4 Ἀλκιβιάδης δ' ἐπεὶ ἧκεν εἰς τὸ στρατόπεδον τήν τε λείαν ἔχων καὶ πίστεις πεποιημένος, ἀπετείχιζε τὴν Καλχηδόνα παντὶ τῷ στρατοπέδῳ ἀπὸ θαλάττης εἰς θάλατταν καὶ τοῦ ποταμοῦ ὅσον οἷόν τ' ἦν ξυλίνῳ τείχει. 5 ἐνταῦθα Ἱπποκράτης μὲν ὁ Λακεδαιμόνιος ἁρμοστὴς ἐκ τῆς πόλεως ἐξήγαγε τοὺς στρατιώτας, ὡς μαχούμενος· οἱ δὲ Ἀθηναῖοι ἀντιπαρετάξαντο αὐτῷ, Φαρνάβαζος δὲ ἔξω τῶν περιτειχισμάτων προσεβοήθει στρατιᾷ τε καὶ ἵπποις πολλοῖς. 6 Ἱπποκράτης μὲν οὖν καὶ Θράσυλλος ἐμάχοντο ἑκάτερος τοῖς ὁπλίταις χρόνον πολύν, μέχρι Ἀλκιβιάδης ἔχων ὁπλίτας τέ τινας καὶ τοὺς ἱππέας ἐβοήθησε. καὶ Ἱπποκράτης μὲν ἀπέθανεν, οἱ δὲ μετ' αὐτοῦ ὄντες ἔφυγον εἰς τὴν πόλιν. 7 ἅμα δὲ καὶ Φαρνάβαζος, οὐ δυνάμενος συμμεῖξαι πρὸς τὸν Ἱπποκράτην διὰ τὴν στενοπορίαν[1], τοῦ ποταμοῦ καὶ τῶν ἀποτειχισμάτων ἐγγὺς ὄντων, ἀπεχώρησεν εἰς τὸ Ἡράκλειον τὸ τῶν Καλχηδονίων, οὗ ἦν αὐτῷ τὸ στρατόπεδον.

8 Ἐκ τούτου δὲ Ἀλκιβιάδης μὲν ᾤχετο εἰς τὸν Ἑλλήσποντον καὶ εἰς Χερρόνησον χρήματα πράξων· οἱ δὲ λοιποὶ στρατηγοὶ συνεχώρησαν πρὸς Φαρνάβαζον ὑπὲρ Καλχηδόνος εἴκοσι τάλαντα δοῦναι Ἀθηναίοις Φαρνάβαζον καὶ ὡς βασιλέα πρέσβεις Ἀθηναίων ἀναγαγεῖν, 9 καὶ ὅρκους ἔδοσαν καὶ ἔλαβον παρὰ Φαρναβάζου ὑποτελεῖν τὸν φόρον Καλχηδονίους Ἀθηναίοις ὅσονπερ εἰώθεσαν καὶ τὰ ὀφειλόμενα χρήματα ἀποδοῦναι, Ἀθηναίους δὲ μὴ πολεμεῖν Καλχηδονίοις[2], ἕως ἂν οἱ παρὰ βασιλέως πρέσβεις ἔλθωσιν.

10 Ἀλκιβιάδης δὲ τοῖς [τε][3] ὅρκοις οὐκ ἐτύγχανε παρών, ἀλλὰ περὶ Σηλυμβρίαν ἦν· κείνην δ' ἑλὼν πρὸς τὸ Βυζάντιον ἧκεν, ἔχων Χερρονησίτας τε πανδημεὶ καὶ ἀπὸ Θρᾴκης στρατιώτας καὶ ἱππέας πλείους τριακοσίων. 11 Φαρνάβαζος δὲ ἀξιῶν δεῖν κἀκεῖνον ὀμνύναι, περιέμενεν ἐν Καλχηδόνι, μέχρι ἔλθοι ἐκ τοῦ Βυζαντίου· ἐπειδὴ δὲ ἧκεν, οὐκ ἔφη ὀμεῖσθαι, εἰ μὴ κἀκεῖνος αὐτῷ ὀμεῖται. 12 μετὰ ταῦτα ὤμοσεν ὁ μὲν ἐν Χρυσοπόλει οἷς Φαρνάβαζος ἔπεμψε Μιτροβάτει καὶ Ἀρνάπει, ὁ δ' ἐν Καλχηδόνι τοῖς παρ' Ἀλκιβιάδου Εὐρυπτολέμῳ καὶ Διοτίμῳ τόν τε κοινὸν ὅρκον καὶ ἰδίᾳ ἀλλήλοις

---

[1] στενοπορίαν Β: στενωπορίαν Π στενοξορίαν rell.
[2] Καλχηδονίοις: Φαρναβάζῳ Hatzfeld
[3] τε del. Dindorf

they set out against Kalchedon and Byzantion and made their camp near Kalchedon. When the Kalchedonians realized that the Athenians were attacking, they gave all their movable goods to the Bithynian Thracians, their neighbors, for safekeeping. **3** Alkibiades, taking a few of the hoplites and the cavalry and ordering the ships to sail along the coast, went to the Bithynians and asked for the Kalchedonians' property; otherwise, he said, he would make war on them. So they handed it over. **4** When he returned to the camp with the booty, after making a treaty with the Bithynians, he employed the entire army in blockading Kalchedon from sea to sea, and as much of the river as possible, with a wooden stockade. **5** Then Hippokrates, the Lakedaimonian governor, led the soldiers out of the city, with the intention of fighting. The Athenians drew up in battle formation opposite him, and outside the stockade Pharnabazos came up to help him with an army and a large cavalry force. **6** Hippokrates and Thrasyllos fought with their hoplites for a long time, until Alkibiades with a few hoplites and the cavalry came to Thrasyllos' aid. Hippokrates died and his men fled into the city. **7** At the same time Pharnabazos, unable to join Hippokrates because of the narrow space between the river and the fortifications, retreated to the Herakleion of the Kalchedonians, where he had his camp.

8 After that Alkibiades went to the Hellespont and the Cherronesos to raise money, and the other generals agreed with Pharnabazos on the subject of Kalchedon: Pharnabazos was to pay twenty talents to the Athenians and to conduct Athenian ambassadors to the King, **9** and they exchanged oaths that the Kalchedonians would pay their customary tribute to the Athenians and would repay the amount they owed, and that the Athenians would not make war on the Kalchedonians until the ambassadors returned from the King.

10 Alkibiades was not present for the oaths, but was at Selymbria. After capturing that city he came to Byzantion with the Cherronesians in full force and soldiers and more than three hundred cavalry from Thrace. **11** Pharnabazos thought that Alkibiades should also give his oath, so he waited in Kalchedon for him to return from Byzantion. When he arrived, he refused to swear unless Pharnabazos also swore to him. **12** Then Alkibiades swore in Chrysopolis to the representatives Pharnabazos sent, Mitrobates and Arnapes, and Pharnabazos swore in Kalchedon to the representatives from Alkibiades, Euryptolemos and Diotimos; they not only swore the common oath but also gave assurances to each other personally.

13 Φαρνάβαζος μὲν οὖν εὐθὺς ἀπῄει, καὶ τοὺς παρὰ βασιλέα ορευομένους πρέσβεις ἀπαντᾶν ἐκέλευσεν εἰς Κύζικον. ἐπέμφθησαν δὲ Ἀθηναίων μὲν Δωρόθεος, Φιλοκύδης[1], Θεογένης, Εὐρυπτόλεμος, Μαντίθεος, σὺν δὲ τούτοις Ἀργεῖοι Κλεόστρατος, Πυρρόλοχος· ἐπορεύοντο δὲ καὶ Λακεδαιμονίων πρέσβεις[2] Πασιππίδας καὶ ἕτεροι, μετὰ δὲ τούτων καὶ Ἑρμοκράτης, ἤδη φεύγων ἐκ Συρακουσῶν, καὶ ὁ ἀδελφὸς αὐτοῦ Πρόξενος.

14 καὶ Φαρνάβαζος μὲν τούτους ἦγεν· οἱ δὲ Ἀθηναῖοι τὸ Βυζάντιον ἐπολιόρκουν περιτειχίσαντες, καὶ πρὸς τὸ τεῖχος ἀκροβολισμοὺς καὶ προσβολὰς ἐποιοῦντο. 15 ἐν δὲ τῷ Βυζαντίῳ ἦν Κλέαρχος Λακεδαιμόνιος ἁρμοστὴς καὶ σὺν αὐτῷ τῶν περιοίκων τινὲς καὶ τῶν νεοδαμώδων οὐ πολλοὶ καὶ Μεγαρεῖς καὶ ἄρχων αὐτῶν Ἕλιξος Μεγαρεὺς καὶ Βοιωτοὶ καὶ τούτων ἄρχων Κοιρατάδας. 16 οἱ δ᾽ Ἀθηναῖοι ὡς οὐδὲν ἐδύναντο διαπράξασθαι κατ᾽ ἰσχύν, ἔπεισάν τινας τῶν Βυζαντίων προδοῦναι τὴν πόλιν. 17 Κλέαρχος δὲ ὁ ἁρμοστὴς οἰόμενος οὐδένα ἂν τοῦτο ποιῆσαι, καταστήσας δὲ ἅπαντα ὡς ἐδύνατο κάλλιστα καὶ ἐπιτρέψας τὰ ἐν τῇ πόλει Κοιρατάδᾳ καὶ Ἑλίξῳ, διέβη παρὰ τὸν Φαρνάβαζον εἰς τὸ πέραν, μισθόν τε τοῖς στρατιώταις παρ᾽ αὐτοῦ ληψόμενος καὶ ναῦς συλλέξων, αἳ ἦσαν ἐν τῷ Ἑλλησπόντῳ ἄλλαι ⟨ἄλλη⟩[3] καταλελειμμέναι φρουρίδες ὑπὸ Πασιππίδου καὶ ἃς Ἀγησανδρίδας εἶχεν ἐπὶ Θρᾴκης, ἐπιβάτης ὢν Μινδάρου, καὶ ὅπως καὶ ἐν Ἀντάνδρῳ[4] ἄλλαι ναυπηγηθείησαν, ἁθρόαι δὲ γενόμεναι πᾶσαι κακῶς τοὺς συμμάχους τῶν Ἀθηναίων ποιοῦσαι ἀποσπάσειαν τὸ στρατόπεδον ἀπὸ τοῦ Βυζαντίου. 18 ἐπεὶ δ᾽ ἐξέπλευσεν ὁ Κλέαρχος, οἱ προδιδόντες τὴν πόλιν τῶν Βυζαντίων, Κύδων καὶ Ἀρίστων καὶ Ἀναξικράτης καὶ Λυκοῦργος καὶ Ἀναξίλαος 19 (ὃς ὑπαγόμενος θανάτου ὕστερον ἐν Λακεδαίμονι διὰ τὴν προδοσίαν ἀπέφυγεν, ἀπολογούμενος[5] ὅτι οὐ προδοίη τὴν πόλιν, ἀλλὰ σώσαι, παῖδας ὁρῶν καὶ γυναῖκας λιμῷ ἀπολλυμένους, Βυζάντιος ὢν καὶ οὐ Λακεδαιμόνιος· τὸν γὰρ ἐνόντα σῖτον Κλέαρχον τοῖς Λακεδαιμονίων στρατιώταις διδόναι· διὰ ταῦτ᾽ οὖν τοὺς πολεμίους ἔφη εἰσέσθαι, οὐκ ἀργυρίου ἕνεκα οὐδὲ διὰ τὸ μισεῖν Λακεδαιμονίους)· 20 ἐπεὶ δὲ αὐτοῖς παρεσκεύαστο, νυκτὸς ἀνοίξαντες τὰς πύλας τὰς ἐπὶ τὸ Θρᾴκιον καλουμένον[6] εἰσήγαγον τὸ στράτευμα καὶ τὸν Ἀλκιβιάδην. 21 ὁ δὲ Ἕλιξος καὶ ὁ Κοιρατάδας οὐδὲν τούτων εἰδότες ἐβοήθουν μετὰ πάντων εἰς τὴν ἀγοράν· ἐπεὶ δὲ πάντῃ οἱ πολέμιοι κατεῖχον,

[1] Φιλοκύδης Dindorf: Φιλοδίκης ΒΡΜΠ Φιλοδίκος Riemann
[2] πρέσβεις del. Kurz Dindorf
[3] ⟨ἄλλη⟩ add. Schaefer
[4] καὶ ἐν Ἀντάνδρῳ hic pos. Trieber, post Πασιππίδου codd. Π
[5] ἀπολογούμενος Π: om. ΒΡΜ
[6] καλούμενον Dindorf: καλουμένας codd.

13 Pharnabazos departed immediately, telling the ambassadors going to the King to meet him in Kyzikos. Of the Athenians were sent Dorotheos, Philokydes, Theogenes, Euryptolemos, and Mantitheos; with them went the Argives Kleostratos and Pyrrolochos; ambassadors of the Lakedaimonians, Pasippidas and others, also went, and with them Hermokrates, now an exile from Syracuse, and his brother Proxenos.

14 So Pharnabazos was conducting these ambassadors, and the Athenians continued the siege of Byzantion by building a stockade around the city; they also attacked the city wall both at long range and at close quarters. **15** In Byzantion the Lakedaimonian governor, Klearchos, had some *perioikoi*, a few *neodamodeis*, a contingent of Megarians under the command of Helixos the Megarian and a contingent of Boiotians under the command of Koiratadas. **16** Since the Athenians could not accomplish anything by force, they persuaded some of the Byzantines to betray the city. **17** Klearchos the governor thought no one would do such a thing, and after arranging everything as best he could and entrusting affairs in the city to Koiratadas and Helixos, he crossed over to Pharnabazos on the mainland in order to get pay for the troops from him and to collect ships. Some ships had been left as guards in various places in the Hellespont by Pasippidas, and Agesandridas (Mindaros' lieutenant) had some in the Thraceward region. He intended to have still others built at Antandros and to draw the army away from Byzantion by attacking Athens' allies with his combined fleet. **18** When Klearchos sailed away, the Byzantines who were betraying the city completed their preparations. They included Kydon, Ariston, Anaxikrates, Lykourgos and Anaxilaos **19** (who was later put on trial for his life in Lakedaimon because of the betrayal, but was acquitted; he defended himself by saying that he did not betray the city, but saved it when he saw children and women dying from hunger--he was a Byzantine and not a Lakedaimonian--for Klearchos gave the food in the city to the soldiers of the Lakedaimonians; he let in the enemy for this reason, he said, not for money or because he hated the Lakedaimonians). **20** During the night they let in the army and Alkibiades by opening the gates to the so-called Thrakion. **21** Helixos and Koiratadas, who knew nothing of what was going on, came with all their forces to the agora to defend the city. But when their enemies prevailed everywhere, they had no choice but to

οὐδὲν ἔχοντες ὅ τι ποιήσαιεν, παρέδοσαν σφᾶς αὐτούς. 22 καὶ οὗτοι μὲν ἀπεπέμφθησαν εἰς Ἀθήνας, καὶ ὁ Κοιρατάδας ἐν τῷ ὄχλῳ ἀποβαινόντων ἐν Πειραιεῖ ἔλαθεν ἀποδρὰς καὶ ἀπεσώθη εἰς Δεκέλειαν.

4

1 Φαρνάβαζος δὲ καὶ οἱ πρέσβεις τῆς Φρυγίας ἐν Γορδίῳ ὄντες τὸν χειμῶνα τὰ περὶ τὸ Βυζάντιον πεπραγμένα ἤκουσαν. 2 ἀρχομένου δὲ τοῦ ἔαρος πορευομένοις αὐτοῖς παρὰ βασιλέα ἀπήντησαν καταβαίνοντες οἵ τε Λακεδαιμονίων πρέσβεις Βοιώτιος [ὄνομα]¹ καὶ οἱ μετ' αὐτοῦ καὶ οἱ ἄλλοι ἄγγελοι, καὶ ἔλεγον ὅτι Λακεδαιμόνιοι πάντων ὧν δέονται πεπραγότες εἶεν παρὰ βασιλέως, 3 καὶ Κῦρος, ἄρξων πάντων τῶν ἐπὶ θαλάττῃ καὶ συμπολεμήσων Λακεδαιμονίοις, ἐπιστολήν τε ἔφερε τοῖς κάτω πᾶσι τὸ βασίλειον σφράγισμα ἔχουσαν, ἐν ᾗ ἐνῆν καὶ τάδε· Καταπέμπω Κῦρον κάρανον τῶν εἰς Καστωλὸν ἀθροιζομένων. τὸ δὲ κάρανον ἔστι κύριον. 4 Ταῦτ' οὖν ἀκούοντες οἱ τῶν Ἀθηναίων πρέσβεις, καὶ ἐπειδὴ Κῦρον εἶδον, ἐβούλοντο μὲν μάλιστα παρὰ βασιλέα ἀναβῆναι· εἰ δὲ μή, οἴκαδε ἀπελθεῖν. 5 Κῦρος δὲ Φαρναβάζῳ εἶπεν ἢ παραδοῦναι τοὺς πρέσβεις ἑαυτῷ ἢ μὴ οἴκαδέ πω ἀποπέμψαι, βουλόμενος τοὺς Ἀθηναίους μὴ εἰδέναι τὰ πραττόμενα. 6 Φαρνάβαζος δὲ τέως μὲν κατεῖχε τοὺς πρέσβεις, φάσκων τοτὲ μὲν ἀνάξειν αὐτοὺς παρὰ βασιλέα, τοτὲ δὲ οἴκαδε ἀποπέμψειν, ὡς μηδὲν μέμψησθε²· 7 ἐπειδὴ δὲ ἐνιαυτοὶ τρεῖς ἦσαν, ἐδεήθη τοῦ Κύρου ἀφεῖναι αὐτούς, φάσκων ὀμωμοκέναι καὶ³ ἀπάξειν ἐπὶ θάλατταν, ἐπειδὴ οὐ παρὰ βασιλέα. πέμψαντες δὲ Ἀριοβαρζάνει παρακομίσαι αὐτοὺς ἐκέλευον· ὁ δὲ ἀπήγαγεν εἰς Κίον τῆς Μυσίας, ὅθεν πρὸς τὸ ἄλλο στρατόπεδον ἀπέπλευσαν.

8 Ἀλκιβιάδης δὲ βουλόμενος μετὰ τῶν στρατιωτῶν ἀποπλεῖν οἴκαδε, ἀνήχθη εὐθὺς ἐπὶ Σάμου· ἐκεῖθεν δὲ λαβὼν τῶν νεῶν εἴκοσιν ἔπλευσε τῆς Καρίας εἰς τὸν Κεραμικὸν κόλπον. ἐκεῖθεν δὲ συλλέξας ἑκατὸν τάλαντα ἧκεν εἰς τὴν Σάμον.

9 Θρασύβουλος δὲ σὺν τριάκοντα ναυσὶν ἐπὶ Θρᾴκης ᾤχετο, ἐκεῖ⁴ δὲ τά τε ἄλλα χωρία τὰ πρὸς Λακεδαιμονίους μεθεστηκότα κατεστρέψατο καὶ Θάσον, ἔχουσαν κακῶς ὑπό τε τῶν πολέμων καὶ στάσεων καὶ λιμοῦ.

---

¹ ὄνομα del. Kurz
² μέμψησθε Π: πέμψηται Β μέμψηται rell.
³ καὶ Π: om. codd.
⁴ ἐκεῖ Herwerden: ἐκεῖθεν codd. ἐκεῖθι Hude

surrender themselves. **22** They were sent to Athens, and while they were disembarking in Peiraieus Koiratadas slipped into the crowd and escaped safely to Dekeleia.

4

1 Pharnabazos and the ambassadors were at Gordion in Phrygia for the winter when they heard what had happened at Byzantion. **2** At the beginning of the spring, when they were continuing their journey to the King they met, going in the other direction, both the Lakedaimonian ambassadors, Boiotios and his colleagues, and the other messengers, who said that the Lakedaimonians had gained everything they asked for from the King, **3** and Kyros, who was to command all the men on the coast and to fight together with the Lakedaimonians. He carried a letter with the royal seal to all the inhabitants of the coast. It said, among other things, "I am sending Kyros as *karanon* of those who marshal at Kastolos." *Karanon* means "lord."

4 When the Athenian ambassadors heard this news and saw Kyros, they wanted more than ever to go to the King, or else to return home. **5** But Kyros commanded Pharnabazos either to hand the ambassadors over to him or not to send them home yet, since he wanted the Athenians to remain ignorant of what was going on. **6** Pharnabazos held the ambassadors for a while, sometimes saying that he would take them to the King, and other times that he would send them home, in order that Kyros would not find fault with him. **7** But when three years had passed, he asked Kyros to release them, saying that he had sworn to bring them back to the sea if he could not take them to the King. So they sent the ambassadors to Ariobarzanes and told him to conduct them. He brought them to Kios in Mysia, and from there they sailed to rejoin the rest of the army.

8 Alkibiades, wishing to sail home with the troops, set out immediately for Samos, and from there, taking twenty of the ships, he sailed to the Gulf of Keramos in Karia. After collecting one hundred talents there he returned to Samos.

9 Thrasyboulos went in the direction of Thrace with thirty ships, and there he subdued the places that had revolted to the Lakedaimonians, including Thasos, which was suffering from wars and civil disorders and famine.

10 Θράσυλλος δὲ σὺν τῇ ἄλλῃ στρατιᾷ εἰς Ἀθήνας κατέπλευσε· πρὶν δὲ ἥκειν αὐτὸν οἱ Ἀθηναῖοι στρατηγοὺς εἵλοντο Ἀλκιβιάδην μὲν φεύγοντα καὶ Θρασύβουλον ἀπόντα, Κόνωνα δὲ τρίτον ἐκ τῶν οἴκοθεν. 11 Ἀλκιβιάδης δὲ ἐκ τῆς Σάμου ἔχων τὰ χρήματα κατέπλευσεν εἰς Πάρον ναυσὶν εἴκοσιν, ἐκεῖθεν δ' ἀνήχθη εὐθὺ Γυθείου ἐπὶ κατασκοπὴν τῶν τριήρων, ἃς ἐπυνθάνετο Λακεδαιμονίους αὐτόθι παρασκευάζειν τριάκοντα, καὶ τοῦ οἴκαδε κατάπλου ὅπως ἡ πόλις πρὸς αὐτὸν ἔχει. 12 ἐπειδὴ δ'[1] ἑώρα ἑαυτῷ εὔνουν οὖσαν καὶ στρατηγὸν αὐτὸν ᾑρημένους καὶ ἰδίᾳ μεταπεμπομένους τοὺς ἐπιτηδείους, κατέπλευσεν εἰς τὸν Πειραιᾶ ἡμέρᾳ ᾗ Πλυντήρια ἦγεν ἡ πόλις, τοῦ ἕδους κατακεκαλυμμένου τῆς Ἀθηνᾶς, ὅ τινες οἰωνίζοντο ἀνεπιτήδειον εἶναι καὶ αὐτῷ καὶ τῇ πόλει. Ἀθηναίων γὰρ οὐδεὶς ἐν ταύτῃ τῇ ἡμέρᾳ οὐδενὸς σπουδαίου ἔργου τολμήσαι ἂν ἅψασθαι. 13 καταπλέοντος δ' αὐτοῦ ὅ τε ἐκ τοῦ Πειραιῶς καὶ ὁ ἐκ τοῦ ἄστεως ὄχλος ἠθροίσθη πρὸς τὰς ναῦς, θαυμάζοντες καὶ ἰδεῖν βουλόμενοι τὸν Ἀλκιβιάδην, λέγοντες [ὅτι][2] οἱ μὲν ὡς κράτιστος εἴη τῶν πολιτῶν καὶ μόνος [ἀπελογήθη ὡς][3] οὐ δικαίως φύγοι, ἐπιβουλευθεὶς δὲ ὑπὸ τῶν ἔλαττον ἐκείνου δυναμένων μοχθηρότερά τε λεγόντων καὶ πρὸς τὸ αὑτῶν ἴδιον κέρδος πολιτευόντων, ἐκείνου [δ'][4] ἀεὶ τό [τε][5] κοινὸν αὔξοντος καὶ ἀπὸ τῶν αὑτοῦ καὶ ἀπὸ τοῦ τῆς πόλεως δυνατοῦ· 14 ἐθέλοντος δὲ τότε κρίνεσθαι παραχρῆμα τῆς αἰτίας ἄρτι γεγενημένης ὡς ἠσεβηκότος εἰς τὰ μυστήρια, ὑπερβαλλόμενοι οἱ ἐχθροὶ τὰ δοκοῦντα δίκαια εἶναι ἀπόντα αὐτὸν ἐστέρησαν τῆς πατρίδος· 15 ἐν ᾧ χρόνῳ ὑπὸ ἀμηχανίας δουλεύων ἠναγκάσθη μὲν θεραπεύειν τοὺς ἐχθίστους, κινδυνεύων ἀεὶ παρ' ἑκάστην ἡμέραν ἀπολέσθαι· τοὺς δὲ οἰκειοτάτους πολίτας τε καὶ συγγενεῖς καὶ τὴν πόλιν ἅπασαν ὁρῶν ἐξαμαρτάνουσαν, οὐκ εἶχεν ὅπως ὠφελοίη φυγῇ ἀπειργόμενος. 16 οὐκ ἔφασαν δὲ τῶν οἵωνπερ αὐτὸς ὄντων εἶναι καινῶν δεῖσθαι πραγμάτων οὐδὲ μεταστάσεως· ὑπάρχειν γὰρ ἐκ τοῦ δήμου αὐτῷ[6] μὲν τῶν τε ἡλικιωτῶν πλέον ἔχειν τῶν τε πρεσβυτέρων μὴ ἐλαττοῦσθαι, τοῖς δ' αὐτοῦ ἐχθροῖς τοιοῦτος δοκεῖν εἶναι οἷόσπερ[7] πρότερον†, ὕστερον δὲ δυνασθεῖσιν ἀπολλύναι τοὺς βελτίστους, αὐτοὺς δὲ μόνους λειφθέντας δι'

---

[1] ἐπειδὴ δ' Π: ἐπεὶ δὲ codd.
[2] ὅτι del. Schneider
[3] ἀπελογήθη ὡς del. Brückner, lacunam ante haec verba Riemann statuit
[4] δ' del. Iuntina
[5] τε del. Morus γε Delebecque
[6] αὐτῷ Morus: ἑαυτῷ codd.
[7] τοιοῦτος . . . οἷόσπερ: τοιούτοις . . . οἷοισπερ Morus, post πρότερον lacunam statuerunt Breitenbach Riemann

10 Thrasvllos sailed to Athens with the rest of the fleet. Before he arrived the Athenians chose as generals Alkibiades, who was in exile, and Thrasyboulos, who was away from home, and third, from those at home, Konon. **11** Alkibiades now sailed with the money and twenty ships from Samos to Paros, and from there he set out straight to Gytheion to see the thirty triremes that he learned the Lakedaimonians were preparing there, and to see how the city felt about his return home. **12** When he saw that it was favorably disposed to him, that the Athenians had chosen him general, and that his friends were summoning him privately, he sailed into the Peiraieus on the day when the city was celebrating the Plynteria and the statue of Athena was covered, which some people considered inauspicious both for him and for the city, for no Athenian would dare to begin any serious task on this day. **13** As he sailed in, a crowd from Peiraieus and from the city gathered at the ships, admiring and wishing to see Alkibiades. Some people said that he was the best of the citizens and that he alone had been exiled unjustly. He had been the victim of men less powerful than he, scoundrels who acted politically for their own private gain, although he always improved the state, using both his own resources and the city's power. **14** At the time he had wanted to be tried immediately on the charge just then brought against him, that he had desecrated the Mysteries, but by postponing what seemed to be a just demand his enemies deprived him of his fatherland when he was absent. **15** During his exile, helpless as a slave, he had been forced to serve the enemy, in daily danger of losing his life. Though he saw his fellow citizens and relatives and the entire city making mistakes, he was prevented by his exile from helping them. **16** It was not the character, they said, of men like Alkibiades to want change or revolution, for under the democracy he excelled his contemporaries and was not inferior to his elders; and to his enemies he seemed the same as he was before† . . . later they destroyed the best persons during

αὐτὸ τοῦτο ἀγαπᾶσθαι ὑπὸ τῶν πολιτῶν ὅτι ἑτέροις βελτίοσιν οὐκ εἶχον χρῆσθαι· 17 οἱ δέ, ὅτι τῶν παροιχομένων αὐτοῖς κακῶν μόνος αἴτιος εἴη, τῶν τε φοβερῶν ὄντων τῇ πόλει γενέσθαι μόνος κινδυνεῦσαι ἡγεμὼν καταστῆναι.

18 Ἀλκιβιάδης δὲ πρὸς τὴν γῆν ὁρμισθεὶς ἀπέβαινε μὲν οὐκ εὐθύς[1], φοβούμενος τοὺς ἐχθρούς· ἐπαναστὰς δὲ ἐπὶ τοῦ καταστρώματος ἐσκόπει τοὺς αὑτοῦ ἐπιτηδείους, εἰ παρείησαν. 19 κατιδὼν δὲ Εὐρυπτόλεμον τὸν Πεισιάνακτος, ἑαυτοῦ[2] δὲ ἀνεψιόν, καὶ τοὺς ἄλλους οἰκείους καὶ τοὺς φίλους μετ' αὐτῶν, τότε ἀποβὰς ἀναβαίνει εἰς τὴν πόλιν μετὰ τῶν παρεσκευασμένων, εἴ τις ἅπτοιτο, μὴ ἐπιτρέπειν 20 ἐν δὲ τῇ βουλῇ καὶ τῇ ἐκκλησίᾳ ἀπολογησάμενος ὡς οὐκ ἠσεβήκει, εἰπὼν δὲ ὡς ἠδίκηται, λεχθέντων δὲ καὶ ἄλλων τοιούτων καὶ οὐδενὸς ἀντειπόντος διὰ τὸ μὴ ἀνασχέσθαι ἂν τὴν ἐκκλησίαν, ἀναρρηθεὶς ἁπάντων ἡγεμὼν αὐτοκράτωρ, ὡς οἷός τε ὢν σῶσαι τὴν προτέραν τῆς πόλεως δύναμιν, πρότερον μὲν τὰ μυστήρια τῶν Ἀθηναίων κατὰ θάλατταν ἀγόντων διὰ τὸν πόλεμον, κατὰ γῆν ἐποίησεν ἐξαγαγὼν τοὺς στρατιώτας ἅπαντας. 21 μετὰ δὲ ταῦτα κατελέξατο στρατιάν, ὁπλίτας μὲν πεντακοσίους καὶ χιλίους, ἱππέας δὲ πεντήκοντα καὶ ἑκατόν, ναῦς δ' ἑκατόν. καὶ μετὰ τὸν κατάπλουν τρίτῳ[3] μηνὶ ἀνήχθη ἐπ' Ἄνδρον ἀφεστηκυῖαν τῶν Ἀθηναίων, καὶ μετ' αὐτοῦ Ἀριστοκράτης καὶ Ἀδείμαντος ὁ Λευκολοφίδου συνεπέμφθησαν ᾑρημένοι κατὰ γῆν στρατηγοί. 22 Ἀλκιβιάδης δὲ ἀπεβίβασε τὸ στράτευμα τῆς Ἀνδρίας χώρας εἰς Γαύριον· ἐκβοηθήσαντας δὲ τοὺς Ἀνδρίους ἐτρέψαντο καὶ κατέκλεισαν εἰς τὴν πόλιν καί τινας ἀπέκτειναν οὐ πολλούς, καὶ τοὺς Λάκωνας οἳ αὐτόθι ἦσαν. 23 Ἀλκιβιάδης δὲ τροπαῖόν τε ἔστησε καὶ μείνας αὐτοῦ ὀλίγας ἡμέρας ἔπλευσεν εἰς Σάμον, κἀκεῖθεν ὁρμώμενος ἐπολέμει.

5

1 Οἱ δὲ Λακεδαιμόνιοι πρότερον τούτων οὐ πολλῷ χρόνῳ Κρατησιππίδα τῆς ναυαρχίας παρεληλυθυίας Λύσανδρον ἐξέπεμψαν ναύαρχον. ὁ δὲ ἀφικόμενος εἰς Ῥόδον καὶ ναῦς ἐκεῖθεν λαβών, εἰς Κῶ καὶ Μίλητον ἔπλευσεν, ἐκεῖθεν δ' εἰς Ἔφεσον, καὶ ἐκεῖ ἔμεινε ναῦς ἔχων ἑβδομήκοντα μέχρι οὗ Κῦρος εἰς Σάρδεις ἀφίκετο. ἐπεὶ δ' ἧκεν, ἀνέβη πρὸς αὐτὸν σὺν τοῖς ἐκ Λακεδαίμονος πρέσβεσιν. 2 ἐνταῦθα δὴ κατά τε τοῦ Τισσαφέρνους ἔλεγον ἃ πεποιηκὼς εἴη, αὐτοῦ τε Κύρου ἐδέοντο ὡς προθυμοτάτου πρὸς τὸν

---

[1] εὐθύς Π: εὐθέως codd.
[2] ἑαυτοῦ cu: αὐτοῦ rell. Π
[3] τρίτῳ: πέμπτῳ Breitenbach τετάρτῳ Clinton

he oligarchical government, and since only they remained they were tolerated by the
itizens because they had no other leaders any better.

17 Others said that he alone was responsible for their past troubles, and that
he might be the sole cause for the disasters that threatened the city in the future.

18 Alkibiades anchored near the shore, but did not disembark immediately, as
he feared his enemies. Instead he stood on deck and looked to see if his friends were
present. 19 When he saw Euryptolemos the son of Peisianax, his cousin, and his
other relatives and with them his friends, then he disembarked and went up to the
city with his friends prepared to prevent any attempted arrest. 20 In the Council
and the Assembly he defended himself, saying that he had committed no impiety,
that he had been treated unjustly and other similar things. No one spoke in
opposition since the Assembly would not have permitted it. He was chosen
commander-in-chief, in the belief that he could recover the city's previous power.
Although the Athenians had previously been making the procession of the Mysteries
by sea because of the war, he conducted it by land, leading out all the soldiers.

21 Then he enlisted an army of 1500 hoplites, 150 horsemen, and one hundred
ships. In the third month after his return he set out for Andros, which had revolted
from Athens; with him were sent Aristokrates and Adeimantos the son of
Leukolophides, who had been chosen as generals for fighting on land. 22
Alkibiades disembarked the army at Gaurion in Andrian territory. They routed the
Andrians who came out to repulse the attack and shut them in the city, killing some
but not many, along with the Lakonians who were there. 23 Alkibiades erected a
trophy and, after remaining there a few days, sailed to Samos, from which base he
carried on the war.

5

1 Not long before these events the Lakedaimonians had sent out Lysandros as
admiral, since Kratesippidas' admiralship had expired. When he arrived at Rhodes he
took the ships there to Kos and Miletos, and sailed from there to Ephesos, where he
remained with seventy ships until Kyros reached Sardis. When Kyros arrived,
Lysandros went inland to visit him with the Lakedaimonian ambassadors. 2 Then
they accused Tissaphernes for what he had done, and they asked Kyros himself to be

πόλεμον γενέσθαι. 3 Κῦρος δὲ τόν τε πατέρα ἔφη ταῦτα ἐπεσταλκέναι καὶ αὐτὸς οὐκ ἄλλ' ἐγνωκέναι, ἀλλὰ πάντα ποιήσειν· ἔχων δὲ ἥκειν τάλαντα πεντακόσια· ἐὰν δὲ ταῦτα ἐπιλίπῃ[1], τοῖς ἰδίοις χρήσεσθαι ἔφη, ἃ ὁ πατὴρ αὐτῷ ἔδωκεν· ἐὰν δὲ καὶ ταῦτα, καὶ τὸν θρόνον κατακόψειν ἐφ' οὗ ἐκάθητο, ὄντα ἀργυροῦν καὶ χρυσοῦν. 4 οἱ δὲ ταῦτά τε[2] ἐπῄνουν καὶ ἐκέλευον αὐτὸν τάξαι τῷ ναύτῃ δραχμὴν Ἀττικήν, διδάσκοντες ὅτι, ἂν οὗτος ὁ μισθὸς γένηται, οἱ τῶν Ἀθηναίων ναῦται ἀπολείψουσι τὰς ναῦς, καὶ μείω χρήματα ἀναλώσει. 5 ὁ δὲ καλῶς μὲν ἔφη αὐτοὺς λέγειν, οὐ δυνατὸν δ' εἶναι παρ' ἃ βασιλεὺς ἐπέστειλεν[3] αὐτῷ ἄλλα ποιεῖν. εἶναι δὲ καὶ τὰς συνθήκας οὕτως ἐχούσας, τριάκοντα μνᾶς ἑκάστῃ νηὶ τοῦ μηνὸς διδόναι, ὁπόσας ἂν βούλωνται τρέφειν Λακεδαιμόνιοι. 6 ὁ δὲ Λύσανδρος τότε μὲν ἐσιώπησε· μετὰ δὲ τὸ δεῖπνον, ἐπεὶ αὐτῷ προπιὼν ὁ Κῦρος ἤρετο τί ἂν μάλιστα χαρίζοιτο ποιῶν, εἶπεν ὅτι Εἰ πρὸς τὸν μισθὸν ἑκάστῳ ναύτῃ ὀβολὸν προσθείης. 7 ἐκ δὲ τούτου τέτταρες ὀβολοὶ ἦν ὁ μισθός, πρότερον δὲ τριώβολον. καὶ τόν τε προοφειλόμενον[4] ἀπέδωκε καὶ ἔτι μηνὸς προέδωκεν, ὥστε τὸ στράτευμα πολὺ προθυμότερον εἶναι.

8 Οἱ δὲ Ἀθηναῖοι ἀκούοντες ταῦτα ἀθύμως μὲν εἶχον, ἔπεμπον δὲ πρὸς τὸν Κῦρον πρέσβεις διὰ Τισσαφέρνους. 9 ὁ δὲ οὐ προσεδέχετο, δεομένου Τισσαφέρνους καὶ λέγοντος, ἅπερ αὐτὸς ἐποίει πεισθεὶς ὑπ' Ἀλκιβιάδου, σκοπεῖν ὅπως τῶν Ἑλλήνων μηδὲ οἵτινες ἰσχυροὶ ὦσιν, ἀλλὰ πάντες ἀσθενεῖς, αὐτοὶ ἐν αὐτοῖς στασιάζοντες.

10 καὶ ὁ μὲν Λύσανδρος, ἐπεὶ αὐτῷ τὸ ναυτικὸν συνετέτακτο, ἀνελκύσας τὰς ἐν τῇ Ἐφέσῳ οὔσας ναῦς ἐνενήκοντα ἡσυχίαν ἦγεν, ἐπισκευάζων καὶ ἀναψύχων αὐτάς[5].

11 Ἀλκιβιάδης δὲ ἀκούσας Θρασύβουλον ἔξω Ἑλλησπόντου ἥκοντα τειχίζειν[6] Φώκαιαν διέπλευσε πρὸς αὐτόν, καταλιπὼν ἐπὶ ταῖς ναυσὶν Ἀντίοχον τὸν αὐτοῦ κυβερνήτην, ἐπιστείλας μὴ ἐπιπλεῖν ἐπὶ τὰς Λυσάνδρου ναῦς. 12 ὁ δὲ Ἀντίοχος τῇ τε αὐτοῦ νηὶ καὶ ἄλλῃ ἐκ Νοτίου εἰς τὸν λιμένα τῶν Ἐφεσίων εἰσπλεύσας παρ' αὐτὰς τὰς πρῴρας τῶν Λυσάνδρου νεῶν παρέπλει. 13 ὁ δὲ Λύσανδρος τὸ μὲν πρῶτον ὀλίγας τῶν νεῶν καθελκύσας ἐδίωκεν αὐτόν, ἐπεὶ δὲ οἱ Ἀθηναῖοι τῷ Ἀντιόχῳ ἐβοήθουν πλείοσι ναυσί, τότε δὴ καὶ πάσας συντάξας ἐπέπλει. μετὰ δὲ ταῦτα καὶ οἱ Ἀθηναῖοι ἐκ τοῦ Νοτίου καθελκύσαντες τὰς λοιπὰς τριήρεις ἀνήχθησαν, ὡς

---

[1] ἐπιλίπῃ Π: ἐκλίπῃ codd.
[2] ταῦτά τε Π: ταῦτ' codd.
[3] ἐπέστειλεν Loewenklau: ἀπέστειλεν codd. Π
[4] προοφειλόμενον Loewenklau: προσοφειλόμενον codd.
[5] post αὐτάς lacunam statuit Delebecque
[6] τειχίζειν: ἀποτειχίζειν Holwerda περιτειχίζειν Krüger

as enthusiastic as possible toward the war. **3** Kyros said that his father had given him these very instructions, and that he himself had no other intentions, but would do everything he had been ordered. He had come with five hundred talents, and if these did not suffice, he said that he would use his own money which his father had given him, and if this too was not enough, he would coin into money the silver and gold throne on which he sat. **4** The ambassadors applauded these promises and urged him to fix the pay at one Attic drachma for each sailor, explaining that if this were the wage the sailors of the Athenians would desert, and he would spend less money. **5** He said this was a good suggestion, but that it was impossible for him to act contrary to the King's orders. Also the agreement said that the King would provide thirty mnai for each ship each month, for however many ships the Lakedaimonians wanted to maintain.

6 At that time Lysandros kept quiet, but after dinner, when Kyros toasted him and asked what favor he could do that would please Lysandros most, Lysandros said, "If you would add an obol to each sailor's wage." **7** Thereafter the wage was four obols, having previously been three. Kyros paid what was owed and a month's wage in advance, with the result that the army became much more enthusiastic.

8 When the Athenians heard what had happened they were depressed, and they sent ambassadors to Kyros through Tissaphernes. **9** Kyros, however, refused to see them, although Tissaphernes asked him to do so and advised him to see to it (as he himself was doing, on Alkibiades' advice) that none of the Greeks whatever be strong, but all weak, fighting among themselves.

10 After Lysandros had reorganized the fleet, he dragged ashore the ninety ships at Ephesos and remained quiet while he repaired and dried them out.

11 Leaving his pilot Antiochos in charge of the ships with orders not to attack Lysandros' ships, Alkibiades sailed across to Thrasyboulos, who he heard had come out of the Hellespont to fortify Phokaia. **12** But having sailed from Notion into the harbor of Ephesos with his own ship and one other, Antiochos sailed past the very prows of Lysandros' ships. **13** At first Lysandros launched a few ships and pursued him, but when the Athenians came to Antiochos' aid with more ships, then Lysandros arranged all his ships in formation and attacked. Then the Athenians also launched their remaining triremes and put to sea one by one, as each got clear of the

ἕκαστος ἤνοιξεν¹. **14** ἐκ τούτου δ' ἐναυμάχησαν οἱ μὲν ἐν τάξει, οἱ δὲ Ἀθηναῖοι διεσπαρμέναις ταῖς ναυσί, μέχρι οὗ ἔφυγον ἀπολέσαντες πεντεκαίδεκα τριήρεις. τῶν δὲ ἀνδρῶν οἱ μὲν πλεῖστοι ἐξέφυγον, οἱ δ' ἐζωγρήθησαν. Λύσανδρος δὲ τάς τε ναῦς ἀναλαβὼν καὶ τροπαῖον στήσας ἐπὶ τοῦ Νοτίου διέπλευσεν εἰς Ἔφεσον, οἱ δ' Ἀθηναῖοι εἰς Σάμον.

15 Μετὰ δὲ ταῦτα Ἀλκιβιάδης ἐλθὼν εἰς Σάμον ἀνήχθη ταῖς ναυσὶν ἁπάσαις ἐπὶ τὸν λιμένα τῶν Ἐφεσίων, καὶ πρὸ τοῦ στόματος παρέταξεν, εἴ τις βούλοιτο ναυμαχεῖν. ἐπειδὴ δὲ Λύσανδρος οὐκ ἀντανήγαγε διὰ τὸ πολλαῖς ναυσὶν ἐλαττοῦσθαι, ἀπέπλευσεν εἰς Σάμον. Λακεδαιμόνιοι δὲ ὀλίγῳ ὕστερον αἱροῦσι Δελφίνιον καὶ Ἠιόνα².

16 Οἱ δὲ ἐν οἴκῳ Ἀθηναῖοι, ἐπειδὴ ἠγγέλθη ἡ ναυμαχία, χαλεπῶς εἶχον τῷ Ἀλκιβιάδῃ, οἰόμενοι δι' ἀμέλειάν τε καὶ ἀκράτειαν ἀπολωλεκέναι τὰς ναῦς, καὶ στρατηγοὺς εἵλοντο ἄλλους δέκα, Κόνωνα, Διομέδοντα, Λέοντα, Περικλέα, Ἐρασινίδην, Ἀριστοκράτην, Ἀρχέστρατον, Πρωτόμαχον, Θράσυλλον, Ἀριστογένην. **17** Ἀλκιβιάδης μὲν οὖν πονηρῶς καὶ ἐν τῇ στρατιᾷ φερόμενος, λαβὼν τριήρη μίαν ἀπέπλευσεν εἰς Χερρόνησον εἰς τὰ ἑαυτοῦ τείχη.

18 Μετὰ δὲ ταῦτα Κόνων ἐκ τῆς Ἄνδρου σὺν αἷς εἶχε ναυσὶν εἴκοσι ψηφισαμένων Ἀθηναίων εἰς Σάμον ἔπλευσεν ἐπὶ τὸ ναυτικόν. ἀντὶ δὲ Κόνωνος εἰς Ἄνδρον ἔπεμψαν Φανοσθένην, τέτταρας ναῦς ἔχοντα. **19** οὗτος περιτυχὼν δυοῖν τριήροιν Θουρίαιν ἔλαβεν αὐτοῖς ἀνδράσι· καὶ τοὺς μὲν αἰχμαλώτους ἅπαντας ἔδησαν Ἀθηναῖοι, τὸν δὲ ἄρχοντα αὐτῶν Δωριέα, ὄντα μὲν Ῥόδιον, πάλαι δὲ φυγάδα ἐξ Ἀθηνῶν καὶ Ῥόδου ὑπὸ Ἀθηναίων κατεψηφισμένων αὐτοῦ θάνατον καὶ τῶν ἐκείνου συγγενῶν, πολιτεύοντα παρ' αὐτοῖς, ἐλεήσαντες ἀφεῖσαν οὐδὲ χρήματα πραξάμενοι. **20** Κόνων δ' ἐπεὶ εἰς τὴν Σάμον ἀφίκετο καὶ τὸ ναυτικὸν κατέλαβεν ἀθύμως ἔχον, συμπληρώσας τριήρεις ἑβδομήκοντα ἀντὶ τῶν προτέρων, οὐσῶν πλέον ἢ ἑκατόν, καὶ ταύταις ἀναγαγόμενος³ μετὰ τῶν ἄλλων στρατηγῶν, ἄλλοτε ἄλλη ἀποβαίνων τῆς τῶν πολεμίων χώρας ἐλῄζετο.

21 [Καὶ ὁ ἐνιαυτὸς ἔληγεν, ἐν ᾧ Καρχηδόνιοι εἰς Σικελίαν στρατεύσαντες εἴκοσι καὶ ἑκατὸν τριήρεσι καὶ πεζῆς στρατιᾶς δώδεκα μυριάσιν εἷλον Ἀκράγαντα λιμῷ, μάχῃ μὲν ἡττηθέντες, προσκαθεζόμενοι δὲ ἑπτὰ μῆνας.]⁴

---

¹ ἤνοιξεν: ἤνυσεν Riemann ἤνυτεν Kondos
² Ἠιόνα: Τέων Schneider
³ ἀναγαγόμενος Hertlein: ἀναγόμενος codd.
⁴ Καὶ . . . μῆνας del. Unger

land. **14** After that they fought a naval battle, the Peloponnesians in formation, the Athenians with their ships scattered, until they fled after losing fifteen triremes. Most of the men escaped, but some were captured. After taking over the ships and erecting a trophy on Notion, Lysandros sailed across to Ephesos, while the Athenians returned to Samos.

15 After this Alkibiades came to Samos and set out with all the ships for the harbor of Ephesos. He drew them up in formation in front of the harbor mouth as a challenge to fight a naval battle. But when Lysandros did not put out against them because he was outnumbered by many ships, Alkibiades sailed back to Samos. A little later the Lakedaimonians took Delphinion and Eion.

16 When the news about the battle arrived, the Athenians at home were angry with Alkibiades, thinking that he had lost the ships through carelessness and dissolute behavior. They chose ten other generals: Konon, Diomedon, Leon, Perikles, Erasinides, Aristokrates, Archestratos, Protomachos, Thrasyllos and Aristogenes. **17** So Alkibiades, who was unpopular even in the army, took one trireme and sailed away to his forts in the Cherronesos.

18 Then Konon, with the twenty ships he had, sailed from Andros to Samos to take over the command of the fleet, in accordance with the Athenians' decree. To replace Konon at Andros they sent Phanosthenes with four ships. **19** He met two Thourian triremes and captured them with their crews. The Athenians bound all the prisoners, but they had pity on their commander Dorieus, a Thourian citizen who had been born Rhodian but had long ago been exiled from Athens and Rhodes and condemned to death, along with his relatives, by the Athenians. They released him without ransom. **20** When Konon arrived at Samos and took over the discouraged fleet, he put crews aboard seventy triremes (previously there had been more than one hundred) and with these he set out with the other generals. He disembarked at various places and plundered the enemy's territory.

21 [So the year ended, in which the Carthaginians invaded Sicily with 120 triremes and 120,000 infantry. They were defeated in a battle, but starved Akragas into submission after besieging it for seven months.]

6

1 Τῷ δ' ἐπιόντι ἔτει, ᾧ ἥ τε σελήνη ἐξέλιπεν ἑσπέρας καὶ ὁ παλαιὸς τῆς Ἀθηνᾶς νεὼς ἐν Ἀθήναις ἐνεπρήσθη[1], [Πιτύα[2] μὲν ἐφορεύοντος, ἄρχοντος δὲ Καλλίου Ἀθήνησιν,][3] οἱ Λακεδαιμόνιοι τῷ Λυσάνδρῳ παρεληλυθότος ἤδη τοῦ χρόνου [καὶ τῷ πολέμῳ τεττάρων καὶ εἴκοσιν ἐτῶν][4] ἔπεμψαν ἐπὶ τὰς ναῦς Καλλικρατίδαν. 2 ὅτε δὲ παρεδίδου ὁ Λύσανδρος τὰς ναῦς, ἔλεγε τῷ Καλλικρατίδᾳ ὅτι θαλαττοκράτωρ τε παραδιδοίη καὶ ναυμαχίᾳ νενικηκώς. ὁ δὲ αὐτὸν ἐκέλευσεν ἐξ Ἐφέσου ἐν ἀριστερᾷ Σάμου παραπλεύσαντα, οὗ ἦσαν αἱ τῶν Ἀθηναίων νῆες, ἐν Μιλήτῳ παραδοῦναι τὰς ναῦς, καὶ ὁμολογήσειν θαλαττοκρατεῖν. 3 οὐ φαμένου δὲ τοῦ Λυσάνδρου πολυπραγμονεῖν ἄλλου ἄρχοντος, αὐτὸς ὁ Καλλικρατίδας πρὸς αἷς παρὰ Λυσάνδρου ἔλαβε ναυσὶ προσεπλήρωσεν ἐκ Χίου καὶ Ῥόδου καὶ ἄλλοθεν ἀπὸ τῶν συμμάχων πεντήκοντα ναῦς. ταύτας δὲ πάσας ἀθροίσας, οὔσας τετταράκοντα καὶ ἑκατόν, παρεσκευάζετο ὡς ἀπαντησόμενος τοῖς πολεμίοις.

4 Καταμαθὼν δ' ὑπὸ τῶν Λυσάνδρου φίλων καταστασιαζόμενος, οὐ μόνον ἀπροθύμως ὑπηρετούντων, ἀλλὰ καὶ διαθροούντων ἐν ταῖς πόλεσιν ὅτι Λακεδαιμόνιοι μέγιστα παραπίπτοιεν ἐν τῷ διαλλάττειν τοὺς ναυάρχους, πολλάκις †ἀνεπιτηδείων γιγνομένων καὶ ἄρτι συνιέντων τὰ ναυτικὰ καὶ ἀνθρώποις ὡς χρηστέον οὐ γιγνωσκόντων ἀπείρους θαλάττης πέμποντες καὶ ἀγνῶτας τοῖς ἐκεῖ, κινδυνεύοιέν τι παθεῖν διὰ τοῦτο†[5], ἐκ τούτου δὲ ὁ Καλλικρατίδας συγκαλέσας τοὺς Λακεδαιμονίων ἐκεῖ παρόντας ἔλεγεν αὐτοῖς τοιάδε.

5 Ἐμοὶ ἀρκεῖ οἴκοι μένειν, καὶ εἴτε Λύσανδρος εἴτε ἄλλος τις ἐμπειρότερος περὶ τὰ ναυτικὰ βούλεται εἶναι, οὐ κωλύω τὰ κατ' ἐμέ· ἐγὼ δ' ὑπὸ τῆς πόλεως ἐπὶ τὰς ναῦς πεμφθεὶς οὐκ ἔχω τί ἄλλο ποιῶ ἢ τὰ κελευόμενα ὡς ἂν δύνωμαι κράτιστα. ὑμεῖς δὲ πρὸς ἃ ἐγώ τε φιλοτιμοῦμαι καὶ ἡ πόλις ἡμῶν αἰτιάζεται (ἴστε γὰρ αὐτὰ ὥσπερ καὶ ἐγώ), συμβουλεύετε[6] τὰ ἄριστα ὑμῖν δοκοῦντα εἶναι περὶ τοῦ ἐμὲ ἐνθάδε μένειν ἢ

---

[1] ᾧ . . . ἐνεπρήσθη del. Keller
[2] Πιτύα Dindorf ex II.3.10: Πίτιος codd.
[3] Πιτύα . . . Ἀθήνησιν del. Dindorf
[4] καὶ . . . ἐτῶν del. Dindorf
[5] Locus totus ἀνεπιτηδείων . . . ἀπείρους varie tractatus est ab edd.: ἀντ ἐπιτηδείων Jacobs ἀντ' ἐπιτηδείων γενομένων καὶ ἀκριβούντων τὰ ναυτικὰ καὶ ἀνθρώποις ὡς χρηστέον εὖ γιγνωσκόντων ἀπείρους Cobet καὶ ante ἀπείρους add. Hatzfeld ἀπείρους . . . τοῦτο del. Keller
[6] συμβουλεύετε manus recens in margine M: συμβουλεύω codd.

6

1 In the next year, in which there was an eclipse of the moon one evening and the old temple of Athena in Athens was burned, [when Pityas was ephor, and Kallias was archon at Athens, and the war had lasted twenty-four years,] the Lakedaimonians sent Kallikratidas to take command of the ships since Lysandros' term of office had expired. **2** When Lysandros handed over the ships, he said to Kallikratidas that he handed them over as master of the sea and victor in a naval battle. Kallikratidas told him to hand over the ships in Miletos after sailing along the coast from Ephesos, on the left of Samos where the Athenian ships were, and he would agree that Lysandros controlled the sea. **3** When Lysandros replied that he was not in the habit of meddling when another held the command, Kallikratidas himself manned--in addition to the ships he received from Lysandros--fifty ships from Chios and Rhodes and other allies. Gathering them together, 140 in all, he prepared to meet the enemy.

4 But when he learned that Lysandros' friends were conspiring against him-- not only carrying out his orders without enthusiasm, but also spreading in the cities their view that the Lakedaimonians made a serious mistake by changing the admirals; since often the admirals were unqualified, inexperienced in naval affairs, and ignorant of how to handle human beings, by sending men without experience of the sea and unknown to the people there, the Lakedaimonians risked a defeat--then Kallikratidas called together the Lakedaimonians present and spoke to them as follows:

5 "I am content to stay at home, and if Lysandros or anyone else claims to be more experienced in naval matters, I will not hinder him on my own account. But since I have been sent by the city to command the ships I cannot do anything other than obey my orders to the best of my ability. You, however, in regard to the objects of my ambition and the criticisms made against our city, for you know these as well as I, advise me whether it seems best to you for me to remain here or to sail

οἴκαδε ἀποπλεῖν ἐροῦντα τὰ καθεστῶτα ἐνθάδε.

6 Οὐδενὸς δὲ τολμήσαντος ἄλλο τι εἰπεῖν ἢ τοῖς οἴκοι πείθεσθαι ποιεῖν τε ἐφ' ἃ ἥκει, ἐλθὼν παρὰ Κῦρον ᾔτει μισθὸν τοῖς ναύταις· ὁ δὲ αὐτῷ εἶπε δύο ἡμέρας ἐπισχεῖν. 7 Καλλικρατίδας δὲ ἀχθεσθεὶς τῇ ἀναβολῇ καὶ ταῖς ἐπὶ ταῖς θύραις φοιτήσεσιν ὀργισθεὶς καὶ εἰπὼν ἀθλιωτάτους εἶναι τοὺς Ἕλληνας, ὅτι βαρβάρους κολακεύουσιν ἕνεκα ἀργυρίου, φάσκων τε, ἂν σωθῇ οἴκαδε, κατά γε τὸ αὑτοῦ δυνατὸν διαλλάξειν Ἀθηναίους καὶ Λακεδαιμονίους, ἀπέπλευσεν εἰς Μίλητον· 8 κἀκεῖθεν πέμψας τριήρεις εἰς Λακεδαίμονα ἐπὶ χρήματα, ἐκκλησίαν ἀθροίσας τῶν Μιλησίων τάδε εἶπεν.

Ἐμοὶ μέν, ὦ Μιλήσιοι, ἀνάγκη τοῖς οἴκοι ἄρχουσι πείθεσθαι· ὑμᾶς δὲ ἐγὼ ἀξιῶ προθυμοτάτους εἶναι εἰς τὸν πόλεμον διὰ τὸ οἰκοῦντας ἐν βαρβάροις πλεῖστα κακὰ ἤδη ὑπ' αὐτῶν πεπονθέναι. 9 δεῖ δ' ὑμᾶς ἐξηγεῖσθαι τοῖς ἄλλοις συμμάχοις ὅπως ἂν τάχιστά τε καὶ μάλιστα βλάπτωμεν τοὺς πολεμίους, ἕως ἂν οἱ ἐκ Λακεδαίμονος ἥκωσιν, οὓς ἐγὼ ἔπεμψα χρήματα ἄξοντας, 10 ἐπεὶ τὰ ἐνθάδε ὑπάρχοντα Λύσανδρος Κύρῳ ἀποδοὺς ὡς περιττὰ ὄντα οἴχεται· Κῦρος δὲ ἐλθόντος ἐμοῦ ἐπ' αὐτὸν ἀεὶ ἀνεβάλλετό μοι διαλεχθῆναι, ἐγὼ δ' ἐπὶ τὰς ἐκείνου θύρας φοιτᾶν οὐκ ἐδυνάμην ἐμαυτὸν πεῖσαι. 11 ὑπισχνοῦμαι δ' ὑμῖν ἀντὶ τῶν συμβάντων ἡμῖν ἀγαθῶν ἐν τῷ χρόνῳ ᾧ ἂν ἐκεῖνα προσδεχώμεθα χάριν ἀξίαν ἀποδώσειν. ἀλλὰ σὺν τοῖς θεοῖς δείξωμεν τοῖς βαρβάροις ὅτι καὶ ἄνευ τοῦ ἐκείνους θαυμάζειν δυνάμεθα τοὺς ἐχθροὺς τιμωρεῖσθαι.

12 Ἐπεὶ δὲ ταῦτ' εἶπεν, ἀνιστάμενοι πολλοὶ καὶ μάλιστα οἱ αἰτιαζόμενοι ἐναντιοῦσθαι δεδιότες εἰσηγοῦντο πόρον χρημάτων καὶ αὐτοὶ ἐπαγγελλόμενοι ἰδίᾳ. λαβὼν δὲ ταῦτα ἐκεῖνος καὶ ἐκ Χίου πεντεδραχμίαν ἑκάστῳ τῶν ναυτῶν ἐφοδιασάμενος ἔπλευσε τῆς Λέσβου ἐπὶ Μήθυμναν πολεμίαν οὖσαν.

13 Οὐ βουλομένων δὲ τῶν Μηθυμναίων προσχωρεῖν, ἀλλ' ἐμφρούρων ὄντων Ἀθηναίων καὶ τῶν τὰ πράγματα ἐχόντων ἀττικιζόντων, προσβαλὼν αἱρεῖ τὴν πόλιν κατὰ κράτος. 14 τὰ μὲν οὖν χρήματα πάντα διήρπασαν οἱ στρατιῶται, τὰ δὲ ἀνδράποδα πάντα συνήθροισεν ὁ Καλλικρατίδας εἰς τὴν ἀγοράν, καὶ κελευόντων τῶν συμμάχων ἀποδόσθαι καὶ τοὺς Μηθυμναίους οὐκ ἔφη ἑαυτοῦ γε ἄρχοντος οὐδέν' ἂν[1] Ἑλλήνων εἰς τὸ κείνου δυνατὸν ἀνδραποδισθῆναι. 15 τῇ δ' ὑστεραίᾳ τοὺς μὲν ἐλευθέρους ἀφῆκε, τοὺς δὲ τῶν Ἀθηναίων φρουροὺς καὶ τὰ ἀνδράποδα τὰ δοῦλα πάντα ἀπέδοτο· Κόνωνι δὲ εἶπεν ὅτι παύσει αὐτὸν μοιχῶντα τὴν θάλατταν.

Κατιδὼν δὲ αὐτὸν ἀναγόμενον ἅμα τῇ ἡμέρᾳ, ἐδίωκεν ὑποτεμνόμενος τὸν εἰς Σάμον πλοῦν, ὅπως μὴ ἐκεῖσε φύγοι. 16 Κόνων δ' ἔφευγε ταῖς

---

[1] οὐδέν' ἂν Naber: οὐδένα codd.

home and report the situation here."

6 Since no one dared to say anything other than that he should obey the authorities at home and do what he had come to do, he went to Kyros and asked for pay for the sailors. Kyros told him to wait for two days. **7** Kallikratidas was irritated at the delay and furious at having to attend the court. Saying that the Greeks were in a wretched situation, because they flattered the barbarians for the sake of money, and claiming that if he reached home safely he would do everything he could to reconcile the Athenians and Lakedaimonians, he sailed off to Miletos. **8** From there he sent triremes to Lakedaimon for money, and he called an assembly of the Milesians, at which he spoke as follows:

"I, men of Miletos, must obey the authorities at home. As for you, I think you should be extremely enthusiastic in the war, since you have suffered the greatest harm from the barbarians because you live among them. **9** You must show the other allies how we can do the most damage to the enemy in the shortest time, until the men whom I sent to bring money return from Lakedaimon. **10** Lysandros left after giving the remaining money back to Kyros as if it were a surplus, and Kyros, when I went to see him, always postponed talking with me, and I was unable to persuade myself to attend his court. **11** But I promise you that I will repay you suitably for whatever successes we have during the time in which we await the money. With the gods' help let us show the barbarians that even without fawning on them we can punish the enemy."

12 When he said this, many men, rising one after another in fear, particularly those who were accused of opposing him, proposed a grant of money and offered to make private contributions themselves. After taking this money and securing from Chios five drachmai for each sailor's travel expenses, Kallikratidas sailed against Methymna, a hostile city, in Lesbos.

13 Since the men of Methymna refused to join his side, for there was an Athenian garrison and those who had power favored Athens, he attacked and took the city by force. **14** The soldiers seized all the property, but Kallikratidas gathered all the captives in the agora, and although the allies urged him to sell the men of Methymna also, he said that while he was in command none of the Greeks would be enslaved, so far as it was in his power. **15** On the next day he released the free men, but he sold the troops of the Athenian garrison and all the captured slaves.

To Konon he sent word that he would stop him from fornicating with the sea. When he saw him putting out to sea at dawn, he set out in pursuit, attempting to cut off the route to Samos, so that Konon could not flee there. **16** Konon fled,

ναυσὶν εὖ πλεούσαις διὰ τὸ ἐκ πολλῶν πληρωμάτων εἰς ὀλίγας ἐκλελέχθαι τοὺς ἀρίστους ἐρέτας, καὶ καταφεύγει εἰς Μυτιλήνην τῆς Λέσβου καὶ σὺν αὐτῷ τῶν δέκα στρατηγῶν Λέων καὶ Ἐρασινίδης. Καλλικρατίδας δὲ συνεισέπλευσεν εἰς τὸν λιμένα, διώκων ναυσὶν ἑκατὸν καὶ ἑβδομήκοντα[1]. 17 Κόνων δὲ ὡς ἔφθη ὑπὸ τῶν πολιτῶν[2] κατακωλυθείς, ἠναγκάσθη ναυμαχῆσαι πρὸς τῷ λιμένι, καὶ ἀπώλεσε ναῦς τριάκοντα· οἱ δὲ ἄνδρες εἰς τὴν γῆν ἀπέφυγον· τὰς δὲ λοιπὰς τῶν νεῶν, τετταράκοντα οὔσας, ὑπὸ τῷ τείχει ἀνείλκυσε. 18 Καλλικρατίδας δὲ ἐν τῷ λιμένι ὁρμισάμενος ἐπολιόρκει ἐνταῦθα, τὸν ἔκπλουν ἔχων. καὶ κατὰ γῆν μεταπεμψάμενος τοὺς Μηθυμναίους πανδημεὶ καὶ ἐκ τῆς Χίου τὸ στράτευμα διεβίβασε· χρήματά τε παρὰ Κύρου αὐτῷ ἦλθεν.

19 Ὁ δὲ Κόνων ἐπεὶ ἐπολιορκεῖτο καὶ κατὰ γῆν καὶ κατὰ θάλατταν, καὶ σίτων οὐδαμόθεν ἦν εὐπορῆσαι, οἱ δὲ ἄνθρωποι πολλοὶ ἐν τῇ πόλει ἦσαν καὶ οἱ Ἀθηναῖοι οὐκ ἐβοήθουν διὰ τὸ μὴ πυνθάνεσθαι ταῦτα, καθελκύσας τῶν νεῶν τὰς ἄριστα πλεούσας δύο ἐπλήρωσε πρὸ ἡμέρας, ἐξ ἁπασῶν τῶν νεῶν τοὺς ἀρίστους ἐρέτας ἐκλέξας καὶ τοὺς ἐπιβάτας εἰς κοίλην ναῦν μεταβιβάσας καὶ τὰ παραρύματα παραβαλών[3]. 20 τὴν μὲν οὖν ἡμέραν οὕτως ἀνεῖχον, εἰς δὲ τὴν ἑσπέραν, ἐπεὶ σκότος εἴη, ἐξεβίβαζεν, ὡς μὴ καταδήλους εἶναι τοῖς πολεμίοις ταῦτα ποιοῦντας. πέμπτῃ δὲ ἡμέρᾳ εἰσθέμενοι σῖτα μέτρια, ἐπειδὴ ἤδη μέσον ἡμέρας ἦν καὶ οἱ ἐφορμοῦντες ὀλιγώρως εἶχον καὶ ἔνιοι ἀνεπαύοντο, ἐξέπλευσαν ἔξω τοῦ λιμένος, καὶ ἡ μὲν ἐπὶ Ἑλλησπόντου ὥρμησεν, ἡ δὲ εἰς τὸ πέλαγος. 21 τῶν δ᾽ ἐφορμούντων ὡς ἕκαστοι ἤνοιγον[4] τάς τε ἀγκύρας ἀποκόπτοντες καὶ ἐγειρόμενοι ἐβοήθουν τεταραγμένοι, τυχόντες ἐν τῇ γῇ ἀριστοποιούμενοι· εἰσβάντες δὲ ἐδίωκον τὴν εἰς τὸ πέλαγος ἀφορμήσασαν[5], καὶ ἅμα τῷ ἡλίῳ δύνοντι κατέλαβον, καὶ κρατήσαντες μάχῃ, ἀναδησάμενοι ἀπῆγον εἰς τὸ στρατόπεδον αὐτοῖς ἀνδράσιν. 22 ἡ δ᾽ ἐπὶ τοῦ Ἑλλησπόντου φυγοῦσα ναῦς διέφυγε, καὶ ἀφικομένη εἰς τὰς Ἀθήνας ἐξαγγέλλει τὴν πολιορκίαν.

Διομέδων δὲ βοηθῶν Κόνωνι πολιορκουμένῳ δώδεκα ναυσὶν ὡρμίσατο εἰς τὸν εὔριπον τὸν τῶν Μυτιληναίων. 23 ὁ δὲ Καλλικρατίδας ἐπιπλεύσας αὐτῷ ἐξαίφνης δέκα μὲν τῶν νεῶν ἔλαβε, Διομέδων δ᾽ ἔφυγε τῇ τε αὐτοῦ καὶ ἄλλῃ.

---

[1] ἑβδομήκοντα: τετταράκοντα Cobet τετταράκοντα ναῦς ante ἑβδομήκοντα add. Hatzfeld
[2] πολιτῶν: πολεμίων Portus κατὰ τον εὔριπον πλοῦ post πολιτῶν add. Delebecque
[3] παραβαλών Stephanus: παραλαβών codd.
[4] ἤνοιγον: ἤνυτον Riemann cf. I.5.13
[5] ἀφορμήσασαν: Dindorf ἐφορμήσασαν codd.

with his ships sailing fast because he had selected the best rowers from many crews and put them into a few ships, and he took refuge in Mytilene in Lesbos. Of the ten generals Leon and Erasinides were with him. Kallikratidas sailed along with the Athenians into the harbor, pursuing with 170 ships. **17** As Konon arrived first he was prevented by the citizens . . . and he was forced to fight near the harbor, and lost thirty ships; the men escaped to the land. He dragged the remaining forty ships up under the wall. **18** Kallikratidas anchored in the harbor and besieged the city, controlling the entrance. As for the land, he summoned the full forces of the Methymnians and even brought over the army from Chios, and money came to him from Kyros.

19 Konon now found himself blockaded by land and sea; he had no source of grain, many men were in the city, and the Athenians were doing nothing to help since they knew nothing of what had happened. He therefore launched his two fastest ships and manned them before dawn, selecting the best rowers from all the ships. He sent the marines to the hold of the ship, and put up the side-screens. **20** They continued in this position throughout the day, and he made them disembark in the evening when it was dark, so that the enemy would not see what they were doing. On the fifth day they loaded a moderate amount of food, and when it was midday and the blockaders were off their guard and some were asleep, they sailed out of the harbor, and one ship set out for the Hellespont, the other into the open sea. **21** The blockaders, cutting their anchors and rousing themselves from sleep, responded in disorder as each ship got clear of land, for they had been eating breakfast. When they were aboard, they chased the ship that set out into the open sea and overtook it at sunset. After winning a fight they took it in tow and brought it back to the camp, with its crew. **22** But the ship fleeing for the Hellespont escaped, reached Athens and reported the news about the blockade.

Diomedon came to help Konon with twelve ships and anchored at the straits of Mytilene. **23** Kallikratidas attacked him suddenly and captured ten ships, while Diomedon fled with his own and one other.

24 Οἱ δὲ Ἀθηναῖοι τὰ γεγενημένα καὶ τὴν πολιορκίαν ἐπεὶ ἤκουσαν, ἐψηφίσαντο βοηθεῖν ναυσὶν ἑκατὸν καὶ δέκα, εἰσβιβάζοντες τοὺς ἐν τῇ ἡλικίᾳ ὄντας ἅπαντας καὶ δούλους καὶ ἐλευθέρους· καὶ πληρώσαντες τὰς[1] δέκα καὶ ἑκάτον ἐν τριάκοντα ἡμέραις ἀπῆραν. εἰσέβησαν δὲ καὶ τῶν ἱππέων πολλοί. 25 μετὰ ταῦτα ἀνήχθησαν εἰς Σάμον, κἀκεῖθεν Σαμίας ναῦς ἔλαβον δέκα· ἤθροισαν δὲ καὶ ἄλλας πλείους ἢ τριάκοντα παρὰ τῶν ἄλλων συμμάχων, εἰσβαίνειν ἀναγκάσαντες ἅπαντας, ὁμοίως δὲ καὶ εἴ τινες αὐτοῖς ἔτυχον ἔξω οὖσαι. ἐγένοντο δὲ αἱ πᾶσαι πλείους ἢ πεντήκοντα καὶ ἑκατόν.

26 Ὁ δὲ Καλλικρατίδας ἀκούων τὴν βοήθειαν ἤδη ἐν Σάμῳ οὖσαν, αὐτοῦ μὲν κατέλιπε πεντήκοντα ναῦς καὶ ἄρχοντα Ἐτεόνικον, ταῖς δὲ εἴκοσι καὶ ἑκατὸν ἀναχθεὶς ἐδειπνοποιεῖτο τῆς Λέσβου ἐπὶ τῇ Μαλέᾳ ἄκρᾳ [ἀντίον τῆς Μυτιλήνης][2]. 27 τῇ δ' αὐτῇ ἡμέρᾳ ἔτυχον καὶ οἱ Ἀθηναῖοι δειπνοποιούμενοι ἐν ταῖς Ἀργινούσαις· αὗται δ' εἰσὶν [ἀντίον τῆς Λέσβου ἐπὶ τῇ Μαλέᾳ ἄκρᾳ][3] ἀντίον τῆς Μυτιλήνης. 28 τῆς δὲ νυκτὸς ἰδὼν τὰ πυρά, καί τινων αὐτῷ ἐξαγγειλάντων ὅτι οἱ Ἀθηναῖοι εἶεν, ἀνήγετο περὶ μέσας νύκτας, ὡς ἐξαπιναίως προσπέσοι· ὕδωρ δ' ἐπιγενόμενον πολὺ καὶ βρονταὶ διεκώλυσαν τὴν ἀναγωγήν. ἐπεὶ δὲ ἀνέσχεν, ἅμα τῇ ἡμέρᾳ ἔπλει ἐπὶ τὰς Ἀργινούσας.

29 Οἱ δ' Ἀθηναῖοι ἀντανήγοντο εἰς τὸ πέλαγος τῷ εὐωνύμῳ, παρατεταγμένοι ὧδε. Ἀριστοκράτης μὲν τὸ εὐώνυμον ἔχων ἡγεῖτο πεντεκαίδεκα ναυσί, μετὰ δὲ ταῦτα Διομέδων ἑτέραις πεντεκαίδεκα· ἐπετέτακτο δὲ Ἀριστοκράτει μὲν Περικλῆς, Διομέδοντι δὲ Ἐρασινίδης· παρὰ δὲ Διομέδοντα οἱ Σάμιοι δέκα ναυσὶν ἐπὶ μιᾶς τεταγμένοι· ἐστρατήγει δὲ αὐτῶν Σάμιος ὀνόματι Ἱππεύς· ἐχόμεναι δ' (αἱ)[4] τῶν ταξιάρχων δέκα, καὶ αὐταὶ ἐπὶ μιᾶς· ἐπὶ δὲ ταύταις αἱ τῶν ναυάρχων τρεῖς, καὶ εἴ τινες ἄλλαι ἦσαν συμμαχίδες. 30 τὸ δὲ δεξιὸν κέρας Πρωτόμαχος εἶχε πεντεκαίδεκα ναυσί· παρὰ δ' αὐτὸν Θράσυλλος ἑτέραις πεντεκαίδεκα· ἐπετέτακτο δὲ Πρωτομάχῳ μὲν Λυσίας, ἔχων τὰς ἴσας ναῦς, Θρασύλλῳ δὲ Ἀριστογένης. 31 οὕτω δ' ἐτάχθησαν, ἵνα μὴ διέκπλουν διδοῖεν· χεῖρον γὰρ ἔπλεον. αἱ δὲ τῶν Λακεδαιμονίων ἀντιτεταγμέναι ἦσαν ἅπασαι ἐπὶ μιᾶς ὡς πρὸς διέκπλουν καὶ περίπλουν παρεσκευασμέναι, διὰ τὸ βέλτιον πλεῖν. 32 εἶχε δὲ τὸ δεξιὸν κέρας Καλλικρατίδας. Ἕρμων δὲ Μεγαρεὺς ὁ τῷ Καλλικρατίδᾳ κυβερνῶν εἶπε πρὸς αὐτὸν ὅτι εἴη καλῶς ἔχον ἀποπλεῦσαι· αἱ γὰρ τριήρεις

---

[1] τὰς a: om. rell.
[2] ἀντίον τῆς Μυτιλήνης del. Krüger
[3] ἀντίον τῆς Λέσβου ἐπὶ τῇ Μαλέᾳ ἄκρᾳ del. Krüger ἐπὶ . . . Μυτιλήνης del. Gomme
[4] αἱ add. Stephanus

24 When the Athenians heard about what had happened and about the blockade, they voted to send a relief force of 110 ships, embarking everyone of military age, both slave and free. After manning the 110 ships in thirty days they sailed away. Many horsemen also embarked. **25** After this they sailed to Samos and from there added ten Samian ships to the fleet; they also collected more than thirty from the other allies, compelling everyone to embark, and whatever ships they happened to have abroad. They amounted in all to more than 150.

26 When Kallikratidas heard that the relief force was already in Samos, he left fifty ships at Mytilene under the command of Eteonikos and set out with 120. He ate the evening meal on Lesbos at Cape Malea [opposite Mytilene]. **27** On the same day the Athenians were eating at the Arginousai; these are [opposite Lesbos at Cape Malea] opposite Mytilene. **28** During the night he saw the fires, and when some men informed him that it was the Athenians, he attempted to put to sea around midnight in order to attack unexpectedly. But heavy rain and thunder prevented him from setting out. When they stopped, he sailed at dawn against the Arginousai.

29 The Athenians put out to the open sea with their left, arranged as follows. Aristokrates commanded the left with fifteen ships, and next to him was Diomedon with fifteen others; Perikles was stationed behind Aristokrates and Erasinides behind Diomedon. Next to Diomedon were the Samians with ten ships formed in a single line; a Samian by the name of Hippeus commanded them. Then came the ten of the division commanders, also in a single line. Behind these were the three of the admirals and whatever other allied ships were present. **30** Protomachos commanded the right wing with fifteen ships, and next to him was Thrasyllos with fifteen others. Lysias was stationed behind Protomachos with an equal number of ships, and Aristogenes behind Thrasyllos. **31** They were arranged in this way in order not to give the enemy a chance of breaking through their line, for the Athenian ships were slower. The opposing ships of the Lakedaimonians were all drawn up in a single line in preparation for breaking through and sailing round the enemy line, since the Lakedaimonian ships were quicker. Kallikratidas commanded the right wing. **32** Hermon the Megarian, Kallikratidas' pilot, said to him that it would be a good idea to sail away since the Athenian triremes were much more numerous. But

τῶν Ἀθηναίων πολλῷ πλείους ἦσαν. Καλλικρατίδας δὲ εἶπεν ὅτι ἡ Σπάρτη οὐδὲν μὴ¹ κάκιον οἰκεῖται² αὐτοῦ ἀποθανόντος, φεύγειν δὲ αἰσχρὸν ἔφη εἶναι.

33 Μετὰ δὲ ταῦτα ἐναυμάχησαν χρόνον πολύν, πρῶτον μὲν ἀθρόαι, ἔπειτα δὲ διεσκεδασμέναι. ἐπεὶ δὲ Καλλικρατίδας τε ἐμβαλούσης τῆς νεὼς ἀποπεσὼν εἰς τὴν θάλατταν ἠφανίσθη Πρωτόμαχός τε καὶ οἱ μετ' αὐτοῦ τῷ δεξιῷ τὸ εὐώνυμον ἐνίκησαν, ἐντεῦθεν φυγὴ τῶν³ Πελοποννησίων ἐγένετο εἰς Χίον πλείστων, ⟨τινῶν⟩⁴ δὲ καὶ εἰς Φώκαιαν· οἱ δὲ Ἀθηναῖοι πάλιν εἰς τὰς Ἀργινούσας κατέπλευσαν. **34** ἀπώλοντο δὲ τῶν μὲν Ἀθηναίων νῆες πέντε καὶ εἴκοσιν αὐτοῖς ἀνδράσιν ἐκτὸς ὀλίγων τῶν πρὸς τὴν γῆν προσενεχθέντων, τῶν δὲ Πελοποννησίων Λακωνικαὶ μὲν ἐννέα, ⟨τῶν⟩⁵ πασῶν οὐσῶν δέκα, τῶν δ' ἄλλων συμμάχων πλείους ἢ ἑξήκοντα.

35 Ἔδοξε δὲ καὶ τοῖς τῶν Ἀθηναίων στρατηγοῖς ἕξ⁶ μὲν καὶ τετταράκοντα ναυσὶ Θηραμένην τε καὶ Θρασύβουλον τριηράρχους ὄντας καὶ τῶν ταξιάρχων τινὰς πλεῖν ἐπὶ τὰς καταδεδυκυίας ναῦς καὶ τοὺς ἐπ' αὐτῶν ἀνθρώπους, ταῖς δὲ ἄλλαις ἐπὶ τὰς μετ' Ἐτεονίκου τῇ Μυτιλήνῃ ἐφορμούσας. ταῦτα δὲ βουλομένους ποιεῖν ἄνεμος καὶ χειμὼν διεκώλυσεν αὐτοὺς μέγας γενόμενος· τροπαῖον δὲ στήσαντες αὐτοῦ ηὐλίζοντο.

36 Τῷ δ' Ἐτεονίκῳ ὁ ὑπηρετι.ὸς κέλης πάντα ἐξήγγειλε τὰ περὶ τὴν ναυμαχίαν. ὁ δὲ αὐτὸν πάλιν ἐξέπεμψεν εἰπὼν τοῖς ἐνοῦσι σιωπῇ ἐκπλεῖν καὶ μηδενὶ διαλέγεσθαι, παραχρῆμα δὲ αὖθις πλεῖν εἰς τὸ ἑαυτῶν στρατόπεδον ἐστεφα.ωμένους καὶ βοῶντας ὅτι Καλλικρατίδας νενίκηκε ναυμαχῶν καὶ ὅτι αἱ τῶν Ἀθηναίων νῆες ἀπολώλασιν ἅπασαι. **37** καὶ οἱ μὲν τοῦτ' ἐποίουν· αὐτὸς δ', ἐπειδὴ ἐκεῖνοι κατέπλεον, ἔθυε τὰ εὐαγγέλια, καὶ τοῖς στρατιώταις παρήγγειλε δειπνοποιεῖσθαι, καὶ τοῖς ἐμπόροις τὰ χρήματα σιωπῇ ἐνθεμένους εἰς τὰ πλοῖα ἀποπλεῖν εἰς Χίον (ἦν δὲ τὸ πνεῦμα οὔριον) καὶ τὰς τριήρεις τὴν ταχίστην. **38** αὐτὸς δὲ τὸ πεζὸν ἀπῆγεν εἰς τὴν Μήθυμναν, τὸ στρατόπεδον ἐμπρήσας.

Κόνων δὲ καθελκύσας τὰς ναῦς, ἐπεὶ οἵ τε πολέμιοι ἀπεδεδράκεσαν καὶ ὁ ἄνεμος εὐδιαίτερος ἦν, ἀπαντήσας τοῖς Ἀθηναίοις ἤδη ἀνηγμένοις ἐκ τῶν Ἀργινουσῶν ἔφρασε τὰ περὶ τοῦ Ἐτεονίκου. οἱ δὲ Ἀθηναῖοι κατέπλευσαν εἰς τὴν Μυτιλήνην, ἐκεῖθεν δ' ἐπανήχθησαν εἰς τὴν Χίον, καὶ οὐδὲν διαπραξάμενοι ἀπέπλευσαν ἐπὶ Σάμου.

---

¹ οὐδὲν μή: οὐδαμῇ Jacobᵉ οὐδὲν μὲν Schneider οὐ δέος μὴ Liebhold del. Büchsenschütz μὴ om. cu
² οἰκεῖται: οἰκήσεται Schneider οἰκῆται Hermann διακέηται Delebecque
³ τῶν: ἐνίων Delebecque
⁴ τινῶν add. Madvig
⁵ τῶν add. Cobet
⁶ ἕξ: ἑπτὰ D

Kallikratidas said that Sparta would fare just the same if he died, but to flee, he said, is disgraceful.

33 After this they fought for a long time, in close order at first and then spread out. When Kallikratidas fell overboard as his ship rammed another and disappeared into the sea, and Protomachos and those with him on the right defeated the left, then the Peloponnesians fled to Chios, and most of them to Phokaia. The Athenians sailed back again to the Arginousai. **34** The Athenians lost twenty-five ships with their men, except for a few who were carried to land; the Peloponnesians lost nine of the ten Lakonian ships and more than sixty allied ships.

35 The Athenian generals decided that Theramenes and Thrasyboulos, who were captains, and some of the division commanders should sail with forty-six ships to the aid of the disabled ships and the men on them, while they themselves went with the others against the ships anchored with Eteonikos in Mytilene. But the wind and a great storm came and prevented them from doing what they wanted to do, so they erected a trophy and made camp there.

36 The dispatch-boat reported all the news about the naval battle to Eteonikos. He sent it out again, telling the crew to sail out silently and to speak to no one, and then immediately to sail back to his fleet wearing garlands and shouting that Kallikratidas had won a naval victory and that all the Athenian ships had been destroyed. **37** They carried out these instructions, and when they sailed back, he sacrificed for the good news. He ordered the troops to eat dinner, the traders to put their goods quietly into the merchant ships and sail away to Chios for the wind was favorable, and the triremes to sail as quickly as possible. **38** He himself led the infantry away to Methymna after burning the camp.

When the enemy had run away and the wind was calmer, Konon launched the ships and met the Athenians, who had already set out from Arginousai. He informed them about what Eteonikos had done. They sailed to Mytilene, and from there they went to Chios, and without accomplishing anything they sailed back towards Samos.

7

1 Οἱ δ᾽ ἐν οἴκῳ τούτους μὲν τοὺς στρατηγοὺς ἔπαυσαν πλὴν Κόνωνος· πρὸς δὲ τούτῳ εἵλοντο Ἀδείμαντον καὶ τρίτον Φιλοκλέα. τῶν δὲ ναυμαχησάντων στρατηγῶν Πρωτόμαχος μὲν καὶ Ἀριστογένης οὐκ ἀπῆλθον εἰς Ἀθήνας, 2 τῶν δὲ ἓξ καταπλευσάντων, Περικλέους καὶ Διομέδοντος καὶ Λυσίου καὶ Ἀριστοκράτους καὶ Θρασύλλου καὶ Ἐρασινίδου, Ἀρχέδημος ὁ τοῦ δήμου τότε προεστηκὼς ἐν Ἀθήναις καὶ τῆς διωβελίας[1] ἐπιμελόμενος Ἐρασινίδῃ ἐπιβολὴν ἐπιβαλὼν κατηγόρει ἐν δικαστηρίῳ, φάσκων ἐξ Ἑλλησπόντου αὐτὸν ἔχειν χρήματα ὄντα τοῦ δήμου· κατηγόρει δὲ καὶ περὶ τῆς στρατηγίας. καὶ ἔδοξε τῷ δικαστηρίῳ δῆσαι τὸν Ἐρασινίδην. 3 μετὰ δὲ ταῦτα ἐν τῇ βουλῇ διηγοῦντο οἱ στρατηγοὶ περί τε τῆς ναυμαχίας καὶ τοῦ μεγέθους τοῦ χειμῶνος. Τιμοκράτους δ᾽ εἰπόντος ὅτι καὶ τοὺς ἄλλους χρὴ δεθέντας εἰς τὸν δῆμον παραδοθῆναι, ἡ βουλὴ ἔδησε.

4 Μετὰ δὲ ταῦτα ἐκκλησία ἐγένετο, ἐν ᾗ τῶν στρατηγῶν κατηγόρουν ἄλλοι τε καὶ Θηραμένης μάλιστα, δικαίους εἶναι λόγον ὑποσχεῖν διότι οὐκ ἀνείλοντο τοὺς ναυαγούς. ὅτι μὲν γὰρ οὐδενὸς ἄλλου καθήπτοντο, ἐπιστολὴν ἐπεδείκνυε μαρτύριον ἣν[2] ἔπεμψαν οἱ στρατηγοὶ εἰς τὴν βουλὴν καὶ εἰς τὸν δῆμον, ἄλλο οὐδὲν αἰτιώμενοι ἢ τὸν χειμῶνα. 5 μετὰ ταῦτα δὲ οἱ στρατηγοὶ βραχέως ἕκαστος ἀπελογήσατο (οὐ γὰρ προυτέθη σφίσι λόγος κατὰ τὸν νόμον), καὶ τὰ πεπραγμένα διηγοῦντο, ὅτι αὐτοὶ μὲν ἐπὶ τοὺς πολεμίους πλέοιεν, τὴν δὲ ἀναίρεσιν τῶν ναυαγῶν προστάξαιεν τῶν τριηράρχων ἀνδράσιν ἱκανοῖς καὶ ἐστρατηγηκόσιν ἤδη, Θηραμένει καὶ Θρασυβούλῳ καὶ ἄλλοις τοιούτοις· 6 καὶ εἴπερ γέ τινας δέοι, περὶ τῆς ἀναιρέσεως οὐδένα ἄλλον ἔχειν αὐτοὺς αἰτιάσασθαι ἢ τούτους οἷς προσετάχθη. καὶ οὐχ ὅτι γε κατηγοροῦσιν ἡμῶν, ἔφασαν, ψευσόμεθα φάσκοντες αὐτοὺς αἰτίους εἶναι, ἀλλὰ τὸ μέγεθος τοῦ χειμῶνος εἶναι τὸ κωλῦσαν τὴν ἀναίρεσιν. 7 τούτων δὲ μάρτυρας παρείχοντο τοὺς κυβερνήτας καὶ ἄλλους τῶν συμπλεόντων πολλούς. τοιαῦτα λέγοντες ἔπειθον τὸν δῆμον· ἐβούλοντο δὲ πολλοὶ τῶν ἰδιωτῶν ἐγγυᾶσθαι ἀνιστάμενοι· ἔδοξε δὲ ἀναβαλέσθαι εἰς ἑτέραν ἐκκλησίαν (τότε γὰρ ὀψὲ ἦν καὶ τὰς χεῖρας οὐκ ἂν καθεώρων), τὴν δὲ βουλὴν προβουλεύσασαν εἰσενεγκεῖν ὅτῳ τρόπῳ οἱ ἄνδρες κρίνοιντο. 8 μετὰ δὲ ταῦτα ἐγίγνετο Ἀπατούρια, ἐν οἷς οἵ τε πατέρες[3] καὶ οἱ συγγενεῖς σύνεισι σφίσιν αὐτοῖς. οἱ οὖν περὶ τὸν Θηραμένη παρεσκεύασαν ἀνθρώπους μέλανα ἱμάτια ἔχοντας

---

[1] διωβελίας Dindorf: διωκελίας BPM
[2] ἣν Stephanus: καὶ codd.
[3] πατέρες: φράτερες Dindorf

7

1 The Athenians at home deposed these generals except Konon. In addition to him they elected Adeimantos and, thirdly, Philokles. Of the generals who fought in the naval battle Protomachos and Aristogenes did not return to Athens. **2** When six --Perikles, Diomedon, Lysias, Aristokrates, Thrasyllos and Erasinides--did saii back, Archedemos (who was the leader of the people in Athens at the time and was in charge of the two-obol fund) imposed an administrative fine on Erasinides, and accused him in a jury court, charging that he had public money from the Hellespont; he also accused him with regard to his conduct as general. The court decided that Erasinides should be imprisoned. **3** After this the generals spoke at a meeting of the Council about the naval battle and the size of the storm. When Timokrates said that the others must also be imprisoned and handed over to the people, the Council imprisoned them.

4 After this there was a meeting of the assembly in which speakers, particularly Theramenes, accused the generals; he said that they ought to undergo the official audit for their failure to pick up the shipwrecked men. As evidence that they blamed no one else, he showed a letter which the generals sent to the Council and the assembly, blaming nothing other than the storm. **5** Then each of the generals defended himself briefly (for in conformity with the law no opportunity was given them to make a speech), and they recounted what had happened: they themselves were trying to sail against the enemy, and they delegated the task of picking up the shipwrecked men to capable captains, men who had served as generals in the past, Theramenes and Thrasyboulos and others of comparable quality. **6** If it was necessary to blame someone about the recovery, they had no one other than those to whom it was delegated. "We will not claim that they were at fault because they accuse us," they said, "rather the size of the storm was what prevented the recovery." As witnesses they offered the pilots and others who had sailed with them, and their arguments were persuading the people. **7** Many private individuals stood up and volunteered to be sureties. It was decided to adjourn until another meeting, for by then it was late and they could not have counted the hands, and that the Council should discuss the matter and bring in a motion about the manner in which the men should be judged. **8** After this occurred the Apatouria festival, at which fathers and relatives meet together. Accordingly Theramenes' faction arranged for many men

καὶ εν χρῷ κεκαρμένους πολλοὺς ἐν ταύτῃ τῇ ἑορτῇ, ἵνα πρὸς τὴν ἐκκλησίαν ἥκοιεν, ὡς δὴ συγγενεῖς ὄντες τῶν ἀπολωλότων, καὶ Καλλίξενον ἔπεισαν ἐν τῇ βουλῇ κατηγορεῖν τῶν στρατηγῶν.

9 Ἐντεῦθεν ἐκκλησίαν ἐποίουν, εἰς ἣν ἡ βουλὴ εἰσήνεγκε τὴν ἑαυτῆς γνώμην Καλλιξένου εἰπόντος τήνδε· Ἐπειδὴ τῶν τε κατηγορούντων κατὰ τῶν στρατηγῶν καὶ ἐκείνων ἀπολογουμένων ἐν τῇ προτέρᾳ[1] ἐκκλησίᾳ ἀκηκόασι, διαψηφίσασθαι Ἀθηναίους ἅπαντας κατὰ φυλάς· θεῖναι δὲ εἰς τὴν φυλὴν ἑκάστην δύο ὑδρίας· ἐφ᾽ ἑκάστῃ δὲ τῇ φυλῇ κήρυκα κηρύττειν, ὅτῳ δοκοῦσιν ἀδικεῖν οἱ στρατηγοὶ οὐκ ἀνελόμενοι τοὺς νικήσαντας ἐν τῇ ναυμαχίᾳ, εἰς τὴν προτέραν ψηφίσασθαι, ὅτῳ δὲ μή, εἰς τὴν ὑστέραν· 10 ἂν δὲ δόξωσιν ἀδικεῖν, θανάτῳ ζημιῶσαι καὶ τοῖς ἕνδεκα παραδοῦναι καὶ τὰ χρήματα δημεῦσαι[2], τὸ δ᾽ ἐπιδέκατον τῆς θεοῦ εἶνι

11 Παρῆλθε δέ τις εἰς τὴν ἐκκλησίαν φάσκων ἐπὶ τεύχους ἀλφίτων σωθῆναι· ἐπιστέλλειν δ᾽ αὐτῷ τοὺς ἀπολλυμένους, ἐὰν σωθῇ, ἀπαγγεῖλαι τῷ δήμῳ ὅτι οἱ στρατηγοὶ οὐκ ἀνείλοντο τοὺς ἀρίστους ὑπὲρ τῆς πατρίδος γενομένους.

12 Τὸν δὲ Καλλίξενον προσεκαλέσαντο[3] παράνομα φάσκοντες συγγεγραφέναι Εὐρυπτόλεμός τε ὁ Πεισιάνακτος καὶ ἄλλοι τινές. τοῦ δὲ δήμου ἔνιοι ταῦτα ἐπῄνουν, τὸ δὲ πλῆθος ἐβόα δεινὸν εἶναι εἰ μή τις ἐάσει τὸν δῆμον πράττειν ὃ ἂν βούληται. 13 καὶ ἐπὶ τούτοις εἰπόντος Λυκίσκου καὶ τούτους τῇ αὐτῇ ψήφῳ κρίνεσθαι ἧπερ καὶ τοὺς στρατηγούς, ἐὰν μὴ ἀφῶσι τὴν κλῆσιν,[4] ἐπεθορύβησε πάλιν ὁ ὄχλος, καὶ ἠναγκάσθησαν ἀφιέναι τὰς κλήσεις. 14 τῶν δὲ πρυτάνεών τινων οὐ φασκόντων προθήσειν τὴν διαψήφισιν παρὰ τὸν νόμον, αὖθις Καλλίξενος ἀναβὰς κατηγόρει αὐτῶν τὰ αὐτά. οἱ δὲ ἐβόων καλεῖν τοὺς οὐ φάσκοντας. 15 οἱ δὲ πρυτάνεις φοβηθέντες ὡμολόγουν πάντες προθήσειν πλὴν Σωκράτους τοῦ Σωφρονίσκου· οὗτος δ᾽ οὐκ ἔφη ἀλλ᾽ ἢ κατὰ νόμον πάντα ποιήσειν.

16 Μετὰ δὲ ταῦτα ἀναβὰς Εὐρυπτόλεμος ἔλεξεν ὑπὲρ τῶν στρατηγῶν τάδε.

Τὰ μὲν κατηγορήσων, ὦ ἄνδρες Ἀθηναῖοι, ἀνέβην ἐνθάδε Περικλέους ἀναγκαίου μοι ὄντος καὶ ἐπιτηδείου καὶ Διομέδοντος φίλου, τὰ δ᾽ ὑπεραπολογησόμενος, τὰ δὲ συμβουλεύσων ἅ μοι δοκεῖ ἄριστα εἶναι ἁπάσῃ τῇ πόλει. 17 κατηγορῶ μὲν οὖν αὐτῶν ὅτι ἔπεισαν τοὺς συνάρχοντας βουλομένους πέμπειν γράμματα τῇ τε βουλῇ καὶ ὑμῖν ὅτι ἐπέταξαν τῷ Θηραμένει καὶ Θρασυβούλῳ τετταράκοντα καὶ ἑπτὰ τριήρεσιν ἀνελέσθαι

---

[1] προτέρᾳ: προτεραίᾳ BPM
[2] δημεῦσαι Riemann: δημοσιεῦσαι codd. δημόσι᾽ εἶναι Cobet
[3] προσεκαλέσαντο Morus: προεκαλέσαντο codd.
[4] κλῆσιν Dobree: ἐκκλησίαν codd.

with black garments and close-shaven hair to be present at the festival, so that they could attend the assembly pretending to be relatives of those who had died. They also persuaded Kallixenos to bring accusations against the generals in the Council.

9 Then they held the assembly at which the Council brought in its motion, moved by Kallixenos, as follows: "Since they heard the men accusing the generals and the generals defending themselves in the previous assembly, that all Athenians vote, by tribes; that two jars be placed for each tribe; that in each tribe a herald announce that whoever thinks the generals did wrong by not picking up the men who won the naval battle should deposit his pebble in the first jar, and whoever thinks that they did not do wrong should deposit his pebble in the second jar; **10** if they are judged guilty, that they be punished with death and handed over to the Eleven and their property confiscated and the tenth part of it given to the goddess."

11 And a man came forward in the assembly, saying that he had been saved on a grain-barrel, and that the dying men had told him, if he should survive, to report to the people that the generals had not rescued the men who had acted most courageously on behalf of the country.

12 Saying that Kallixenos had made an illegal proposal, Euryptolemos the son of Peisianax and some others served a summons against him. Some of the people praised their action, but the majority shouted that it would be a terrible thing if someone did not allow the people to do what it wished. **13** When Lykiskos added that these men should be judged by the same vote as the generals, unless they withdrew the summons, the mob broke into shouts again, and they were compelled to withdraw the summonses. **14** Some members of the presiding committee refused to put the motion to the vote contrary to the law, but Kallixenos mounted the platform again and made the same accusations against them. The Athenians shouted that those who refused should be prosecuted. **15** As a result all the members of the committee were frightened and agreed to put the motion to the vote, except Sokrates the son of Sophroniskos. He said he would not act in any way other than according to the law.

16 Then Euryptolemos mounted the platform and spoke as follows in defense of the generals:

"I have mounted the platform, men of Athens, partly to accuse Perikles my relative and Diomedon my friend, and partly to defend them, and partly to recommend what I believe is best for the whole city. **17** I accuse them because they changed the minds of their colleagues, who wanted to send a letter to the Council and to you saying that they had ordered Theramenes and Thrasyboulos to pick up the

τοὺς ναυαγούς, οἱ δὲ οὐκ ἀνείλοντο. 18 εἶτα νῦν τὴν αἰτίαν κοινὴν ἔχουσιν ἐκείνων ἰδίᾳ ἁμαρτόντων, καὶ ἀντὶ τῆς τότε φιλανθρωπίας νῦν ὑπ' ἐκείνων τε καί τινων ἄλλων ἐπιβουλευόμενοι κινδυνεύουσιν ἀπολέσθαι;

19 Οὔκ, ἂν ὑμεῖς γέ μοι πείθησθε τὰ δίκαια καὶ ὅσια ποιοῦντες, καὶ ὅθεν μάλιστ' ἀληθῆ πεύσεσθε καὶ οὐ μετανοήσαντες ὕστερον εὑρήσετε σφᾶς αὐτοὺς ἡμαρτηκότας τὰ μέγιστα εἰς[1] θεούς τε καὶ ὑμᾶς αὐτούς. συμβουλεύω δ' ὑμῖν, ἐν οἷς οὔθ' ὑπ' ἐμοῦ οὔθ' ὑπ' ἄλλου οὐδενὸς ἔστιν ἐξαπατηθῆναι ὑμᾶς, καὶ τοὺς ἀδικοῦντας εἰδότας κολάσασθαι ᾗ ἂν βούλησθε δίκῃ, καὶ ἅμα πάντας καὶ καθ' ἕνα ἕκαστον, εἰ μὴ πλέον, ἀλλὰ ⟨κἂν⟩[2] μίαν ἡμέραν δόντες αὐτοῖς ὑπὲρ αὐτῶν ἀπολογήσασθαι, μὴ ἄλλοις μᾶλλον πιστεύοντες ἢ ὑμῖν αὐτοῖς.

20 Ἴστε δέ, ὦ ἄνδρες Ἀθηναῖοι, πάντες ὅτι τὸ Καννωνοῦ ψήφισμά ἐστιν ἰσχυρότατον, ὃ κελεύει, ἐάν τις τὸν τῶν Ἀθηναίων δῆμον ἀδικῇ, δεδεμένον[3] ἀποδικεῖν ἐν τῷ δήμῳ, καὶ ἐὰν καταγνωσθῇ ἀδικεῖν, ἀποθανόντα εἰς τὸ βάραθρον ἐμβληθῆναι[4], τὰ δὲ χρήματα αὐτοῦ δημευθῆναι καὶ τῆς θεοῦ τὸ ἐπιδέκατον εἶναι. 21 κατὰ τοῦτο τὸ ψήφισμα κελεύω κρίνεσθαι τοὺς στρατηγοὺς καὶ νὴ Δία, ἂν ὑμῖν γε δοκῇ, πρῶτον Περικλέα τὸν ἐμοὶ προσήκοντα· αἰσχρὸν μοί ἐστιν ἐκεῖνον περὶ πλείονος ποιεῖσθαι ἢ τὴν ὅλην πόλιν. 22 τοῦτο δ' εἰ βούλεσθε, κατὰ τόνδε τὸν νόμον κρίνατε, ὅς ἐστιν ἐπὶ τοῖς ἱεροσύλοις καὶ προδόταις, ἐάν τις ἢ τὴν πόλιν προδιδῷ ἢ τὰ ἱερὰ κλέπτῃ, κριθέντα ἐν δικαστηρίῳ, ἂν καταγνωσθῇ, μὴ ταφῆναι ἐν τῇ Ἀττικῇ, τὰ δὲ χρήματα αὐτοῦ δημόσια εἶναι.

23 Τούτων ὁποτέρῳ βούλεσθε, ὦ ἄνδρες Ἀθηναῖοι, τῷ νόμῳ κρινέσθων[5] οἱ ἄνδρες κατὰ ἕνα ἕκαστον διῃρημένης τῆς ἡμέρας τριῶν μερῶν[6], ἑνὸς μὲν ἐν ᾧ συλλέγεσθαι ὑμᾶς δεῖ καὶ διαψηφίζεσθαι, ἐάν τε ἀδικεῖν δοκῶσιν ἐάν τε μή, ἑτέρου δ' ἐν ᾧ κατηγορῆσαι, ἑτέρου δ' ἐν ᾧ ἀπολογήσασθαι. 24 τούτων δὲ γιγνομένων οἱ μὲν ἀδικοῦντες τεύξονται τῆς μεγίστης τιμωρίας, οἱ δ' ἀναίτιοι ἐλευθερωθήσονται ὑφ' ὑμῶν, ὦ Ἀθηναῖοι, καὶ οὐκ ἀδίκως[7] ἀπολοῦνται. 25 ὑμεῖς δὲ κατὰ τὸν νόμον εὐσεβοῦντες καὶ εὐορκοῦντες κρινεῖτε καὶ οὐ συμπολεμήσετε Λακεδαιμονίοις τοὺς ἐκείνους ἑβδομήκοντα ναῦς ἀφελομένους καὶ νενικηκότας, τούτους ἀπολλύντες ἀκρίτους παρὰ τὸν νόμον. τί δὲ καὶ δεδιότες σφόδρα οὕτως ἐπείγεσθε; 26 ἢ

---

[1] τὰ μέγιστα εἰς Morus: εἰς τὰ μέγιστα codd.
[2] κἂν schol. in Demosth. Patm. (BCH 1877, 10): om. codd.
[3] δεδεμένον: διαλελημμένον Bamberg ex. Aristoph. Ekkl. 1090
[4] ἀποθανόντα . . . ἐμβληθῆναι: ἀποθανεῖν . . . ἐμβληθέντα Dobree
[5] κρινέσθων Cobet: κρινέσθωσαν codd.
[6] μερῶν DV: ἡμερῶν BPM
[7] ἀδίκως Löwenklau: ἀδικοῦντες codd.

shipwrecked men with forty-seven triremes, but they failed to pick them up. **18** Are they now to share the blame for those individuals' mistakes, and in return for their kindness at that time are they now in danger of losing their lives, the victims of plots by those men and a few others?

19 "No, if you will listen to me and do what is just and right. In this way you will best learn the truth and will not find yourselves later realizing that you have made the greatest errors against the gods and against yourselves. I advise you to follow the procedure in which neither I nor anyone else can deceive you, and through which you may recognize the wrong-doers and punish them however you like, either all of them as a group or individually: give them one day, if not more, to defend themselves, and do not trust others more than yourselves.

20 "You all know, men of Athens, that the decree of Kannonos is extremely severe. It provides that if anyone has wronged the people of Athens he shall defend himself in fetters before the people, and if he is found guilty he shall be executed and thrown into the chasm, and his property shall be confiscated and a tenth of it given to the goddess. **21** I urge you to judge the generals according to this decree and, by Zeus, my relative Perikles first, if that seems best to you; it is disgraceful for me to place his interests above those of the entire city. **22** If you prefer, judge them according to this other law, which is against temple-robbers and traitors: If anyone betrays the city or steals sacred property, he shall be tried in a jury court, and if he is convicted, he shall not be buried in Attika and his property shall be confiscated.

23 "By whichever of these laws you wish, men of Athens, let the men be tried, individually and with the day divided into three parts, one for you to gather and vote whether they seem to have done wrong or not, another for the prosecution, and another for the defense. **24** If this happens the wrong-doers will be punished and the innocent will be set free by you, Athenians, and, not being guilty, will not die. **25** You will judge according to the law, with reverence for the gods and your oaths, and you will not be fighting on the side of the Lakedaimonians by executing without a trial, contrary to the law, these victorious men who destroyed seventy ships. What do you fear that you are in such a hurry? **26** Is it that you will not be able to

μὴ οὐχ ὑμεῖς ὃν ἂν βούλησθε ἀποκτείνητε καὶ ἐλευθερώσητε, ἂν κατὰ τὸν νόμον κρίνητε, ἀλλ' οὐκ ἂν παρὰ τὸν νόμον, ὥσπερ Καλλίξενος τὴν βουλὴν ἔπεισεν εἰς τὸν δῆμον εἰσενεγκεῖν μιᾷ ψήφῳ; **27** ἀλλ' ἴσως ἄν τινα καὶ οὐκ αἴτιον ὄντα ἀποκτείνητε, μεταμελήσει· (μεταμελῆσαι)[1] δὲ ὕστερον ἀναμνήσθητε ὡς ἀλγεινὸν καὶ ἀνωφελὲς ἤδη ἐστί, πρὸς δ' ἔτι καὶ περὶ θανάτου ἀνθρώπου[2] ἡμαρτηκότας. **28** δεινὰ δ' ἂν ποιήσαιτε[3], εἰ Ἀριστάρχῳ μὲν πρότερον τὸν δῆμον καταλύοντι, εἶτα δ' Οἰνόην προδιδόντι Θηβαίοις πολεμίοις οὖσιν, ἔδοτε ἡμέραν ἀπολογήσασθαι ᾗ ἐβούλετο καὶ τἆλλα κατὰ τὸν νόμον προύθετε[4], τοὺς δὲ στρατηγοὺς τοὺς πάντα ὑμῖν κατὰ γνώμην πράξαντας, νικήσαντας δὲ τοὺς πολεμίους, τῶν αὐτῶν τούτων ἀποστερήσετε. **29** μὴ ὑμεῖς γε, ὦ Ἀθηναῖοι, ἀλλ' ἑαυτῶν ὄντες[5] τοὺς νόμους, δι' οὓς μάλιστα μέγιστοί ἐστε, φυλάττοντες, ἄνευ τούτων μηδὲν πράττειν πειρᾶσθε.

Ἐπανέλθετε δὲ καὶ ἐπ'[6] αὐτὰ τὰ πράγματα καθ' ἃ καὶ αἱ ἁμαρτίαι δοκοῦσι γεγενῆσθαι τοῖς στρατηγοῖς. ἐπεὶ γὰρ κρατήσαντες τῇ ναυμαχίᾳ εἰς τὴν γῆν κατέπλευσαν, Διομέδων μὲν ἐκέλευεν ἀναχθέντας ἐπὶ κέρως ἅπαντας ἀναιρεῖσθαι τὰ ναυάγια καὶ τοὺς ναυαγούς, Ἐρασινίδης δ' ἐπὶ τοὺς πρὸς Μυτιλήνην πολεμίους τὴν ταχίστην πλεῖν ἅπαντας· Θράσυλλος δὲ ἀμφότερα ἔφη γενέσθαι, ἂν τὰς μὲν αὐτοῦ καταλίπωσι, ταῖς δὲ ἐπὶ τοὺς πολεμίους πλέωσι· **30** καὶ δοξάντων τούτων καταλιπεῖν τρεῖς ναῦς ἕκαστον ἐκ τῆς αὐτοῦ συμμορίας, τῶν στρατηγῶν ὀκτὼ ὄντων, καὶ τὰς τῶν ταξιάρχων δέκα καὶ τὰς Σαμίων δέκα καὶ τὰς τῶν ναυάρχων τρεῖς, αὗται ἅπασαι γίγνονται ἑπτὰ καὶ τετταράκοντα, τέτταρες περὶ ἑκάστην ναῦν τῶν ἀπολωλυιῶν δώδεκα οὐσῶν. **31** τῶν δὲ καταλειφθέντων τριηράρχων ἦσαν καὶ Θρασύβουλος καὶ Θηραμένης, ὃς ἐν τῇ προτέρᾳ ἐκκλησίᾳ κατηγόρει τῶν στρατηγῶν. ταῖς δὲ ἄλλαις ναυσὶν ἔπλεον ἐπὶ τὰς πολεμίας. τί τούτων οὐχ ἱκανῶς καὶ καλῶς ἔπραξαν; οὐκοῦν δίκαιον τὰ μὲν πρὸς τοὺς πολεμίους μὴ καλῶς πραχθέντα τοὺς πρὸς τούτους[7] ταχθέντας ὑπέχειν λόγον, τοὺς δὲ πρὸς τὴν ἀναίρεσιν μὴ ποιήσαντας ἃ οἱ στρατηγοὶ ἐκέλευσαν, διότι οὐκ ἀνείλοντο κρίνεσθαι. **32** τοσοῦτον δ' ἔχω εἰπεῖν ὑπὲρ ἀμφοτέρων, ὅτι ὁ χειμὼν διεκώλυσε μηδὲν πρᾶξαι ὧν οἱ στρατηγοὶ παρεσκευάσαντο. τούτων δὲ μάρτυρες οἱ σωθέντες ἀπὸ τοῦ αὐτομάτου, ὧν εἷς τῶν ἡμετέρων

---

[1] ⟨μεταμελῆσαι⟩ Hatzfeld
[2] ἀνθρώπου Stephanus: ἀνθρώπους codd.
[3] ποιήσαιτε Zeune: ποιήσητε BP ποιήσοιτε M
[4] προύθετε f[2]: προύθετο rell.
[5] ὄντες Peter: ὄντας codd.
[6] ἐπ': ὑπ' BPM
[7] τούτους edd. plerique: τούτοις codd. τοῦτο Hartmann

execute and acquit whom you wish if you judge them legally, but you are not afraid if you judge them illegally, as Kallixenos persuaded the Council to propose to the people, with a single vote? **27** But perhaps you will put to death an innocent man, and you will regret it later. Remember that regret is painful and useless, especially when you have made a mistake about a man's life. **28** You would be doing a terrible thing if, after giving Aristarchos--who first destroyed the democracy and then betrayed Oinoe to the Thebans, our enemies--a day to defend himself in whatever way he wished and allowing him all his other legal rights, you deprived the generals--who have done everything according to your wishes and defeated the enemy--of these same rights. **29** Do not act like this, Athenians, but guard your own laws, which above all have made you great, and try to do nothing without them.

"Return now to the matters themselves in which the generals seem to have made mistakes. For when they had sailed back to land after winning the naval battle, Diomedon proposed that they set out in single file and pick up the wreckage and the shipwrecked men, Erasinides that they all sail as fast as possible against the enemy at Mytilene. Thrasyllos said that they could do both, if they left some ships there and sailed with the rest against the enemy; **30** if this proposal were accepted he suggested that they leave behind three ships from each of the eight generals' own contingents, the ten of the division commanders and the ten Samian and the three of the admirals: forty-seven in all, four for each of the twelve lost ships. **31** Among the captains left behind were Thrasyboulos and Theramenes, the man who accused the generals in the earlier assembly. With the rest of the ships they were attempting to sail against the enemy. Which of these things did they not do adequately and well? It is just, therefore, that those appointed to sail against the enemy undergo an audit for what they did not do well, and that those appointed to pick up the shipwrecked men be tried because they did not carry out the rescue the generals had ordered. **32** This much, however, I have to say on behalf of both: the storm prevented them from carrying out any of the generals' plans. Witnesses for these events are the men who were saved by chance, among whom is one of our generals

στρατηγῶν ἐπὶ καταδύσης νεὼς διασωθείς, ὃν κελεύουσι τῇ αὐτῇ ψήφῳ κρίνεσθαι, καὶ αὐτὸν τότε δεόμενον ἀναιρέσεως, ᾗπερ τοὺς οὐ πράξαντας τὰ προσταχθέντα. **33** μὴ τοίνυν, ὦ ἄνδρες Ἀθηναῖοι, ἀντὶ μὲν τῆς νίκης καὶ τῆς εὐτυχίας ὅμοια ποιήσητε τοῖς ἡττημένοις τε καὶ ἀτυχοῦσιν, ἀντὶ δὲ τῶν ἐκ θεοῦ ἀναγκαίων ἀγνωμονεῖν δόξητε, προδοσίαν καταγνόντες ἀντὶ τῆς ἀδυναμίας οὐχ ἱκανοὺς γενομένους διὰ τὸν χειμῶνα πρᾶξαι τὰ προσταχθέντα· ἀλλὰ πολὺ δικαιότερον στεφάνοις γεραίρειν τοὺς νικῶντας ἢ θανάτῳ ζημιοῦν πονηροῖς ἀνθρώποις πειθομένους.

34 Ταῦτ’ εἰπὼν Εὐρυπτόλεμος ἔγραψε γνώμην κατὰ τὸ Καννωνοῦ ψήφισμα κρίνεσθαι τοὺς ἄνδρας δίχα ἕκαστον· ἡ δὲ τῆς βουλῆς ἦν μιᾷ ψήφῳ ἅπαντας κρίνειν. τούτων δὲ διαχειροτονουμένων τὸ μὲν πρῶτον ἔκριναν τὴν Εὐρυπτολέμου· ὑπομοσαμένου δὲ Μενεκλέους καὶ πάλιν διαχειροτονίας γενομένης ἔκριναν τὴν τῆς βουλῆς. καὶ μετὰ ταῦτα κατεψηφίσαντο τῶν ναυμαχησάντων στρατηγῶν ὀκτὼ ὄντων· ἀπέθανον δὲ οἱ παρόντες ἕξ.

35 Καὶ οὐ πολλῷ χρόνῳ ὕστερον μετέμελε τοῖς Ἀθηναίοις, καὶ ἐψηφίσαντο, οἵτινες τὸν δῆμον ἐξηπάτησαν, προβολὰς αὐτῶν εἶναι, καὶ ἐγγυητὰς καταστῆσαι, ἕως ἂν[1] κριθῶσιν, εἶναι δὲ καὶ Καλλίξενον τούτων. προυβλήθησαν δὲ καὶ ἄλλοι τέτταρες, καὶ ἐδέθησαν ὑπὸ τῶν ἐγγυησαμένων, ὕστερον δὲ στάσεώς τινος γενομένης, ἐν ᾗ Κλεοφῶν ἀπέθανεν, ἀπέδρασαν οὗτοι, πρὶν κριθῆναι· Καλλίξενος δὲ κατελθὼν ὅτε καὶ οἱ ἐκ Πειραιῶς εἰς τὸ ἄστυ, μισούμενος ὑπὸ πάντων λιμῷ ἀπέθανεν.

[1] ἕως ἂν Stephanus: ἐὰν codd.

who survived on a wrecked ship. Now they want to judge him, a man who needed rescue himself at the time, by the same vote as those who did not carry out their instructions. **33** Do not, then, men of Athens, in the face of victory and good fortune behave similarly to men defeated and unfortunate. Do not in the face of divine compulsion seem to be unreasonable by giving a verdict of treason rather than helplessness, because they were incapable of carrying out the instructions because of the storm. It would be more just to reward the victors with garlands than to punish them with death due to the persuasions of bad men."

34 After making this speech Euryptolemos proposed that the men be judged separately, according to the decree of Kannonos; the Council's proposal was to judge them all with a single vote. When the assembly voted between these two proposals, at first it chose that of Euryptolemos. But when Menekles lodged an objection under oath and another vote was taken, it chose the Council's proposal. And after this they condemned the eight generals who had fought in the naval battle; the six who were present were executed.

35 Not much later the Athenians regretted what they had done and voted that complaints should be brought against those who deceived the people, that they should give sureties until they could be tried, and that Kallixenos should be one of them. Complaints were brought against four others as well, and they were confined by the sureties. Later, however, during the civil disorder in which Kleophon died, they escaped, before they were tried. Kallixenos came back when those from Peiraieus returned to the city, but was universally despised and died of hunger.

II

1

1 Οἱ δ' ἐν τῇ Χίῳ μετὰ τοῦ Ἐτεονίκου στρατιῶται ὄντες, ἕως μὲν θέρος ἦν, ἀπό τε τῆς ὥρας ἐτρέφοντο καὶ ἐργαζόμενοι μισθοῦ κατὰ τὴν χώραν· ἐπεὶ δὲ χειμὼν ἐγένετο καὶ τροφὴν οὐκ εἶχον γυμνοί τε ἦσαν καὶ ἀνυπόδητοι, συνίσταντο ἀλλήλοις καὶ συνετίθεντο ὡς τῇ Χίῳ ἐπιθησόμενοι· οἷς δὲ ταῦτα ἀρέσκοι κάλαμον φέρειν ἐδόκει, ἵνα ἀλλήλους μάθοιεν ὁπόσοι εἴησαν. 2 πυθόμενος δὲ τὸ σύνθημα ὁ Ἐτεόνικος, ἀπόρως μὲν εἶχε τί χρῷτο τῷ πράγματι διὰ τὸ πλῆθος τῶν καλαμηφόρων· τό τε γὰρ ἐκ τοῦ ἐμφανοῦς ἐπιχειρῆσαι σφαλερὸν ἐδόκει εἶναι, μὴ εἰς τὰ ὅπλα ὁρμήσωσι καὶ τὴν πόλιν κατασχόντες καὶ πολέμιοι γενόμενοι ἀπολέσωσι πάντα τὰ πράγματα, ἂν κρατήσωσι, τό τ' αὖ ἀπολλύναι ἀνθρώπους συμμάχους πολλοὺς δεινὸν ἐφαίνετο εἶναι, μή τινα καὶ εἰς τοὺς ἄλλους Ἕλληνας διαβολὴν σχοῖεν καὶ οἱ στρατιῶται δύσνοοι πρὸς τὰ πράγματα ὦσιν. 3 ἀναλαβὼν δὲ μεθ' ἑαυτοῦ ἄνδρας πεντεκαίδεκα ἐγχειρίδια ἔχοντας ἐπορεύετο κατὰ τὴν πόλιν, καὶ ἐντυχὼν τινι ὀφθαλμιῶντι ἀνθρώπῳ ἀπιόντι ἐξ ἰατρείου, κάλαμον ἔχοντι, ἀπέκτεινε. 4 θορύβου δὲ γενομένου καὶ ἐρωτώντων τινῶν διὰ τί ἀπέθανεν ὁ ἄνθρωπος, παραγγέλλειν ἐκέλευεν ὁ Ἐτεόνικος, ὅτι τὸν κάλαμον εἶχε. κατὰ δὲ τὴν παραγγελίαν ἐρρίπτουν πάντες ὅσοι εἶχον τοὺς καλάμους, ἀεὶ ὁ ἀκούων δεδιὼς μὴ ὀφθείη ἔχων. 5 μετὰ δὲ ταῦτα ὁ Ἐτεόνικος συγκαλέσας τοὺς Χίους χρήματα ἐκέλευσε συνενεγκεῖν, ὅπως οἱ ναῦται λάβωσι μισθὸν καὶ μὴ νεωτερίσωσί τι· οἱ δὲ εἰσήνεγκαν· ἅμα δὲ εἰς τὰς ναῦς ἐσήμανεν εἰσβαίνειν· προσιὼν δὲ ἐν μέρει παρ' ἑκάστην ναῦν παρεθάρρυνέ τε καὶ παρῄνει πολλά, ὡς τοῦ γεγενημένου οὐδὲν εἰδώς, καὶ μισθὸν ἑκάστῳ μηνὸς διέδωκε. 6 Μετὰ δὲ ταῦτα οἱ Χῖοι καὶ οἱ ἄλλοι σύμμαχοι συλλεγέντες εἰς Ἔφεσον ἐβουλεύσαντο περὶ τῶν ἐνεστηκότων πραγμάτων πέμπειν εἰς Λακεδαίμονα πρέσβεις ταῦτά τε ἐροῦντας καὶ Λύσανδρον αἰτήσοντας ἐπὶ τὰς ναῦς, εὖ φερόμενον παρὰ τοῖς συμμάχοις κατὰ τὴν προτέραν ναυαρχίαν, ὅτε καὶ τὴν ἐν Νοτίῳ ἐνίκησε ναυμαχίαν. 7 καὶ ἀπεπέμφθησαν πρέσβεις, σὺν αὐτοῖς δὲ καὶ παρὰ Κύρου ταὐτὰ λέγοντες ἄγγελοι. οἱ δὲ Λακεδαιμόνιοι ἔδοσαν τὸν Λύσανδρον ὡς ἐπιστολέα, ναύαρχον δὲ Ἄρακον·

II

1

1 The troops in Chios with Eteonikos subsisted during the summer on seasonal produce and by working for pay on the land. But when it was winter and they lacked food and clothing and footwear, they got together and agreed to make an attack on Chios. They decided that whoever approved of this plan should carry a reed so that they could learn how many they were. **2** Eteonikos discovered the plot, but was uncertain how to handle it because of the large number of men carrying reeds. It seemed dangerous to try to suppress it openly, for fear that they would rush to arms, gain control of the city, become hostile and ruin everything, if they won; it also seemed terrible to kill many allied men, for fear he would be criticized by the other Greeks and the troops become disaffected. **3** Taking with him fifteen men with daggers he went through the city, and when he met a man suffering from an eye disease coming out of a doctor's office with a reed, he killed him. **4** A commotion arose and some asked why the man had died. Eteonikos instructed his followers to say that it was because he had a reed. As this report spread everyone who had a reed threw it away out of fear that he would be seen with it. **5** After this Eteonikos called the Chians together and told them to raise money, in order that the sailors be paid and not revolt. The Chians brought in the money. At the same time he gave the signal to embark on the ships. He visited each ship in turn and exhorted and encouraged the men in many ways, as if he knew nothing of what had happened, and he gave each man pay for a month.

6 After this the Chians and the other allies assembled at Ephesos consulted about the present situation and decided to send ambassadors to Lakedaimon to report on the situation and ask for Lysandros as commander of the fleet; the allies viewed him favorably from his earlier period of command, when he had also won the naval battle at Notion. **7** Ambassadors were sent, and with them went messengers from Kyros with the same request. The Lakedaimonians sent Lysandros as vice-admiral,

οὐ γὰρ νόμος αὐτοῖς δὶς τὸν αὐτὸν ναυαρχεῖν· τὰς μέντοι ναῦς παρέδοσαν Λυσάνδρῳ [ἐτῶν ἤδη τῷ πολέμῳ πέντε καὶ εἴκοσι παρεληλυθότων]¹.

8 [Τούτῳ δὲ τῷ ἐνιαυτῷ καὶ Κῦρος ἀπέκτεινεν Αὐτοβοισάκην καὶ Μιτραῖον, υἱεῖς ὄντας τῆς Δαρειαίου ἀδελφῆς τῆς τοῦ Ξέρξου τοῦ Δαρείου πατρός, ὅτι αὐτῷ ἀπαντῶντες οὐ διέωσαν διὰ τῆς κόρης τὰς χεῖρας, ὃ ποιοῦσι βασιλεῖ μόνον· ἡ δὲ κόρη ἐστὶ μακρότερον ἢ χειρίς², ἐν ᾗ τὴν χεῖρα ἔχων οὐδὲν ἂν δύναιτο³ ποιῆσαι. **9** Ἱεραμένης μὲν οὖν καὶ ἡ γυνὴ ἔλεγον πρὸς Δαρειαῖον δεινὸν εἶναι εἰ περιόψεται τὴν λίαν ὕβριν τούτου· ὁ δὲ αὐτὸν μεταπέμπεται ὡς ἀρρωστῶν, πέμψας ἀγγέλους.]⁴

10 Τῷ δ' ἐπιόντι ἔτει [ἐπὶ Ἀρχύτα μὲν ἐφορεύοντος. ἄρχοντος δ' ἐν Ἀθήναις Ἀλεξίου]⁵ Λύσανδρος ἀφικόμενος εἰς Ἔφεσον μετεπέμψατο Ἐτεόνικον ἐκ Χίου σὺν ταῖς ναυσί, καὶ τὰς ἄλλας πάσας συνήθροισεν, εἴ πού τις ἦν, καὶ ταύτας τ' ἐπεσκεύαζε καὶ ἄλλας ἐν Ἀντάνδρῳ ἐναυπηγεῖτο. **11** ἐλθὼν δὲ παρὰ Κῦρον χρήματα ᾔτει· ὁ δ' αὐτῷ εἶπεν ὅτι τὰ μὲν παρὰ βασιλέως ἀνηλωμένα εἴη, καὶ ἔτι πλείω πολλῷ, δεικνύων ὅσα ἕκαστος τῶν ναυάρχων ἔχοι, ὅμως δ' ἔδωκε. **12** λαβὼν δὲ ὁ Λύσανδρος τἀργύριον, ἐπὶ τὰς τριήρεις τριηράρχους ἐπέστησε καὶ τοῖς ναύταις τὸν ὀφειλόμενον μισθὸν ἀπέδωκε. παρεσκευάζοντο δὲ καὶ οἱ τῶν Ἀθηναίων στρατηγοὶ ⟨τὰ⟩⁶ πρὸς τὸ ναυτικὸν ἐν τῇ Σάμῳ.

13 Κῦρος δ' ἐπὶ τούτοις μετεπέμψατο Λύσανδρον, ἐπεὶ αὐτῷ παρὰ τοῦ πατρὸς ἧκεν ἄγγελος λέγων ὅτι ἀρρωστῶν ἐκεῖνον καλοίη, ὢν ἐν Θαμνηρίοις τῆς Μηδίας ἐγγὺς Καδουσίων, ἐφ' οὓς ἐστράτευσεν ἀφεστῶτας. **14** ἥκοντα δὲ Λύσανδρον οὐκ εἴα ναυμαχεῖν πρὸς Ἀθηναίους, ἐὰν μὴ πολλῷ πλείους ναῦς ἔχῃ· εἶναι γὰρ χρήματα πολλὰ καὶ βασιλεῖ καὶ ἑαυτῷ, ὥστε τούτου ἕνεκεν πολλὰς πληροῦν. παρέδειξε δ' αὐτῷ πάντας τοὺς φόρους τοὺς ἐκ τῶν πόλεων, οἳ αὐτῷ ἴδιοι ἦσαν, καὶ τὰ περιττὰ χρήματα ἔδωκε· καὶ ἀναμνήσας ὡς εἶχε φιλίας πρός τε τὴν τῶν Λακεδαιμονίων πόλιν καὶ πρὸς Λύσανδρον ἰδίᾳ, ἀνέβαινε παρὰ τὸν πατέρα.

15 Λύσανδρος δ' ἐπεὶ αὐτῷ Κῦρος πάντα παραδοὺς τὰ αὑτοῦ πρὸς τὸν πατέρα ἀρρωστοῦντα μετάπεμπτος ἀνέβαινε, μισθὸν διαδοὺς τῇ στρατιᾷ ἀνήχθη τῆς Καρίας εἰς τὸν Κεραμικὸν⁷ κόλπον. καὶ προσβαλὼν πόλει τῶν Ἀθηναίων συμμάχῳ ὄνομα Κεδρείαις τῇ ὑστεραίᾳ προσβολῇ κατὰ κράτος

---

¹ ἐτῶν . . . παρεληλυθότων del. Unger
² χειρίς Stephanus: χειρός codd.
³ δύναιτο cu: δύναται rell.
⁴ Τούτῳ δὲ τῷ ἐνιαυτῷ . . . ἀγγέλους del. Unger
⁵ ἐπὶ '. . . Ἀλεξίου del. Marsham
⁶ ⟨τὰ⟩Marchant ⟨ἄλλας τριάκοντα ναῦς⟩ πρὸς Breitenbach πρὸς del. Kurz
⁷ Κεραμικὸν Hude (cf. I.4.8): Κεράμιον BP: Κεράμειον Pᶜ rell.

but Arakos as admiral, for they had a law forbidding a man to serve as admiral twice. They handed over the ships, however, to Lysandros, [after twenty-five years of the war had gone by].

8 [Also during this year Kyros executed Autoboisakes and Mitraios, sons of Dareiaios' sister (the daughter of Xerxes, Dareios' father), because when they met him they did not push their hands through the long-sleeved garment known as the *kore*, which they do only for the King. (The *kore* is longer than the *cheiris*; whoever has a hand in the *kore* cannot do anything.) **9** Hieramenes and his wife then told Dareiaios that it would be a terrible thing to overlook Kyros' excessive arrogance; so Dareiaios sent messengers to summon Kyros, on the grounds that he was ill.]

10 In the next year, [when Archytas was ephor and Alexias was archon at Athens,] Lysandros arrived at Ephesos and summoned Eteonikos from Chios with the ships. He also collected all the others, if there were any anywhere, and he repaired these and built others in Antandros. **11** When he went to Kyros to ask for money, Kyros told him that the money from the King had been spent and a great deal more besides, showing him how much each of the admirals had received; nevertheless he gave it to him. **12** After Lysandros received the money he appointed captains for the triremes and gave the sailors their back pay. Meanwhile the Athenian generals were preparing the navy in Samos.

13 Then Kyros summoned Lysandros, since a messenger had arrived from his father saying that he was sick and wanted to see Kyros; his father was in Thamneria in Media near the territory of the Kadousioi, against whom he was campaigning because they had revolted. **14** When Lysandros arrived Kyros urged him not to fight the Athenians in a naval battle unless he far outnumbered them in ships, for the King had a great deal of money and he himself did too, and therefore they could fill many ships. He assigned to Lysandros all the tribute that was his personally from the cities, and he gave Lysandros his remaining funds. And after reminding Lysandros of his friendship toward Sparta and toward Lysandros personally, he set out on the journey inland to his father.

15 After Kyros gave all his money to Lysandros and set out, as requested, to see his sick father, Lysandros distributed pay to the army and set out for the Keramic Gulf in Karia. He attacked the city named Kedreiai, an Athenian ally, and took it by

αἱρεῖ καὶ ἐξηνδραπόδισεν. ἦσαν δὲ μιξοβάρβαροι οἱ ἐνοικοῦντες. ἐκεῖθεν δ' ἀπέπλευσεν εἰς Ῥόδον.

16 οἱ δ' Ἀθηναῖοι ἐκ τῆς Σάμου ὁρμώμενοι τὴν βασιλέως κακῶς ἐποίουν, καὶ ἐπὶ τὴν Χίον καὶ τὴν Ἔφεσον ἐπέπλεον, καὶ παρεσκευάζοντο πρὸς ναυμαχίαν, καὶ στρατηγοὺς πρὸς τοῖς ὑπάρχουσι προσείλοντο Μένανδρον, Τυδέα, Κηφισόδοτον.

17 Λύσανδρος δ' ἐκ τῆς Ῥόδου παρὰ τὴν Ἰωνίαν ἐκπλεῖ πρὸς τὸν Ἑλλήσποντον πρός τε τῶν πλοίων τὸν ἔκπλουν καὶ ἐπὶ τὰς ἀφεστηκυίας αὐτῶν πόλεις. ἀνήγοντο δὲ καὶ οἱ Ἀθηναῖοι ἐπὶ τῆς Χίου πελάγιοι· ἡ γὰρ Ἀσία πολεμία αὐτοῖς ἦν. **18** Λύσανδρος δ' ἐξ Ἀβύδου παρέπλει εἰς Λάμψακον σύμμαχον οὖσαν Ἀθηναίων· καὶ οἱ Ἀβυδηνοὶ καὶ οἱ ἄλλοι παρῆσαν[1] πεζῇ· ἡγεῖτο δὲ Θώραξ Λακεδαιμόνιος. **19** προσβαλόντες δὲ τῇ πόλει αἱροῦσι κατὰ κράτος, καὶ διήρπασαν οἱ στρατιῶται οὖσαν πλουσίαν καὶ οἴνου καὶ σίτου καὶ τῶν ἄλλων ἐπιτηδείων πλήρη· τὰ δὲ ἐλεύθερα σώματα πάντα ἀφῆκε Λύσανδρος. **20** οἱ δ' Ἀθηναῖοι κατὰ πόδας πλέοντες ὡρμίσαντο τῆς Χερρονήσου ἐν Ἐλαιοῦντι ναυσὶν ὀγδοήκοντα καὶ ἑκατόν. ἐνταῦθα δὴ ἀριστοποιουμένοις αὐτοῖς ἀγγέλλεται τὰ περὶ Λάμψακον, καὶ εὐθὺς ἀνήχθησαν εἰς Σηστόν. **21** ἐκεῖθεν δ' εὐθὺς ἐπισιτισάμενοι ἔπλευσαν εἰς Αἰγὸς ποταμοὺς ἀντίον τῆς Λαμψάκου· διεῖχε δ' ὁ Ἑλλήσποντος ταύτῃ σταδίους ὡς πεντεκαίδεκα. ἐνταῦθα δὴ ἐδειπνοποιοῦντο.

22 Λύσανδρος δὲ τῇ ἐπιούσῃ νυκτί, ἐπεὶ ὄρθρος ἦν, ἐσήμανεν εἰς τὰς ναῦς ἀριστοποιησαμένους εἰσβαίνειν, πάντα δὲ παρασκευασάμενος ὡς εἰς ναυμαχίαν καὶ τὰ παραβλήματα παραβάλλων, προεῖπεν ὡς μηδεὶς κινήσοιτο ἐκ τῆς τάξεως μηδὲ ἀνάξοιτο. **23** οἱ δὲ Ἀθηναῖοι ἅμα τῷ ἡλίῳ ἀνίσχοντι ἐπὶ τῷ λιμένι παρετάξαντο ἐν μετώπῳ ὡς εἰς ναυμαχίαν. ἐπεὶ δὲ οὐκ ἀντανήγαγε Λύσανδρος, καὶ τῆς ἡμέρας ὀψὲ ἦν, ἀπέπλευσαν πάλιν εἰς τοὺς Αἰγὸς ποταμούς. **24** Λύσανδρος δὲ τὰς ταχίστας τῶν νεῶν ἐκέλευσεν ἕπεσθαι τοῖς Ἀθηναίοις, ἐπειδὰν δὲ ἐκβῶσι, κατιδόντας ὅ τι ποιοῦσιν ἀποπλεῖν καὶ αὐτῷ ἐξαγγεῖλαι. καὶ οὐ πρότερον ἐξεβίβασεν ἐκ τῶν νεῶν πρὶν αὗται ἧκον. ταῦτα δ' ἐποίει τέτταρας ἡμέρας· καὶ οἱ Ἀθηναῖοι ἐπανήγοντο.

25 Ἀλκιβιάδης δὲ κατιδὼν ἐκ τῶν τειχῶν τοὺς μὲν Ἀθηναίους ἐν αἰγιαλῷ ὁρμοῦντας καὶ πρὸς οὐδεμιᾷ πόλει, τὰ δ' ἐπιτήδεια ἐκ Σηστοῦ μετιόντας πεντεκαίδεκα σταδίους ἀπὸ τῶν νεῶν, τοὺς δὲ πολεμίους ἐν λιμένι καὶ πρὸς πόλει ἔχοντας πάντα, οὐκ ἐν καλῷ ἔφη αὐτοὺς ὁρμεῖν, ἀλλὰ μεθορμίσαι[2] εἰς Σηστὸν παρήνει πρός τε λιμένα καὶ πρὸς πόλιν· οὗ ὄντες ναυμαχήσετε, ἔφη, ὅταν βούλησθε. **26** οἱ δὲ στρατηγοί, μάλιστα δὲ Τυδεὺς

---

[1] παρῆσαν Cobet: παρησαν codd.
[2] μεθορμίσαι f: μεθορμῆσαι rell.

storm on the second day's assault and enslaved it. The inhabitants were half-barbarians. From there he sailed to Rhodes.

16 The Athenians, based at Samos, were ravaging the King's territory, and they sailed against Chios and Ephesos. They also prepared for a naval battle, and they chose Menandros, Tydeus, and Kephisodotos as generals in addition to the ones they had already.

17 Lysandros sailed from Rhodes along the Ionian coast toward the Hellespont, both to intercept the grain ships and to subdue the cities that had revolted from the Peloponnesians. The Athenians also set out in the direction of Chios, sailing on the open sea since Asia was hostile to them. **18** Lysandros sailed along the coast from Abydos to Lampsakos, an Athenian ally. The men of Abydos and the other allies went along on foot, under the command of Thorax the Lakedaimonian. **19** They attacked the city and took it by storm. The soldiers looted the city, which was rich and full of wine and grain and other supplies. Lysandros released all the free persons whom he captured. **20** The Athenians, sailing right behind him, anchored at Elaious in the Cherronesos with 180 ships. The news about Lampsakos was reported to them while they were eating breakfast there, and immediately they set out for Sestos. **21** Immediately after taking provisions there they sailed to Aigospotamoi, opposite Lampsakos, where the Hellespont is about fifteen *stadia* wide. There they ate supper.

22 During the coming night, when it was early dawn, Lysandros gave the signal to eat breakfast and board the ships. He prepared everything as for a naval battle, putting up the side-screens, and announced no one should move from his position or put to sea. **23** At sunrise the Athenians drew up in line facing the harbor, as for a naval battle. But when Lysandros did not put out against them, and it was late in the day, they sailed back again to Aigospotamoi. **24** Lysandros ordered his fastest ships to follow the Athenians and to watch them when they disembarked, and then to sail away and report to him. He did not let his sailors disembark from the ships until these ships had returned. He did the same thing every day for four days, and the Athenians continued to put out against him.

25 From the fort Alkibiades saw that the Athenians were anchored at a beach without a city near by, and that they were bringing their provisions from Sestos, fifteen *stadia* from the ships, while the enemy had everything, being in a harbor in front of a city. He told the Athenians that they were anchored in a poor location, and encouraged them to move to Sestos, to a harbor and a city. "Located there," he said, "you can fight whenever you wish." **26** The generals, however, particularly Tydeus

καὶ Μένανδρος, ἀπιέναι αὐτὸν ἐκέλευσαν· αὐτοὶ γὰρ νῦν στρατηγεῖν, οὐκ ἐκεῖνον. καὶ ὁ μὲν ᾤχετο.

27 Λύσανδρος δ', ἐπεὶ ἦν ἡμέρα πέμπτη ἐπιπλέουσι τοῖς Ἀθηναίοις, εἶπε τοῖς παρ' αὐτοῦ ἑπομένοις, ἐπὰν κατίδωσιν αὐτοὺς ἐκβεβηκότας καὶ ἐσκεδασμένους κατὰ τὴν Χερρόνησον, ὅπερ ἐποίουν πολὺ μᾶλλον καθ' ἑκάστην ἡμέραν, τά τε σιτία πόρρωθεν ὠνούμενοι καὶ καταφρονοῦντες δὴ τοῦ Λυσάνδρου, ὅτι οὐκ ἀντανῆγεν, ἀποπλέοντας τοὔμπαλιν παρ' αὐτὸν ἆραι ἀσπίδα κατὰ μέσον τὸν πλοῦν. οἱ δὲ ταῦτα ἐποίησαν ὡς ἐκέλευσε. 28 Λύσανδρος δ' εὐθὺς ἐσήμηνε τὴν ταχίστην πλεῖν· συμπαρῄει δὲ καὶ Θώραξ τὸ πεζὸν ἔχων. Κόνων δὲ ἰδὼν τὸν ἐπίπλουν, ἐσήμανεν εἰς τὰς ναῦς βοηθεῖν κατὰ κράτος. διεσκεδασμένων δὲ τῶν ἀνθρώπων, αἱ μὲν τῶν νεῶν δίκροτοι ἦσαν, αἱ δὲ μονόκροτοι, αἱ δὲ παντελῶς κεναί· ἡ δὲ Κόνωνος καὶ ἄλλαι περὶ αὐτὸν ἑπτὰ πλήρεις ἀνήχθησαν ἀθρόαι καὶ ἡ Πάραλος, τὰς δ' ἄλλας πάσας Λύσανδρος ἔλαβε πρὸς τῇ γῇ. τοὺς δὲ πλείστους ἄνδρας ἐν τῇ γῇ συνέλεξεν· οἱ δὲ καὶ ἔφυγον εἰς τὰ τειχύδρια.

29 Κόνων δὲ ταῖς ἐννέα ναυσὶ φεύγων, ἐπεὶ ἔγνω τῶν Ἀθηναίων τὰ πράγματα διεφθαρμένα, κατασχὼν ἐπὶ τὴν Ἀβαρνίδα τὴν Λαμψάκου ἄκραν ἔλαβεν αὐτόθεν τὰ μεγάλα τῶν Λυσάνδρου νεῶν ἱστία, καὶ αὐτὸς μὲν ὀκτὼ ναυσὶν ἀπέπλευσε παρ' Εὐαγόραν εἰς Κύπρον, ἡ δὲ Πάραλος εἰς τὰς Ἀθήνας ἀπαγγελοῦσα[1] τὰ γεγονότα.

30 Λύσανδρος δὲ τάς τε ναῦς καὶ τοὺς αἰχμαλώτους καὶ τἆλλα πάντα εἰς Λάμψακον ἀπήγαγεν, ἔλαβε δὲ καὶ τῶν στρατηγῶν ἄλλους τε καὶ Φιλοκλέα καὶ Ἀδείμαντον. ᾗ δ' ἡμέρᾳ ταῦτα κατειργάσατο, ἔπεμψε Θεόπομπον τὸν Μιλήσιον λῃστὴν εἰς Λακεδαίμονα ἀπαγγελοῦντα τὰ γεγονότα, ὃς ἀφικόμενος τριταῖος ἀπήγγειλε. 31 μετὰ δὲ ταῦτα Λύσανδρος ἀθροίσας τοὺς συμμάχους ἐκέλευσε βουλεύεσθαι περὶ τῶν αἰχμαλώτων. ἐνταῦθα δὴ κατηγορίαι ἐγίγνοντο πολλαὶ τῶν Ἀθηναίων, ἅ τε ἤδη παρενενομήκεσαν καὶ ἃ ἐψηφισμένοι ἦσαν ποιεῖν, εἰ κρατήσειαν τῇ ναυμαχίᾳ, τὴν δεξιὰν χεῖρα ἀποκόπτειν τῶν ζωγρηθέντων πάντων, καὶ ὅτι λαβόντες δύο τριήρεις, Κορινθίαν καὶ Ἀνδρίαν, τοὺς ἄνδρας ἐξ αὐτῶν πάντας κατακρημνίσειαν· Φιλοκλῆς δ' ἦν στρατηγὸς τῶν Ἀθηναίων, ὃς τούτους διέφθειρε. 32 ἐλέγετο δὲ καὶ ἄλλα πολλά, καὶ ἔδοξεν ἀποκτεῖναι τῶν αἰχμαλώτων ὅσοι ἦσαν Ἀθηναῖοι πλὴν Ἀδειμάντου, ὅτι μόνος ἐπελάβετο ἐν τῇ ἐκκλησίᾳ τοῦ περὶ τῆς ἀποτομῆς τῶν χειρῶν ψηφίσματος· ᾐτιάθη μέντοι ὑπό τινων προδοῦναι τὰς ναῦς. Λύσανδρος δὲ Φιλοκλέα πρῶτον ἐρωτήσας, [ὃς τοὺς Ἀνδρίους καὶ Κορινθίους

---

[1] ἀπαγγελοῦσα Vᶜ: ἀπαγγέλλουσα BPM

and Menandros, told him to go away, for they were the generals now, not he. So he left.

27 When the Athenians sailed out on the fifth day, Lysandros instructed his men who followed them back that when they saw them disembarked and scattered along the Cherronesos--which they did more and more every day, because they bought provisions far away and because they felt contempt for Lysandros since he did not put out to sea against them--they should sail back again to him and raise a shield in the middle of their journey. They did as they were ordered. **28** Lysandros immediately signalled to sail as fast as possible; Thorax went along with the infantry. When Konon saw the attack, he signalled the ships to go into action as quickly as possible. But since the men were scattered, some of the ships had rowers for only two banks of oars, some only for one, and some were entirely empty. Konon's ship and seven others with him put to sea together, with full complements of rowers, and the Paralos did too; Lysandros took all the rest near land. He also captured most of the men on land, though some escaped to small forts.

29 Konon, fleeing with the nine ships when he recognized that all was lost for the Athenians, put in at Abarnis, the headland of Lampsakos, and there seized the main sails of Lysandros' ships. He himself sailed away with eight ships to Euagoras in Cyprus, while the Paralos went to Athens to report what had happened.

30 Lysandros took the ships and the prisoners and everything else to Lampsakos, including Philokles and Adeimantos and other generals. On the day the battle was fought, he sent Theopompos the Milesian pirate to Lakedaimon to report what had happened; he arrived on the third day and gave his report. **31** After this Lysandros assembled the allies and told them to consult about the prisoners. Then many accusations against the Athenians were made, both with regard to the ways they had already violated custom and with regard to what they had voted to do if they won the naval battle (to cut off the right hand of anyone captured alive), and because when they had captured two triremes, one Korinthian and one Andrian, they had thrown their crews overboard. Philokles was the Athenian general who had killed them. **32** Many other things were also said, and they decided to kill all the Athenians among the captives except for Adeimantos, who alone had objected in the assembly to the decree about cutting off the hands; he was accused by some persons, however, of betraying the ships. Lysandros, after first asking Philokles [who had

κατεκρήμνισε,]¹ τί εἴη ἄξιος παθεῖν ἀρξάμενος εἰς Ἕλληνας παρανομεῖν, ἀπέσφαξεν.

<h2 style="text-align:center">2</h2>

1 Ἐπεὶ δὲ τὰ ἐν τῇ Λαμψάκῳ κατεστήσατο, ἔπλει ἐπὶ τὸ Βυζάντιον καὶ Καλχηδόνα. οἱ δ' αὐτὸν ὑπεδέχοντο, τοὺς τῶν Ἀθηναίων φρουροὺς ὑποσπόνδους ἀφέντες. οἱ δὲ προδόντες Ἀλκιβιάδῃ τὸ Βυζάντιον τότε μὲν ἔφυγον εἰς τὸν Πόντον, ὕστερον δ' εἰς Ἀθήνας καὶ ἐγένοντο Ἀθηναῖοι. **2** Λύσανδρος δὲ τούς τε φρουροὺς τῶν Ἀθηναίων καὶ εἴ τινά που ἄλλον ἴδοι Ἀθηναῖον, ἀπέπεμπεν εἰς τὰς Ἀθήνας, διδοὺς ἐκεῖσε μόνον πλέουσιν ἀσφάλειαν, ἄλλοθι δ' οὔ, εἰδὼς ὅτι ὅσῳ ἂν πλείους συλλεγῶσιν εἰς τὸ ἄστυ καὶ τὸν Πειραιᾶ, θᾶττον τῶν ἐπιτηδείων ἔνδειαν ἔσεσθαι. καταλιπὼν δὲ Βυζαντίου καὶ Καλχηδόνος Σθενέλαον ἁρμοστὴν Λάκωνα, αὐτὸς ἀποπλεύσας εἰς Λάμψακον τὰς ναῦς ἐπεσκεύαζεν.

3 Ἐν δὲ ταῖς Ἀθήναις τῆς Παράλου ἀφικομένης νυκτὸς ἐλέγετο ἡ συμφορά, καὶ οἰμωγὴ ἐκ τοῦ Πειραιῶς διὰ τῶν μακρῶν τειχῶν εἰς ἄστυ διῆκεν, ὁ ἕτερος τῷ ἑτέρῳ παραγγέλλων· ὥστ' ἐκείνης τῆς νυκτὸς οὐδεὶς ἐκοιμήθη, οὐ μόνον τοὺς ἀπολωλότας πενθοῦντες, ἀλλὰ πολὺ μᾶλλον ἔτι αὐτοὶ ἑαυτούς, πείσεσθαι νομίζοντες οἷα ἐποίησαν Μηλίους τε Λακεδαιμονίων ἀποίκους ὄντας, κρατήσαντες πολιορκίᾳ, καὶ Ἱστιαιᾶς² καὶ Σκιωναίους καὶ Τορωναίους καὶ Αἰγινήτας καὶ ἄλλους πολλοὺς τῶν Ἑλλήνων. **4** Τῇ δ' ὑστεραίᾳ ἐκκλησίαν ἐποίησαν, ἐν ᾗ ἔδοξε τούς τε λιμένας ἀποχῶσαι πλὴν ἑνὸς καὶ τὰ τείχη εὐτρεπίζειν καὶ φυλακὰς ἐφιστάναι καὶ τἆλλα πάντα ὡς εἰς πολιορκίαν παρασκευάζειν τὴν πόλιν.

Καὶ οὗτοι μὲν περὶ ταῦτα ἦσαν. **5** Λύσανδρος δ' ἐκ τοῦ Ἑλλησπόντου ναυσὶ διακοσίαις ἀφικόμενος εἰς Λέσβον κατεσκευάσατο τάς τε ἄλλας πόλεις ἐν αὐτῇ καὶ Μυτιλήνην· εἰς δὲ τὰ ἐπὶ Θρᾴκης χωρία ἔπεμψε δέκα τριήρεις ἔχοντα Ἐτεόνικον, ὃς τὰ ἐκεῖ πάντα πρὸς Λακεδαιμονίους μετέστησεν. **6** εὐθὺς δὲ καὶ ἡ ἄλλη Ἑλλὰς ἀφειστήκει Ἀθηναίων μετὰ τὴν ναυμαχίαν πλὴν Σαμίων· οὗτοι δὲ σφαγὰς τῶν γνωρίμων ποιήσαντες κατεῖχον τὴν πόλιν.

7 Λύσανδρος δὲ μετὰ ταῦτα ἔπεμψε πρὸς Ἆγίν τε εἰς Δεκέλειαν καὶ εἰς Λακεδαίμονα ὅτι προσπλεῖ σὺν διακοσίαις ναυσί. Λακεδαιμόνιοι δ' ἐξῇσαν πανδημεὶ καὶ οἱ ἄλλοι Πελοποννήσιοι πλὴν Ἀργείων, παραγγείλαντος τοῦ ἑτέρου Λακεδαιμονίων βασιλέως Παυσανίου. **8** ἐπεὶ

---

¹ ὅς . . . κατεκρήμνισε del. Cobet
² Ἱστιαιᾶς: Ἱστιαίας M² Ἱστιέας rell.

thrown the Andrians and Korinthians overboard,] what he deserved for beginning to violate custom against Greeks, cut his throat.

2

1 When Lysandros had settled matters in Lampsakos, he sailed against Byzantion and Kalchedon. The inhabitants admitted him, allowing the Athenian garrison to depart under a truce. At the time those who had betrayed Byzantion to Alkibiades fled to the Black Sea region; later they reached Athens and became Athenian citizens. **2** Lysandros sent back to Athens the Athenian garrison and any other Athenians he found anywhere, granting safe passage to them only if they went to Athens, because he knew that the more people collected in the city and in Peiraieus, the sooner they would run short of provisions. He left Sthenelaos the Lakonian as governor of Byzantion and Kalchedon and himself sailed back to Lampsakos, where he repaired the ships. **3** At Athens the disaster was reported when the Paralos arrived during the night, and a sound of wailing extended from Peiraieus through the long walls to the city, one man reporting the news to the next; as a result that night no one slept, not only because they were mourning the lost, but much more because they were mourning themselves, believing that they would suffer the same things they had done to the Melians, colonists from Sparta whom they had conquered in a siege, and the Histiaians and Skionaians and Toronaians and Aiginetans and many other Greeks. **4** On the next day they held an assembly, in which they decided to block up the harbors, except for one, and to repair the walls and to establish guards and in every other way to prepare the city for a siege.

While they were occupied with these matters, **5** Lysandros arrived at Lesbos from the Hellespont with two hundred ships. He settled matters in other cities of Lesbos and particularly in Mytilene, and he sent Eteonikos with ten triremes to the Thraceward region. Eteonikos brought all those parts over to the side of the Lakedaimonians. **6** Immediately after the naval battle the rest of Greece revolted from the Athenians, except for the Samians, who were in possession of the city after slaughtering the aristocrats.

7 Then Lysandros sent messages to Agis at Dekeleia and to Lakedaimon saying that he would arrive with two hundred ships. The Lakedaimonians came out in full force along with the other Peloponnesians (except for the Argives), under the command of Pausanias, the other Lakedaimonian king. **8** When all of them had

δ' ἅπαντες ἠθροίσθησαν, ἀναλαβὼν αὐτοὺς πρὸς τὴν πόλιν ἐστρατοπέδευσεν ἐν τῇ Ἀκαδημείᾳ[1] [τῷ καλουμένῳ γυμνασίῳ][2]. **9** Λύσανδρος δὲ ἀφικόμενος εἰς Αἴγιναν ἀπέδωκε τὴν πόλιν Αἰγινήταις, ὅσους ἐδύνατο πλείστους αὐτῶν ἀθροίσας, ὡς δ' αὕτως καὶ Μηλίοις καὶ τοῖς ἄλλοις ὅσοι τῆς αὐτῶν ἐστέροντο. μετὰ δὲ τοῦτο δῃώσας Σαλαμῖνα ὡρμίσατο πρὸς τὸν Πειραιᾶ ναυσὶ πεντήκοντα καὶ ἑκατόν, καὶ τὰ πλοῖα εἶργε τοῦ εἴσπλου.

10 Οἱ δ' Ἀθηναῖοι πολιορκούμενοι κατὰ γῆν καὶ κατὰ θάλατταν ἠπόρουν τί χρὴ ποιεῖν, οὔτε νεῶν οὔτε συμμάχων αὐτοῖς ὄντων οὔτε σίτου· ἐνόμιζον δὲ οὐδεμίαν εἶναι σωτηρίαν [εἰ][3] μὴ παθεῖν ἃ οὐ τιμωρούμενοι ἐποίησαν, ἀλλὰ διὰ τὴν ὕβριν ἠδίκουν ἀνθρώπους μικροπολίτας οὐδ' ἐπὶ μιᾷ αἰτίᾳ ἑτέρᾳ ἢ ὅτι ἐκείνοις συνεμάχουν. **11** διὰ ταῦτα τοὺς ἀτίμους ἐπιτίμους ποιήσαντες ἐκαρτέρουν, καὶ ἀποθνησκόντων ἐν τῇ πόλει λιμῷ πολλῶν οὐ διελέγοντο περὶ διαλλαγῆς. ἐπεὶ δὲ παντελῶς ἤδη ὁ σῖτος ἐπελελοίπει, ἔπεμψαν πρέσβεις παρ' Ἆγιν, βουλόμενοι σύμμαχοι εἶναι Λακεδαιμονίοις ἔχοντες τὰ τείχη καὶ τὸν Πειραιᾶ, καὶ ἐπὶ τούτοις συνθήκας ποιεῖσθαι. **12** ὁ δὲ αὐτοὺς εἰς Λακεδαίμονα ἐκέλευεν ἰέναι· οὐ γὰρ εἶναι κύριος αὐτός. ἐπεὶ δ' ἀπήγγειλαν οἱ πρέσβεις ταῦτα τοῖς Ἀθηναίοις, ἔπεμψαν αὐτοὺς εἰς Λακεδαίμονα. **13** οἱ δ' ἐπεὶ ἦσαν ἐν Σελλασίᾳ [πλησίον τῆς Λακωνικῆς][4] καὶ ἐπύθοντο οἱ ἔφοροι αὐτῶν ἃ ἔλεγον, ὄντα οἷάπερ καὶ πρὸς Ἆγιν, αὐτόθεν αὐτοὺς ἐκέλευον ἀπιέναι, καὶ εἴ τι δέονται εἰρήνης, κάλλιον ἥκειν βουλευσαμένους. **14** οἱ δὲ πρέσβεις ἐπεὶ ἧκον οἴκαδε καὶ ἀπήγγειλαν ταῦτα εἰς τὴν πόλιν, ἀθυμία ἐνέπεσε πᾶσιν· ᾤοντο γὰρ ἀνδραποδισθήσεσθαι, καὶ ἕως ἂν πέμπωσιν ἑτέρους πρέσβεις, πολλοὺς τῷ λιμῷ ἀπολεῖσθαι. **15** περὶ δὲ τῶν τειχῶν τῆς καθαιρέσεως οὐδεὶς ἐβούλετο συμβουλεύειν· Ἀρχέστρατος γὰρ εἰπὼν ἐν τῇ βουλῇ Λακεδαιμονίοις κράτιστον εἶναι ἐφ' οἷς προυκαλοῦντο εἰρήνην ποιεῖσθαι, ἐδέθη· προυκαλοῦντο δὲ τῶν μακρῶν τειχῶν ἐπὶ δέκα σταδίους καθελεῖν ἑκατέρου· ἐγένετο δὲ ψήφισμα μὴ ἐξεῖναι περὶ τούτων συμβουλεύειν.

16 Τοιούτων δὲ ὄντων Θηραμένης εἶπεν ἐν ἐκκλησίᾳ ὅτι εἰ βούλονται αὐτὸν πέμψαι παρὰ Λύσανδρον, εἰδὼς ἥξει Λακεδαιμονίους πότερον ἐξανδραποδίσασθαι τὴν πόλιν βουλόμενοι ἀντέχουσι[5] περὶ τῶν τειχῶν ἢ πίστεως ἕνεκα. πεμφθεὶς δὲ διέτριβε παρὰ Λυσάνδρῳ τρεῖς μῆνας καὶ πλείω, ἐπιτηρῶν ὁπότε Ἀθηναῖοι ἔμελλον διὰ τὸ ἐπιλελοιπέναι τὸν σῖτον ἅπαντα ὅ τι τις λέγοι ὁμολογήσειν. **17** ἐπεὶ δὲ ἧκε τετάρτῳ μηνί,

---

[1] Ἀκαδημείᾳ: Ἀκαδημία(ι) codd.
[2] τῷ καλουμένῳ γυμνασίῳ del. Wolf
[3] εἰ del. Dindorf
[4] πλησίον τῆς Λακωνικῆς del. Cobet
[5] ἀντέχουσι Leonclavius: ἀνέχουσι codd.

gathered, he took them against the city and camped in the Academy [(the name of a *gymnasion*)]. **9** Lysandros arrived at Aigina and gave the city back to the Aiginetans, as many of them as he was able to collect, and he treated similarly the Melians and all the others who had been deprived of their own states. After this he ravaged Salamis and anchored facing Peiraieus with 150 ships, and he prevented the grain ships from entering.

10 Besieged by land and sea, the Athenians did not know what to do. They had neither ships nor allies nor food, and they believed they had no way to avoid suffering the same things they had done when through arrogance they did wrong to persons from small states, not in retaliation but for no reason other than that they had allied with the enemy. **11** Therefore they continued to hold out, restoring their rights to those who had been disenfranchised, and although many were dying in the city from hunger they would not talk about a truce. But when food had entirely given out, they sent ambassadors to Agis, proposing peace on the terms that they become allies of the Lakedaimonians while keeping their walls and Peiraieus. **12** He told them to go to Lakedaimon, for he had, he said, no authority to negotiate. When the ambassadors reported his answer to the Athenians, they sent the ambassadors to Lakedaimon. **13** When they were in Sellasia, [near Lakonia,] and the ephors learned their terms (the same ones they had offered Agis), the ephors told them to depart at once. If they wanted peace, the ephors said, the Athenians should come back after taking better counsel. **14** When the ambassadors arrived home and reported this answer to the city, despair fell on everyone. They thought that they would be sold into slavery, and many would die from hunger by the time they could send other ambassadors. **15** No one wished to recommend the dismantling of the walls, for when Archestratos said in the Council that it would be best to make peace on the Lakedaimonians' terms (they had proposed the dismantling of ten *stadia* of each of the long walls), he was put in prison and a decree was passed forbidding any such proposals.

16 In this situation Theramenes said in the assembly that if the Athenians were willing to send him to Lysandros, he would return knowing whether the Lakedaimonians insisted about the walls in order to enslave the city or for an assurance of good faith. Upon being sent, however, he stayed with Lysandros for more than three months, waiting until the Athenians would agree to any terms whatever because the food was gone. **17** When he returned in the fourth month, he

ἀπήγγειλεν ἐν ἐκκλησίᾳ ὅτι αὐτὸν Λύσανδρος τέως μὲν κατέχοι, εἶτα κελεύοι εἰς Λακεδαίμονα ἰέναι· οὐ γὰρ εἶναι κύριος ὧν ἐρωτῷτο ὑπ' αὐτοῦ, ἀλλὰ τοὺς ἐφόρους. μετὰ ταῦτα ᾑρέθη πρεσβευτὴς εἰς Λακεδαίμονα αὐτοκράτωρ δέκατος αὐτός. 18 Λύσανδρος δὲ τοῖς ἐφόροις ἔπεμψεν ἀγγελοῦντα μετ' ἄλλων Λακεδαιμονίων Ἀριστοτέλην, φυγάδα Ἀθηναῖον ὄντα, ὅτι ἀποκρίναιτο Θηραμένει ἐκείνους κυρίους εἶναι εἰρήνης καὶ πολέμου.

19 Θηραμένης δὲ καὶ οἱ ἄλλοι πρέσβεις ἐπεὶ ἦσαν ἐν Σελλασίᾳ, ἐρωτώμενοι δὲ ἐπὶ τίνι λόγῳ ἥκοιεν εἶπαν ὅτι αὐτοκράτορες περὶ εἰρήνης, μετὰ ταῦτα οἱ ἔφοροι καλεῖν ἐκέλευον αὐτούς. ἐπεὶ δ' ἧκον, ἐκκλησίαν ἐποίησαν, ἐν ᾗ ἀντέλεγον Κορίνθιοι καὶ Θηβαῖοι μάλιστα, πολλοὶ δὲ καὶ ἄλλοι τῶν Ἑλλήνων, μὴ σπένδεσθαι Ἀθηναίοις, ἀλλ' ἐξαιρεῖν. 20 Λακεδαιμόνιοι δὲ οὐκ ἔφασαν πόλιν Ἑλληνίδα ἀνδραποδιεῖν μέγα ἀγαθὸν εἰργασμένην ἐν τοῖς μεγίστοις κινδύνοις γενομένοις τῇ Ἑλλάδι, ἀλλ' ἐποιοῦντο εἰρήνην ἐφ' ᾧ τά τε μακρὰ τείχη καὶ τὸν Πειραιᾶ καθελόντας καὶ τὰς ναῦς πλὴν δώδεκα παραδόντας καὶ τοὺς φυγάδας καθέντας, τὸν αὐτὸν ἐχθρὸν καὶ φίλον νομίζοντας[1] Λακεδαιμονίοις ἕπεσθαι καὶ κατὰ γῆν καὶ κατὰ θάλατταν ὅποι ἂν ἡγῶνται.

21 Θηραμένης δὲ καὶ οἱ σὺν αὐτῷ πρέσβεις ἐπανέφερον ταῦτα εἰς τὰς Ἀθήνας. εἰσιόντας δ' αὐτοὺς ὄχλος περιεχεῖτο πολύς, φοβούμενοι μὴ ἄπρακτοι ἥκοιεν· οὐ γὰρ ἔτι ἐνεχώρει μέλλειν διὰ τὸ πλῆθος τῶν ἀπολλυμένων τῷ λιμῷ. 22 τῇ δὲ ὑστεραίᾳ ἀπήγγελλον οἱ πρέσβεις ἐφ' οἷς οἱ Λακεδαιμόνιοι ποιοῖντο τὴν εἰρήνην· προηγόρει δὲ αὐτῶν Θηραμένης, λέγων ὡς χρὴ πείθεσθαι Λακεδαιμονίοις καὶ τὰ τείχη περιαιρεῖν. ἀντειπόντων δέ τινων αὐτῷ, πολὺ δὲ πλειόνων συνεπαινεσάντων, ἔδοξε δέχεσθαι τὴν εἰρήνην. 23 μετὰ δὲ ταῦτα Λύσανδρός τε κατέπλει εἰς τὸν Πειραιᾶ καὶ οἱ φυγάδες κατῇσαν καὶ τὰ τείχη κατέσκαπτον ὑπ' αὐλητρίδων πολλῇ προθυμίᾳ, νομίζοντες ἐκείνην τὴν ἡμέραν τῇ Ἑλλάδι ἄρχειν τῆς ἐλευθερίας.

24 [Καὶ ὁ ἐνιαυτὸς ἔληγεν, ἐν ᾧ μεσοῦντι Διονύσιος ὁ Ἑρμοκράτους Συρακόσιος ἐτυράννησε, μάχῃ μὲν πρότερον ἡττηθέντων ὑπὸ Συρακοσίων Καρχηδονίων, σπάνει δὲ σίτου ἑλόντων Ἀκράγαντα, ἐκλιπόντων τῶν Σικελιωτῶν τὴν πόλιν.][2]

3

1 Τῷ δ' ἐπιόντι ἔτει, [ᾧ ἦν Ὀλυμπιάς, ᾗ τὸ στάδιον ἐνίκα Κροκίνας Θετταλός, Εὐδίου ἐν Σπάρτῃ ἐφορεύοντος, Πυθοδώρου δ' ἐν Ἀθήναις ἄρχοντος,

[1] νομίζοντας: νομίζοντες BPM[1]
[2] Καὶ ὁ ἐνιαυτὸς ... πόλιν del. Unger

reported in the assembly that Lysandros had detained him all this time and then told him to go to Lakedaimon; he did not have authority, he said, in the matters about which Theramenes asked him--it belonged to the ephors. After this Theramenes was chosen ambassador with full powers, along with nine others, to Lakedaimon. **18** Meanwhile Lysandros sent Aristoteles, an Athenian exile, along with some Lakedaimonians to tell the ephors that he had responded to Theramenes that they had the authority in matters of peace and war.

19 When Theramenes and the other ambassadors were in Sellasia, they were asked the reason for their mission. They said that they came with full powers to negotiate peace; after this the ephors gave instructions to summon the ambassadors. When they arrived, an assembly was held in which the Korinthians and Thebans particularly, but many other Greeks as well, objected to making peace with the Athenians and urged their destruction. **20** The Lakedaimonians, however, refused to enslave a Greek city that had done great good at the time of Greece's greatest dangers; instead they offered to make peace on the following terms: the long walls and the Peiraieus wall to be dismantled, the ships except twelve to be surrendered, the exiles to return, and the Athenians to have the same enemies and friends as the Lakedaimonians and to follow them wherever they might lead on land and sea.

21 Theramenes and the ambassadors with him brought back these terms to Athens. A great mob surrounded them as they entered the city, afraid that they had returned unsuccessful, for because of the great number of people who had died from hunger it was no longer possible to delay. **22** On the following day the ambassadors reported the terms on which the Lakedaimonians offered to make peace. Theramenes spoke for the ambassadors, saying that it was necessary to obey the Lakedaimonians and to dismantle the walls. Although some persons spoke in opposition to him, many more spoke in support and it was decided to accept the peace.

23 After this Lysandros sailed into the Peiraieus and the exiles returned and they began to raze the walls to the music of pipe-girls, with great enthusiasm, thinking that day to be the beginning of freedom for Greece.

24 [So the year ended. In the middle of this year Dionysios the son of Hermokrates, a Syracusan, became tyrant after the Carthaginians were defeated in battle by the Syracusans. The Carthaginians did, however, take Akragas due to a shortage of food, the Sikeliots abandoning the city.]

3

1 In the next year [Krokinas the Thessalian won the *stadion* race at the Olympic games, Eudios was ephor in Sparta, and Pythodoros was archon in Athens;

ὃν Ἀθηναῖοι, ὅτι ἐν ὀλιγαρχίᾳ ᾑρέθη, οὐκ ὀνομάζουσιν, ἀλλ' ἀναρχίαν τὸν ἐνιαυτὸν καλοῦσιν. ἐγένετο δὲ αὕτη ἡ ὀλιγαρχία ὧδε.]¹ 2 ἔδοξε τῷ δήμῳ τριάκοντα ἄνδρας ἑλέσθαι, οἳ τοὺς πατρίους νόμους συγγράψουσι, καθ' οὓς πολιτεύσουσι. καὶ ᾑρέθησαν οἵδε Πολυχάρης, Κριτίας, Μηλόβιος, Ἱππόλοχος, Εὐκλείδης, Ἱέρων, Μνησίλοχος, Χρέμων, Θηραμένης, Ἀρεσίας, Διοκλῆς, Φαιδρίας, Χαιρέλεως, Ἀναίτιος, Πείσων, Σοφοκλῆς, Ἐρατοσθένης, Χαρικλῆς, Ὀνομακλῆς, Θέογνις, Αἰσχίνης, Θεογένης, Κλεομήδης, Ἐρασίστρατος, Φείδων, Δρακοντίδης, Εὐμάθης, Ἀριστοτέλης, Ἱππόμαχος, Μνησιθείδης. τούτων δὲ πραχθέντων ἀπέπλει Λύσανδρος πρὸς Σάμον, Ἆγις δ' ἐκ τῆς Δεκελείας ἀπαγαγὼν τὸ πεζὸν στράτευμα διέλυσε κατὰ πόλεις ἑκάστους.

4 Κατὰ δὲ τοῦτον τὸν καιρὸν περὶ ἡλίου ἔκλειψιν Λυκόφρων ὁ Φεραῖος, βουλόμενος ἄρξαι ὅλης τῆς Θετταλίας, τοὺς ἐναντιουμένους αὐτῷ τῶν Θετταλῶν, Λαρισαίους τε καὶ ἄλλους, μάχῃ ἐνίκησε καὶ πολλοὺς ἀπέκτεινεν.

5 Ἐν δὲ τῷ αὐτῷ χρόνῳ καὶ Διονύσιος ὁ Συρακόσιος τύραννος μάχῃ ἡττηθεὶς ὑπὸ Καρχηδονίων Γέλαν καὶ Καμάριναν ἀπώλεσε. μετ' ὀλίγον δὲ καὶ Λεοντῖνοι Συρακοσίοις συνοικοῦντες ἀπέστησαν εἰς τὴν αὐτῶν πόλιν ἀπὸ Διονυσίου καὶ Συρακοσίων. Παραχρῆμα δὲ καὶ οἱ Συρακόσιοι ἱππεῖς ὑπὸ Διονυσίου εἰς Κατάνην ἀπεστάλησαν.

6 Οἱ δὲ Σάμιοι πολιορκούμενοι ὑπὸ Λυσάνδρου πάντῃ, ἐπεὶ οὐ² βουλομένων αὐτῶν τὸ πρῶτον ὁμολογεῖν προσβάλλειν ἤδη ἔμελλεν ὁ Λύσανδρος, ὡμολόγησαν ἓν ἱμάτιον ἔχων ἕκαστος ἀπιέναι τῶν ἐλευθέρων, τὰ δ' ἄλλα παραδοῦναι· καὶ οὕτως ἐξῆλθον. 7 Λύσανδρος δὲ τοῖς ἀρχαίοις πολίταις παραδοὺς τὴν πόλιν καὶ τὰ ἐνόντα πάντα καὶ δέκα ἄρχοντας καταστήσας φρουρεῖν ἀφῆκε τὸ τῶν συμμάχων ναυτικὸν κατὰ πόλεις, 8 ταῖς δὲ Λακωνικαῖς ναυσὶν ἀπέπλευσεν εἰς Λακεδαίμονα, ἀπάγων τά τε τῶν αἰχμαλώτων νεῶν ἀκρωτήρια καὶ τὰς ἐκ Πειραιῶς τριήρεις πλὴν δώδεκα καὶ στεφάνους, οὓς παρὰ τῶν πόλεων ἐλάμβανε δῶρα ἰδίᾳ, καὶ ἀργυρίου τετρακόσια καὶ ἑβδομήκοντα τάλαντα, ἃ περιεγένοντο τῶν φόρων, οὓς αὐτῷ Κῦρος παρέδειξεν εἰς τὸν πόλεμον, καὶ εἴ τι ἄλλο ἐκτήσατο ἐν τῷ πολέμῳ. 9 ταῦτα δὲ πάντα Λακεδαιμονίοις ἀπέδωκε τελευτῶντος τοῦ θέρους [εἰς ὃ ἑξάμηνος καὶ ὀκτὼ καὶ εἴκοσιν ἔτη τῷ πολέμῳ ἐτελεύτα, ἐν οἷς ἔφοροι οἱ ἀριθμούμενοι οἵδε ἐγένοντο, Αἰνησίας πρῶτος, ἐφ' οὗ ἤρξατο ὁ πόλεμος, πέμπτῳ καὶ δεκάτῳ ἔτει τῶν μετ' Εὐβοίας ἅλωσιν τριακονταετίδων σπονδῶν, μετὰ δὲ τοῦτον οἵδε· 10 Βρασίδας, Ἰσάνωρ, Σωστρατίδας, Ἔξαρχος, Ἀγησίστρατος, Ἀγγενίδας, Ὀνομακλῆς, Ζεύξιππος, Πιτύας, Πλειστόλας, Κλεινόμαχος, Ἴλαρχος, Λέων, Χαιρίλας, Πατησιάδας,

---

¹ ᾧ... ὧδε del. Marsham
² οὐ a: om. rell.

the Athenians do not use his name because he was chosen during the oligarchy, but designate the year as without an archon. This oligarchy came about as follows. **2** The people decided to choose thirty men, who were to draw up the ancestral laws, according to which they would govern. The following men were chosen: Polychares, Kritias, Melobios, Hippolochos, Eukleides, Hieron, Mnesilochos, Chremon, Theramenes, Aresias, Diokles, Phaidrias, Chaireleos, Anaitios, Peison, Sophokles, Eratosthenes, Charikles, Onomakles, Theognis, Aischines, Theogenes, Kleomedes, Erasistratos, Pheidon, Drakontides, Eumathes, Aristoteles, Hippomachos and Mnesitheides.]

3 When these events had occurred Lysandros sailed back to Samos, and Agis led the infantry away from Dekeleia and allowed the various contingents to disperse to their own cities.

4 About this time, near the occurrence of a solar eclipse, Lykophron of Pherai, who wanted to rule all Thessaly, defeated in battle his Thessalian opponents, the Larisaians and others, and killed many of them.

5 At the same time Dionysios the tyrant of Syracuse was defeated in battle by the Carthaginians and lost Gela and Kamarina. A little later, moreover, the people of Leontini, who had been living at Syracuse, revolted from Dionysios and the Syracusans and returned to their own city. And immediately thereafter the Syracusan cavalry were sent by Dionysios to Katana.

6 Despite being under siege by Lysandros from all sides, the Samians did not at first wish to come to terms. But when Lysandros was on the point of assaulting the city, they agreed that every free citizen would leave with a single cloak, but that they would surrender everything else. Thus they left the city. **7** Lysandros gave the city and everything in it back to the former citizens, and he appointed ten rulers to guard it. Then he dismissed the naval contingents of the allies to their own cities **8** and sailed back to Lakedaimon with the Lakonian ships, taking the prows of the captured ships and the triremes from Peiraieus (except twelve) and the crowns, which he had received as personal gifts from the cities, and 470 talents of silver, left over from the tribute which Kyros had assigned to him for the war, and whatever else he had acquired in the war. **9** All these things he handed over to the Lakedaimonians at the end of the summer.

[The war lasted twenty-eight years and six months, during which the following men had been ephors: first Ainesias, in whose term the war began, in the fifteenth year of the Thirty Years' Peace made after the capture of Euboia, and after him **10** Brasidas, Isanor, Sostratidas, Exarchos, Agesistratos, Angenidas, Onomakles, Zeuxippos, Pityas, Pleistolas, Kleinomachos, Ilarchos, Leon, Chairilas, Patesiadas,

Κλεοσθένης, Λυκάριος, Ἐπήρατος, Ὀνομάντιος, Ἀλεξιππίδας, Μισγολαΐδας, Ἰσίας, Ἄρακος, Εὐάρχιππος, Παντακλῆς, Πιτύας, Ἀρχύτας, Εὔδιος, ἐφ' οὗ Λύσανδρος πράξας τὰ εἰρημένα οἴκαδε κατέπλευσεν].[1]

---

[1] εἰς . . . κατέπλευσεν del. Dindorf

Kleosthenes, Lykarios, Eperatos, Onomantios, Alexippidas, Misgolaidas, Isias, Arakos, Euarchippos, Pantakles, Pityas, Archytas, and Eudios, in whose term Lysandros sailed home after doing what has been described.]

COMMENTARY

1.1-7. *The Battle of Abydos*

Xenophon begins with an Athenian defeat and then presents Athenian fortunes as improving gradually until, with the arrival of Alkibiades, the Athenians win a major victory. The story contains dramatic elements and portrays Alkibiades' arrival as decisive. Xenophon also shows he appreciates the Persians' importance, here on land but later for financial aid and naval warfare as well.

In this story Xenophon introduces a series of six characters, five of whom will reappear. Though the *Hellenika*'s organization is not particularly tight, Xenophon uses personalities to link most of his narrative in the continuation.

1.1. Then, not many days later: This abrupt beginning does not link directly to Thucydides, whose narrative breaks off in the summer of 411 BC. Dorieus is now in Rhodes, not Miletos (Thuc. VIII.84); the main Athenian fleet in Madytos, not Kyzikos (Thuc. VIII.107); the Peloponnesians in Abydos, not Elaious (Thuc. VIII.107). At least one major event, a storm off Mt. Athos that sank fifty Peloponnesian ships (Ephoros, *FGrHist* 70 F 199 = Diod. XIII.41), belongs in the gap between Thucydides and Xenophon. Puzzled scholars have suggested that either Thucydides' original ending (Underhill xvii) or Xenophon's original beginning (P. Defosse, "A propos du début insolite des *Helléniques*," *Revue Belge* 46 [1968] 1-24) has been lost. Xenophon's obscurity, however, may be due to ignorance: He may not have read Thucydides' last book before writing the continuation (P. Krentz, "Had Xenophon read Thucydides VIII before he wrote the 'continuation' (*Hell.* I-II.3.10)?", *Ancient World* 19 [1989] 15-18). This hypothesis explains other problematic passages too: The battle between Thymochares and Agesandridas near Euboia (§ 1), Hermokrates' exile (§§ 27-31), and Klearchos' mission to Byzantion (§§ 35-36) might all be independent versions of events treated in Thucydides.

The lack of an introduction has been taken as evidence that Xenophon intended to finish Thucydides' work in Thucydides' manner, but it signals quite the opposite. Xenophon begins with one of his commonest expressions (μετὰ ταῦτα or τοῦτο occurs thirty-nine times in the *Hellenika*), the same one with which he ends ("perhaps someone else will describe what happened then," μετὰ ταῦτα, VII.5.27). This simple start suggests he thought his subject neither great nor distinctive, and it encourages us to look for other contrasts with Thucydides as well.

Thymochares: As general in the summer of 411 (probably selected originally by the oligarchy of the Four Hundred, though perhaps chosen *ad hoc* by the Athenians who sent him, after the oligarchy fell), Thymochares lost twenty-two of his thirty-six triremes in a naval battle at Eretria against Agesandridas, who had forty-two ships (Thuc. VIII.95.2).

fought another naval battle: It is unclear which previous battle Xenophon has in mind. If it is the fight between these two commanders described by Thucydides (see previous n.), this battle may have taken place near Euboia again or in the Hellespont. Alternatively, Xenophon may be thinking of the battle of Kynossema (Thuc. VIII.106), in which case there was only one battle off Euboia and Xenophon has reversed Thucydides' sequence. He may have done this in ignorance of Thucydides.

Agesandridas: Son of the Spartiate Agesandros (Thuc. VIII.91.1), who served on the final Spartan embassy to Athens in 431 (Thuc. I.139.3).

2. at the beginning of winter: I believe, with Gomme (*HCT* 3.699-713) and W. K. Pritchett, "Thucydides' Statement on his Chronology," *Zeitschrift für Papyrologie und Epigraphik* 62 (1986) 205-11, that Thucydides' seasons had astronomically fixed limits, winter beginning no earlier than November 1 and ending not later than the first week of March. For a different view see Andrewes, *HCT* 4.18-21 and 5.147-49. Xenophon, of course, need not have had Thucydides' system in mind. He certainly did not follow it rigorously.

Dorieus the son of Diagoras: Born into an old aristocratic family from Ialysos (Paus.IV.24.2-3), Dorieus was a well-known pankratiast (Paus. VI.7.1-7), with two Olympic victories in addition to the one mentioned by Thuc. III.8.1, plus eight Isthmian, seven Nemean, four Pythian, four Panathenaic, and a number at lesser contests (Dittenberger no. 82). Exiled before 424, he became a citizen of Thouriai in Italy. He brought ten Thourian ships to fight with the Lakedaimonians in the Ionian War (Thuc. VIII.35.1), and probably played a role in Rhodes' defection in 411, the most likely occasion for the Athenians to have condemned him to death (5.19; E. David, "The Diagoreans and the Defection of Rhodes from Athens in 411 B.C.," *Eranos* 84 [1986] 157-64). Subsequently he spoke up to the Spartan commander Astyochos on behalf of his unpaid men (Thuc. VIII.84.2). Diod. XIII.38.5 says that Mindaros, learning of plans for a counter-revolution in Rhodes, sent Dorieus with thirteen ships. Thucydides does not mention this mission, which Dorieus carried out successfully (Diod. XIII.45.1), but his figure of seventy-three ships for the Peloponnesians at VIII.99 seems to take the thirteen into account.

Of nearly 400 persons named in the *Hellenika*, fewer than eight per cent receive any identification beyond a single name (D. Whitehead, "Athenians in Xenophon's *Hellenica*," *Liverpool Classical Monthly* 13 [1988] 145-47). Athletes are sometimes identified as such: Lakrates the Olympic victor in II.4.33 and the Arkadian Antiochos the pankratiast in VII.1.33. But patronymics are the most common choice, and here the patronymic identifies Dorieus' prominent family

fourteen ships: As mentioned in the previous note, Thucydides and Diodoros both give Dorieus only thirteen ships. The upcoming Athenian victory is more striking than in Diodoros' version because Xenophon has fewer Athenian ships fighting more Peloponnesian ships and capturing more Peloponnesian ships. See also §§ 5, 7 nn.

The Athenian lookout on duty for the day saw him and signalled to the generals: The lookout signalled (via intermediaries?) from some high position, perhaps near Elaious. Xenophon does not explain the type of signal. Earlier in the summer of 411, the Athenians at Sestos had learned of the approaching Peloponnesian fleet from fire signals (Thuc. VIII.102.1) . See V.1.27 for lookouts sending a similar message over a similar distance, to Antalkidas at Abydos.

the generals: Since 501/0 the Athenians had normally elected ten generals annually. In Aristotle's day the voting took place in the first prytany "after the sixth in which there are good omens" (Aristot. *Ath. Pol.* 44.4). This rule was not necessarily in force in the late fifth century, but the seventh prytany in March/April would have been an appropriate time to elect commanders for the next campaigning season. Originally one general came from each of the ten Athenian tribes, but by 441/0 it was possible to have more than one general from a single tribe. Probably this happened when no candidate from a tribe received a majority of the votes (M. Piérart, "A propos de l'élection des stratéges Athéniens," *Bulletin de Correspondance Hellénique* 98 [1974] 125-46). The generals had equal rank, but of course the Athenians did not assign them all to command the same forces. When multiple generals served together--as in the case of Alkibiades, Lamachos and Nikias, sent to Sicily in 415--they had to decide strategy together.

The year 411 saw great irregularities, however. After the oligarchic coup, the pro-democratic fleet at Samos, suspicious of some of its officers, elected its own generals (Thuc. VIII.76.2). When the oligarchy fell and the fleet and city were reconciled (Thuc. VIII.97.3), the Athenians must have accepted these generals' position. (For a contrary view see A. Andrewes, "The Generals in the Hellespont, 410-407 B.C.," *Journal of Hellenic Studies* 73 [1953] 2-9.) Thereafter they probably held annual elections as usual. Xenophon gives one full list, the ten elected in spring 406 (5.16). He first names only three elected in spring 407, but his narrative soon adds two others and an inscription a sixth (see 4.10 n.). After the deposition of eight generals in the aftermath of Arginousai, two men were promoted to join

Konon in command of the fleet (7.2)--a temporary measure until the normal elections in 405 could produce a full slate. When Xenophon reports this election he gives only three new names (II.1.16), but we can assume the Athenians elected all ten and Xenophon chose to mention only those sent to the Hellespont. The only certain deviation from normal practice after 411 is the chief command given to Alkibiades in 407 (4.20), a short-lived innovation.

Of the 411 generals we know from Thuc. VIII.104-105 that Thrasyllos and Thrasyboulos were in the Hellespont; Diodoros mentions them specifically in his account of this battle (XIII.45.7).

twenty ships: Diodoros' version of the opening phases of this episode differs widely from Xenophon's. In Diodoros the Athenians send all of their seventy-four ships, which compel Dorieus to land not at Rhoiteion (as in Xenophon) but further east at Dardanos. Some scholars have proposed that both encounters took place and that Dorieus landed twice. That is, twenty Athenian ships forced Dorieus to land at Rhoiteion; when the Athenians departed in order to rejoin the main Athenian fleet, Dorieus proceeded further into the Hellespont; seventy-four Athenian ships then drove him to land again at Dardanos, where Mindaros came to his rescue (Kagan 230). This reconstruction, however, contradicts Xenophon's statement that the main Athenian fleet put to sea against (ἀνταναγαγόμενοι, §5) Mindaros, rather than that Mindaros put to sea against the Athenians.

triremes: On these warships, each powered by 170 rowers, see Morrison and Coates.

as he got clear of the Athenians: Literally only "as he got clear." In 5.13 and 6.21 Xenophon uses this verb in the sense "to get clear (of land)." Dissatisfied with having it refer here to the enemy, Underhill and Kondos have emended the text to "as best he could."

3. Madytos: The trip from Rhoiteion to Madytos, more than twenty km., must have required some hours for tired crews rowing against a current of 2.5 knots or more.

According to Diodoros, the Athenians were at Sestos when they learned about Dorieus near Sigeion (XIII.45.2). The fact that Xenophon first mentions the Athenian fleet as being at Madytos is not necessarily inconsistent with this, since it may have advanced from a base at Sestos.

4. Mindaros: He replaced Astyochos as Spartan admiral (*nauarchos*) in the summer of 411 (Thuc. VIII.85.1), probably because of dissatisfaction with Astyochos' slow progress, rumored to be due to corruption (§ 31 n.). Mindaros soon took the fleet north. He got his ships safely past the Athenian fleet at Eresos on Lesbos, but not much later he lost the battle of Kynossema (Thuc. VIII.104-106.4; Diod. XIII.39-40). Though the Athenians captured only twenty-one ships while losing fifteen (Thuc. VIII.106.3; Diod. XIII.40.5 has eight and five), Thucydides speaks of the victory as a turning point for Athenian morale (VIII.106). The Athenians went on to capture eight Byzantine ships and regain control of Kyzikos (Thuc. VIII.107).

saw the fight while at Ilion sacrificing to Athena: This detail foreshadows the result of the coming battle by recalling *Iliad* 6.297-311, where Athena rejects the Trojan women's prayer, and Hdt. VII.43.2, where Xerxes sacrifices one thousand oxen at Ilion to Athena. It is surprising to find Mindaros sacrificing here, more than thirty km. from his fleet at Abydos. From Ilion, Mindaros could not have seen Rhoiteion itself, about seven km. distant beyond high ground, though perhaps he could have seen part of the Rhoiteion shore (Tuplin 55). Diod. XIII.45.6 avoids this difficulty by locating Mindaros at Abydos when he learned about the fighting.

his triremes: Eighty-four ships, according to Diod. XIII.45.6.

5. round about Abydos: Other evidence indicates the fighting took place downstream from Abydos. Theopompos described "the second naval battle near Kynossema" (*FGrHist* 115 F 5 = Anon. *Vit. Thuc.* 5) and in Diodoros the defeated Peloponnesians flee to land far enough away from Abydos that Mindaros has to put to sea in order to return to Abydos at night (XIII.47.2). At the battle of Kynossema the eighty-six Peloponnesian ships extended from Abydos to Dardanos (Thuc. VIII.104.2). See also § 6 n.

Abydos had the best natural harbor in the straits. It defected from Athens in 411 (Thuc. VIII.62).

shore: ἠών, a poetic word. The ancient critic Hermogenes remarks that it is typical of Xenophon to use at intervals poetic words different from his usual diction (*On Types of Style* 406).

from morning until late afternoon: If Dorieus entered the Hellespont at dawn, and time must be allowed for Mindaros to go from Ilion to Abydos (and for the twenty Athenian ships to go from Rhoiteion to Madytos), how can the main struggle have started in the morning? Three solutions have been proposed: (1) Delete "from morning." (2) Assume that the fighting took place over two days, though Xenophon does not make the division clear and though Diodoros' battle concludes within one day (Underhill 3). (3) Assume that Xenophon heard fighting began at dawn and ended at dusk, and did not interrogate his sources very carefully (H. D. Westlake, "Abydos and Byzantium," *Museum Helveticum* 42 [1985] 315). This last solution is clearly the best, though it does not excuse Xenophon's imprecise reporting and writing.

Alkibiades sailed up: A dramatic entrance (emphasized by the use of the historical present and the fact that Alkibiades is the first Athenian named in describing the fighting at the Hellespont), and the turning point in the battle, as Diod. XIII.46.2-3 and Plut. *Alk.* 27.2-6 agree.

For Alkibiades' family and career see Davies no. 600. Hatzfeld (1940) remains the standard biography; for a recent brief survey see P. J. Rhodes, "What Alcibiades Did or What Happened to Him" (inaugural lecture, Durham 1985). In 415 the Athenians recalled him from the Sicilian expedition to stand trial for profaning the Eleusinian Mysteries, and when he escaped to Sparta they condemned him to death. He played a role in the oligarchical revolution in 411 by offering to bring the Persians into alliance with Athens if the Athenians replaced their democracy with an oligarchy. He proved to have promised more than he could deliver, and the oligarchy of the Four Hundred did not bring him back. The fleet at Samos did elect him general (Thuc. VIII.82.1), but he had not yet returned to Athens, though the government of the Five Thousand recalled him after the oligarchy fell (Thuc. VIII.97.3; Diod. XIII.37.5, 38.2, 42.1-2; Nepos *Alc.* 5.4; Plut. *Alk.* 27.1, 33.1). It appears from Thuc. VIII.108-109 that his most recent attempt to negotiate with the Persian satrap Tissaphernes had also failed. Through the autumn of 411 he had been at Samos, perhaps assigned to watch Dorieus at Rhodes (see § 2 n.) and prevent him from joining Mindaros in the Hellespont.

Xenophon treats Alkibiades favorably throughout the *Hellenika*--see §§ 7, 10, 18, 20; 3.10, 20; 4.13, 5.16 nn. Personal acquaintance may explain his attitude.

with eighteen ships: So too Plut. *Alk.* 27.3; Diod. XIII.46.2 says twenty. Previously Alkibiades had twenty-two ships at Samos (Thuc. VIII.108.2; Diod. XIII.42.2).

6. Pharnabazos: Satrap since at least 412 (Thuc. VIII.6.1) of Hellespontine Phrygia, based at Daskyleion (for a description of Daskyleion see IV.1.15-16, 33; *Hell. Oxy.* XXII.3). The satrapy had become almost hereditary in Pharnabazos' powerful family. His father Pharnakes ruled it from at least 430 (Thuc. II.67.1) to at least 414 (Aristoph. *Birds* 1028-30). Artabazos, who took over the satrapy after 479 (Thuc. I.129.1) and survived perhaps until 449 (if the Artabazos named by Diod. XII.3-4 as the Persian commander in Cyprus is the same man), was probably this Pharnakes' father, since Artabazos' father was also named Pharnakes (or Parnaka). Pharnakes I, known from the Persepolis fortification tablets as a high-ranking official in the late sixth century, was the son of Arsames. Since King Dareios I was the grandson of an Arsames, Pharnakes I may have been an uncle of the king.

Pharnabazos may have been subordinated in some way to Tissaphernes (see § 9 n.). He does not, however, behave like Tissaphernes' inferior (other than possibly in the third Lakedaimonian-Persian treaty [Thuc. VIII.58]--and note that Tissaphernes is involved at Antandros, which ought to be part of Pharnabazos' satrapy, in 411 [Thuc. VIII.108.4]). He had begun trying to persuade the Lakedaimonians to send their fleet to the Hellespont in the winter of 413/12 (Thuc. VIII.6.1, 8.1-2), with limited success (despite his offer of maintenance, Thuc. VIII.80) until the arrival of Mindaros as the new admiral (Thuc. VIII.99-101).

riding his horse as far as possible into the sea: This picturesque image is not found in Diodoros' account, and Plut. *Alk.* 27.5 says only that Pharnabazos fought "along the beach." Xenophon may have heard an exaggerated version of the exploit from Pharnabazos himself, who bragged about it in a meeting with Agesilaos that Xenophon may have attended (IV.1.32). Diodoros (XIII.46.5-6) and Plutarch (*Alk.* 27.5) agree that the Persian land forces played an important role in defending the Peloponnesian ships once they reached shore.

7. capturing thirty enemy ships without their crews and recovering the ships they themselves had lost: In Diodoros, the Athenians capture ten ships immediately after Alkibiades' arrival, but then a storm comes up, and they fail to drag the Peloponnesian ships from shore. They recover their damaged ships only the next day (XIII.46.4-47.1). Therefore the Athenian victory is considerably greater in Xenophon's account. In Diodoros, Mindaros sends for reinforcements but plans aggressive land activity until they arrive (XIII.47.2).

For a defense of Diodoros' tradition on this battle, which presumably goes back to the *Hellenika Oxyrhynchia*, see P. Krentz, "Xenophon and Diodoros on the Battle of Abydos," *Ancient History Bulletin* 3 (1989) 10-14. Xenophon's desire to tell a dramatic story and portray Alkibiades in a favorable light explain many of the divergences. Dramatic elements include Mindaros' sacrifice at Ilion and Pharnabazos' horseback ride into the sea. The story begins not, as it might have, with the destruction of fifty Peloponnesian ships in a storm, but with an Athenian loss in a minor contest. Thereafter the Athenians improve--they accomplish nothing, then win some and lose some--but are not victorious until Alkibiades arrives. The credit for the turn-around is his, and Xenophon (or his source) may have exaggerated the victory's size. For Xenophon's positive attitude toward Alkibiades see § 5 n.

Sestos: Strabo 13.591 calls Sestos the best city in the Cherronesos. He quotes Theopompos to the effect that it was small but well fortified, and controlled the passage (*FGrHist* 115 F 390).

Early in the 411 campaign Strombichides had established a garrison at Sestos to guard the entire Hellespont (Thuc. VIII.62.3). He had to withdraw later in the summer (79.3-5), but shortly thereafter the Athenians at Samos sent an unspecified number of ships to the Hellespont (80.4). When Mindaros arrived there were eighteen Athenian ships at Sestos (102.1).

8-10. *Athenian efforts to raise money and to negotiate with Tissaphernes*

Xenophon now shows the limits of the Athenian victory at Abydos. Money remains a problem, and the Peloponnesian defeat does not dispose the Persians to negotiate.

8. to collect money: For similar expeditions see § 12, 4.9 and Plut. *Alk.* 35.5. Since the Sicilian disaster Athens had been short of money, but money-gathering expeditions were not a new phenomenon (Thucydides mentions "money-collecting ships" three time, II.69, III.19, IV.50.1, and Aristeides 26.45 [Dindorf] refers to "money-collecting over and above the tributes if any special need arose").

Thrasyllos, one of the generals: The Five Thousand must have confirmed his selection as general by the fleet in the summer of 411 (Thuc. VIII.76.2), despite the fact that he had previously served only as an ordinary hoplite. After failing to stop Mindaros from sailing to the Hellespont, perhaps through inexperience, he commanded the Athenian left wing at the battle of Kynossema (Thuc. VIII.104.3; Diod. XIII.39.4 puts him on the right). W. J. McCoy, "Thrasyllus," *American Journal of Philology* 98 (1977) 264-89, surveys Thrasyllos' career.

Xenophon later reveals a negative opinion of Thrasyllos. See 2.1, 9, 12, 13, and 3.6 nn.

troops and ships: Pharnabazos' ability to limit his allies' losses in the battles of Kynossema and Abydos had demonstrated the special importance of land forces for fighting in the narrow Hellespont.

9. Tissaphernes: Dareios II had sent Tissaphernes along with Spithridates and Parmises to suppress Pissouthnes' revolt, perhaps about 416, and thereafter Tissaphernes became satrap of Sardis (Ktesias, *FGrHist* 688 F 15.53 [52]; on the date see Lewis 80-81 and *HCT* 5.12-13). Thucydides describes him as "general of the men near the sea" (VIII.5.4), most likely intending to say that he was commander-in-chief for the war against Athens (see however § 6 n. on Pharnabazos).

His father was named Hydarnes, so he may have been descended from the famous Hydarnes, one of the Seven who killed the false Smerdis and established Dareios I in power. But since Hydarnes is a fairly common name, we cannot say whether Tissaphernes really had such a distinguished ancestry. Nor can we fairly deduce that he was of provincial origin from the fact that in the 390s he had a "home" (*oikos*, III.2.12, 3.12) in Karia, since he may have seized this estate after the revolt of Amorges in 414-412. His membership in the Persian aristocracy is not in doubt, and Diod. XIV.26 says that he later married King Artaxerxes II's daughter.

Tissaphernes had negotiated a series of three treaties with the Spartans in 411 (Thuc. VIII.18, 37, 58), in which he undertook to pay Peloponnesian sailors and (in the third treaty) to bring a fleet from the Persian king. But he also negotiated with the Athenians, and Thucydides tells us that in general he followed Alkibiades' advice not to rush to end the war, but to let the Greeks weaken themselves so he could recover the Greek cities in Asia (VIII.46). The Phoenician fleet never arrived, and there were frequent arguments about pay. Feelings at Miletos, which served as the Peloponnesian base from its revolt in 412 (Thuc. VIII.17) until Mindaros took the fleet to the Hellespont, ran particularly high: The Milesians expelled Tissaphernes' garrison (Thuc. VIII.84.4), interfered with the burial of Lichas, the Spartan who advised them to subject themselves to Tissaphernes while the war lasted (Thuc. VIII.84.5), and sent ambassadors to Sparta to complain about Tissaphernes' conduct (Thuc. VIII.85.2). Finally the Lakedaimonians concluded that unless Tissaphernes fulfilled his treaty obligations, the treaty was void and they could shift their operations to the Hellespont. Thereafter they also helped expel Tissaphernes' garrison at Antandros (Thuc. VIII.108.4; Diod. XIII.42.4) and perhaps that at Knidos (Thuc. VIII.109.1).

to the Hellespont: In his last chapter Thucydides says that Tissaphernes intended to go to the Hellespont to defend himself to the Peloponnesians, and that (as preparation?) he sacrificed to Artemis at Ephesos (VIII.109.1).

in a single trireme bringing friendly gifts and other presents: These details suggest that Alkibiades expected a friendly reception. For his earlier attempts to bring Tissaphernes over to the Athenian side, see Thuc. VIII.45-47, 56, 81-88, 108-109. Lewis (100-102) argues that Tissaphernes (with Alkibiades as his spokesperson) negotiated seriously with the Athenians at VIII.56, just before the third treaty he signed with the Spartans; and Alkibiades alleged that he had later prevented Tissaphernes from using the Phoenician ships brought to Aspendos (VIII.108.1). Now that the Peloponnesians were actively fighting with Pharnabazos' help, Alkibiades might have thought another attempt worthwhile. The Athenians tried to work with Tissaphernes again later (5.8-9). On the other hand, Alkibiades might have been bluffing about his success with Tissaphernes--Thucydides never actually says he met the satrap in regard to the Phoenician ships--and so had little choice but to act as if he and Tissaphernes were still on close terms.

saying that the King had instructed him to fight the Athenians: Here Tissaphernes seems to be playing to the Spartan audience (compare Plut. *Alk.* 27.7), though Xenophon takes us no further into whatever direct negotiations occurred. We cannot tell whether Tissaphernes was speaking truthfully, or--if he was--whethei this directive shows the King disapproved of Pharnabazos' initiative. Tissaphernes did not secure the return of the Peloponnesian ships to the south, and we only hear of him fighting defensively against Thrasyllos' expedition (2.6-11).

10. Mantitheos (who had been captured in Karia): Good storyteller that he is, Xenophon gives just enough detail about Mantitheos to let the story continue. Readers interested in Athenian strategy, curious about activity in the south, will wonder what Mantitheos had been doing in Karia. But Xenophon does not give us a full military narrative. His interests lie elsewhere. See further 2.1, 4.8 nn.

Mantitheos later represented the Athenians on an aborted embassy to the Persian King (3.13), after which he must have returned to the fleet in the Hellespont, where he was left in a position of authority when Alkibiades moved south in 408 (Diod. XIII.68.2). This Mantitheos should probably be identified with the councillor of 415 whom Diokleides accused of mutilating the Herms (Andok. 1.43-44).

secured horses and escaped during the night: Xenophon says nothing about Alkibiades' later claim that Tissaphernes helped his "escape" (Plut. *Alk.* 28.2). Despite Plutarch's belief that Alkibiades was trying to discredit Tissaphernes, such aid would explain how this escape was possible.

Klazomenai: Presumably on good terms with Athens at this time, as it was in 406 when Alkibiades came to protect it from raids by exiles (Diod. XIII.71.1; *Hell. Oxy.* III.1 may refer to this episode, and Meiggs and Lewis no. 88 as well).

Earlier Klazomenai had revolted from Athens, only to be recovered shortly thereafter. A later Spartan assault under Astyochos failed (Thuc. VIII.14.3, 23.6, 31.2-3).

11-26. *The Battle of Kyzikos. Athenian operations in the Propontis. Pharnabazos and the Peloponnesians*

Continuing his emphasis on Alkibiades, Xenophon describes how his aggressiveness won another, still greater victory at Kyzikos. Thereafter the Athenians campaigned successfully in the Propontis, while Pharnabazos helped the Peloponnesians to regroup.

11. The Athenians in Sestos: That is, the forty Athenian ships left at Sestos in § 8.

sixty ships: According to Diod. XIII.50.2, Mindaros had eighty ships; Justin V.4.1 says that eighty were captured. By Diodoros' reckoning, Mindaros had ninety-seven ships at the previous engagement, including Dorieus' thirteen (XIII.45.7). He lost ten (XIII.46.4), and therefore had eighty-seven remaining, some of which needed repair (XIII.47.2). These figures are consistent and may be correct. Xenophon has Mindaros lose thirty ships rather than ten at Abydos, and--for Xenophon too is consistent--Mindaros has twenty fewer now, which helps explain the result of the upcoming battle.

escaped during the night: The repetition of this phrase (see previous sentence) highlights the difference between Alkibiades, who courageously escaped and immediately took the offensive against Mindaros despite being outnumbered, and the other Athenian commanders, who simply fled.

skiff: "The usage of the word *epagein* to which *epaktris* is cognate suggests that these may have been boats hoisted aboard much larger vessels" (Morrison and Williams 245). Aulus Gellius *Noctes Atticae* X.25.5 includes among a list of ships' names "*actuariae*, which the Greeks call *histiokopoi* or *epaktrides*," which ought to mean they at least had masts and oars. Xenophon mentions this small boat, militarily an insignificant addition to the Athenian fleet, to convey the impression that Alkibiades brought every ship he possibly could.

Kyzikos: Kyzikos revolted to Pharnabazos and Klearchos in 411, but the Athenians recovered it after the battle of Kynossema. It had no walls (Thuc. VIII.107.1; Diod. XIII.40.6).

he himself went overland to Sestos and he instructed the ships to sail there: Xenophon represents Alkibiades as prodding the Athenian fleet into aggressive action. Diodoros contradicts Xenophon's portrayal of Athenian movements; see § 18 n.

12. as he was about to put to sea: Note the emphasis on the individual Alkibiades.

for a naval battle: Xenophon has Alkibiades move boldly to the attack, even without the forty ships soon to arrive.

Theramenes: The son of Hagnon of Steiria, Theramenes had helped lead the oligarchic coup in 411 and served as general during the rule of the Four Hundred, but he later opposed the oligarchic extremists and supported the Five Thousand (Thuc. VIII.68.4, 89.2-94.1; Lys. XII.66; Aristot. *Ath. Pol.* 33.2; Diod. XIII.38.2). He advised the recall of Alkibiades (Diod. XIII.38.2, 42.2; Nepos *Alc.* 5).

from Macedonia: Diodoros tells us that Theramenes had gone to Euboia with thirty ships, but failed to halt the joint Chalkidian and Boiotian project of joining Euboia to the mainland near Aulis by means of moles and a wooden bridge. He then moved toward the islands, ravaging enemy territory and collecting money from allies. He overthrew the oligarchy at Paros, and reinforced the Macedonian king Archelaos in his siege of Pydna. Thereafter he joined Thrasyboulos in Thrace

(XIII.47.6-8, 49.1-2). If Diodoros is correct, Theramenes had come from Macedonia
(just as he had come from Paros and, earlier yet, Athens), but Xenophon's phrasing
suggests that mere coincidence brought Theramenes and Thrasyboulos to the
Athenian fleet just in time.

Thrasyboulos: The son of Lykon of Steiria, he had opposed the Four Hundred as
a captain at Samos, where the fleet chose him general (Thuc. VIII.73.4-76.2; Diod.
XIII.38.3). He then persuaded the sailors to recall Alkibiades (Thuc. VIII.81.1). He
commanded the Athenian right wing at the battle of Kynossema (Thuc. VIII.104.3,
105.2; Diod. XIII.39.4 puts him on the left) and again at Abydos (Diod. XIII.45.7).

from Thasos: Thasos had revolted no later than July 411, spurred by Timolaos of
Korinth's arrival with a (probably small) squadron of ships (Thuc. VIII.64.3-4; *Hell.
Oxy.* VII [II].4). Thrasyboulos had therefore been raising money by plundering
enemy territory.

Diodoros places both Theramenes and Thrasyboulos in Thrace when they
receive the summons to join the fleet at Kardia (XIII.49.3).

13. to remove their main sails: As Xenophon explains at VI.2.27, triremes
prepared to fight by leaving their main sails behind. The ships were lighter, then;
rowers did all the work. See also II.1.29, where Konon captures the sails Lysandros
cast off before the battle of Aigospotamoi.

Parion: An odd place for a rendezvous, given the Athenian desire to conceal their
fleet's new size from Mindaros (§ 15). With the battle still some thirty-six hours in
the future, might not news of the reinforcements have reached Mindaros, regardless
of later security precautions? In Diodoros the Athenians carefully sail past Abydos
at night, and no other stops are mentioned before Prokonnesos (XIII.49.5), though it
is unlikely that they covered the 150 or more km. from Elaious to Prokonnesos
without resting.

midday: Originally "breakfast," by Xenophon's day *ariston* meant the midday
meal, as is clear in 6.20-21.

**14. Mindaros was in Kyzikos, along with Pharnabazos and the
infantry:** That is, they had captured the city; Diod. XIII.49.4 states the fact more
explicitly.

against the walls: Odd, since Kyzikos was unwalled (see § 11 n.). Alkibiades
seems to be preparing the men for an all-out assault.

**"For we have no money . . . while the enemy has an unlimited
amount from the King:"** The switch to direct speech emphasizes the point.
Xenophon repeatedly stresses the importance of money, so necessary to maintain the
enthusiasm troops need to win.

15. Xenophon here inserts, rather awkwardly, a sentence describing what Alkibiades did the previous day. The style seems informal, the writing unrevised, as if the narrator of an oral story, realizing he had left something out, simply inserted it when he remembered.

how many ships they had: Alkibiades wanted to conceal not the Athenians' presence, but the fact that they had been reinforced.

16. for a naval battle: The same phrase as in § 12, and, like Alkibiades' speech in § 14, it suggests that he planned a direct assault. Xenophon tells us nothing about a stratagem, though Alkibiades' efforts at secrecy presuppose that he had some deception in mind.

far from the harbor: This phrase explains why Pharnabazos' troops in Kyzikos (§ 14) could not help Mindaros as they had in the previous battle.

cut off by himself: Alkibiades found himself, by chance, between Mindaros and the harbor.

17. to the land: That is, the mainland, where Pharnabazos could bring up his land troops in support.

18. all the ships except those of the Syracusans: The other sources say simply that the Athenians captured all the enemy ships (Diod. XIII.51.8; Plut. *Alk.* 28.9; Ps.-Plato *Menex.* 243).

which the Syracusans burned themselves: The number of ships burned is uncertain. Thucydides says that in the summer of 412 the Sicilians sent twenty-two ships (VIII.26.1). Diodoros, on the other hand, says they sent thirty-five (XIII.34.4, 63.1). Andrewes suggests various ways of handling the discrepancy other than finding one source in error: Thirty-five might be the number decreed, twenty-two the number actually sent; or thirty-five might be the total number including later reinforcements (*HCT* 5.61).

Diodoros (XIII.49-51), Frontinus (II.5.44) and Polyainos (I.40.9) all follow a quite different tradition on this battle, presumably that of the *Hell. Oxy.*, which Plutarch (or Plutarch's source) attempted to combine with Xenophon (*Alk.* 28). This more detailed version has the Athenian generals at Kardia summon Thrasyboulos and Theramenes from Thrace and Alkibiades from Lesbos. They all stopped at Elaious and passed Abydos at night so that their numbers would not be known. The day after they reached Prokonnesos they placed soldiers under Chaireas' command on (mainland) Kyzikene territory and instructed them to march toward the city (Frontinus says the troops landed at night). The fleet divided into three groups, led by Alkibiades, Theramenes and Thrasyboulos. Alkibiades with forty (the figure from Plutarch) ships was to lure the Peloponnesians out to a naval battle, while Theramenes and Thrasyboulos were to emerge from "behind a certain promontory" (Frontinus) and cut off Mindaros' retreat to the city. The plan worked. Mindaros' eighty ships chased Alkibiades only to find Theramenes and Thrasyboulos in their rear. In this version there was enough fighting at sea to be celebrated by a trophy on "Polydoros' island." Mindaros fled to land near Pharnabazos' troops at Kleroi. Alkibiades pursued but had difficulty dragging off the ships because of Pharnabazos' infantry. Thrasyboulos landed too, and urged Theramenes to join the troops under Chaireas and come as quickly as possible. Theramenes and Chaireas arrived in time to defeat those opposed to Thrasyboulos. Then they all helped Alkibiades. Alkibiades' men killed Mindaros, and the enemy fled. The Athenians stopped their pursuit when they heard that Pharnabazos was coming with a large cavalry force. (A. Andrewes, "Notion and Kyzikos," *Journal of Hellenic Studies* 102 [1982] 21-25, identifies plausible sites for the promontory and Polydoros' island.)

The two traditions differ on who took the initiative, where the Athenian reinforcements joined the main fleet, how large the Peloponnesian fleet was, whether the Athenians put a land force on Kyzikene territory, whether they used a stratagem to win the battle, whether there was significant fighting at sea and whether Pharnabazos took part. Xenophon credits Alkibiades for the great victory: Alkibiades initiated the departure from Kardia, Alkibiades told Theramenes and Thrasyboulos what to do, Alkibiades convened the assembly at which only he spoke, Alkibiades led both the naval and land attacks. Andrewes (23) suggested that Xenophon took his entire story from a single source, a partisan of Alkibiades who fought under Thrasyboulos. But this supposition does not explain why the informant failed to report the ambush. Xenophon's own prejudice in favor of Alkibiades (see § 7 n.) cannot explain a deliberate omission of the deception, which he could have credited solely to Alkibiades. But Peloponnesian witnesses can. Friends of Mindaros might have told a story in which the Athenians, who unexpectedly dared to sail through a storm, caught the Lakedaimonian admiral training his rowers and destroyed his fleet--not because he fell into a trap but because the Athenians outnumbered him. They might also have omitted Pharnabazos' involvement to make their defeat less discreditable. For an opposing view see V. J. Gray, who argues that Ephoros invented a conventional ambush scene and then amplified the battle by having Pharnabazos participate ("The value of Diodorus Siculus for the years 411-386 BC," *Hermes* 115 [1987] 80-84).

20. without doing any other harm in the city: This phrase notes Alkibiades' clemency, an important virtue for Xenophon. Note 3.19, 5.19 and II.2.20.

21. the Selymbrians, though not admitting them, gave money: A later agreement between Athens and Selymbria called for the restoration of hostages (see 3.10 n.), presumably also given at this time.

22. Chrysopolis in Kalchedonia: The village of Chrysopolis, modern Scutari, lay on a promontory opposite Byzantion. Kalchedon may have revolted along with Byzantion in 411 (Thuc. VIII.80.3; see also § 35 n.).

ten per cent tax: Sometimes identified with the ten per cent tax mentioned in *IG* 1^3.52 line 7 (variously dated between 434/3 and 418/7). Meiggs and Lewis (161) maintain that ten per cent is a high rate for this kind of tax and that it is therefore unlikely to have been imposed in peace-time. Plb. IV.44.4 implies that Alkibiades first imposed the tax, but may mean only that Alkibiades first imposed the tax at Chrysopolis rather than at Byzantion (B. R. MacDonald, "The Phanosthenes Decree," *Hesperia* 50 [1981] 143 n. 24). Apparently it was collected in addition to the five per cent charge on imports and exports substituted for the tribute in 413 (Thuc. VII.28.4). See 3.9 n. for the question of whether the tribute was restored after the battle of Kyzikos.

The Athenians reimposed the tax at Byzantion in the fourth century (IV.8.27), and the Byzantines collected it themselves in the third (Plb. IV.46.6).

from the Black Sea: So also Diod. XIII.64.2, but Plb. IV.44.4 has "to." F.W. Walbank (498) suggests that "the toll was exacted on goods travelling in either direction."

thirty ships: Diod. XIII.64.3 says fifty, left with Theramenes to besiege Kalchedon and Byzantion.

Eumachos: He may have been elected with Thrasyboulos, Thrasyllos and others by the fleet in 411 (Thuc. VIII.76.2). If *E[umachoi]* is correctly restored in *IG* 1^3.375 lines 35-36, he may have been general again in 410/409.

23. Hippokrates: Probably the Hippokrates, a Lakedaimonian, who took twelve ships to Knidos in 411; and the Hippokrates, a Spartiate, who was at Phaselis later that summer; and the Hippokrates sent with Epikles to Euboia for reinforcements (Thuc. VIII.35.1, 99, 107.2). If so, he was one of only twelve men who survived a storm that destroyed those reinforcements (§ 1 n.). For his death see 3.5-6.

vice-admiral: Normally, as Pollux 1.96 says, the *epistoleus* was "the successor in command of the fleet to the admiral." See VI.2.25, where Mnasippos' *epistoliaphoros* (presumably the same office as *epistoleus*) Hyperomenes took over after the battle of Kerkyra. Lysandros held this office when he in practice commanded the Peloponnesian fleet for a second time in 405 (II.1.7).

The ships are lost: Aristophanes uses κᾶλα as equivalent to ξύλα, "timbers"

(*Lys.* 1253; the scholiast explains the "timbers" as "for the ships"). Pharnabazos reassures the Peloponnesians regarding ξύλα in § 24.

dead: ἀπεσσύα is Doric for ἀπεσύη (aorist passive of ἀποσεύω). Laconic in language as well as length, the message also has the Doric πεινῶντι for πεινῶσι, τῶνδρες for οἱ ἄνδρες and ἀπορίομες for ἀπορούμεν.

Xenophon omits Sparta's request for peace on the basis of the *status quo* (Philochoros, *FGrHist* 328 F 138; Diod. XIII.52.2-53; Aristeid. 1.237 [Lenz-Behr]; Justin V.4.4; Nepos *Alc.* 5), Thrasyboulos' mission to Thrace, where he brought over the cities in that area (see § 9 n.), and Alkibiades' ravaging of Pharnabazos' territory (Diod. XIII.64.3-4). But the intercepted message demonstrates Alkibiades' success vividly and memorably.

24. Pharnabazos: Diod. XIII.51.8 says that the Peloponnesians in Kyzikos as well as the losers in the battle fled to Pharnabazos' camp. Xenophon here presents him as responding to the despair revealed in their message: They have lost their "timbers" (ships), so he gives them money and shows them wood on Mt. Ida; they hunger, so he provides them with money for food; they do not know what to do, so he gives them clothing and puts them to work guarding his coast and building ships. **money to buy food for two months:** Pritchett (2.47) collects the references for Persian subsidies to the Peloponnesians between 412 and 404, of which this is the first specifically mentioned by Xenophon (compare § 14). See also 3.17, 5.5-7, 6.18, II.1.11-12, 14-15, 3.8.

25. Antandros: On the Troad's south shore, south of Mt. Ida. The Athenians took Antandros from Mytilene in 427 after the Mytilenian revolt (Thuc. III.50.3). In 424 Mytilenian exiles seized Antandros for the purpose of building ships, but the Athenians recaptured it (Thuc. IV.52.3, 75.1). It had revolted by 411, when the Antandrians and Peloponnesian hoplites drove out a Persian garrison (Thuc. I.108.4-5), but the revolt's date is unknown: perhaps at or before the time of Derkylidas' northward march at the beginning of summer 411.

Mt. Ida had long been known as a source of timber; it supplied oak for Patroklos' funeral pyre (Homer *Iliad* 23.110-26). Theophrastos included Mt. Ida among the limited number of areas that produced good ship timber: "in Europe Macedon, parts of Thrace, and southern Italy; in Asia the territories of Sinope and Amisos, Mt. Olympos in Mysia, and Mt. Ida, where the supply was not extensive" (*HP* IV.5.5). Strabo 13.606 calls Aspaneos in the Troad the market for the timber of Mt. Ida, "for that is where they bring their timber and display it for those who need it."

26. While the construction was going on: This brief note on the Syracusans reflects well on their commander Hermokrates, whom Xenophon admired. See § 30 n.

27-37. Exile of the Syracusan generals. Civil disorder in Thasos. Thrasyllos in Athens. Klearchos' mission to Byzantion.

These loosely connected episodes introduce several important new themes: the good commander Hermokrates' obedient response to his unjust exile; the Spartans' difficulty in governing new allies; and high Athenian hopes for Thrasyllos, over which Xenophon casts a shadow by noting Klearchos' mission, Sparta's first step toward shutting off Athens' grain supply.

In the first story Xenophon brings out several qualities of the good commander, one of his most frequent themes in other works as well as in the *Hellenika*. For a similar admirable reaction to bad news, see Agesilaos' acceptance of his recall during his Asiatic campaign in 395 (IV.2.1-3).

27. During this time: A vague phrase, but it should mean "in the period after the battle of Kyzikos." Xenophon's account of Hermokrates makes tolerable sense by itself, though the fleet has moved without explanation from Antandros (§ 26) to Miletos (§ 31). But this account contradicts Thuc. VIII.85, where Hermokrates' exile takes place in 411, not 410. Against H. D. Westlake's view that Thuc. VIII.85 anticipates events that took place more than a year later ("Hermokrates the Syracusan," *Bulletin of the John Rylands Library* 41 [1958-59] 239-68 = *Essays on the Greek Historians and Greek History* [Manchester 1969] 174-202), see *HCT* 5.281-85. Thucydides' testimony is preferable to Xenophon's. Two clues that Xenophon has the chronology wrong are (1) Hermokrates' boast in § 28, which sounds odd after the Peloponnesian defeats at Kynossema, Abydos and Kyzikos but would fit the context in Thuc. VIII.85 before the battle of Kynossema, and (2) the presence of the Peloponnesian fleet at Miletos, which is surprising given the Milesians' history of difficult relations with Tissaphernes earlier (§ 9 n.), but again would fit the context in Thuc. VIII.85.

they had been exiled: While we might wish to know why the Syracusans exiled Hermokrates, Xenophon does not muddle the story's point by examining the circumstances in detail. Diod. XIII.63.1 says that Hermokrates "was overpowered by his political opponents."

Hermokrates: The son of Hermon, first known from his speech to the Sicilian congress at Gela in 424, which favored peace so that the Athenians would leave the island (Thuc. IV.58-64). He played a leading role in Syracuse's defense against the

Athenian invasion in 415, though the Syracusans did not always follow his advice and at one point deposed him from the generalship ((Thuc. VI.32-34, 72-73.1, 103.4; VII.21.3-22, 73). He favored treating the Athenian prisoners leniently (Diod. XIII.19.5; Plut. *Nik.* 28.2), but urged the Syracusans to send ships to the Aegean to continue the fight against Athens (Thuc. VIII.26.1). He stood up to Tissaphernes several times regarding the troops' pay (Thuc. VIII.29.2, 45.3, 85.3). Thucydides notes his intelligence, experience and courage (VI.72.2).

unjustly and illegally: We cannot judge whether this claim is correct. Xenophon probably has in mind a parallel between the Syracusan democracy's exile of its generals here and the Athenian democracy's execution of its generals after Arginousai. The Athenians condemned their generals by a single vote, which may be the force of "all of them" here. Xenophon also draws a parallel between Syracuse and Athens at 2.14 and II.3.5. Syracusans and Athenians both treat their generals unjustly; Syracusans and Athenians both confine prisoners in quarries; by 404 a tyrant rules Syracuse and a tyrannical oligarchy rules Athens. Xenophon wants his reader to learn that unjust and cruel behavior has its own reward. For further examples see 7.1 n.

28. the captains and the marines and the pilots: A trireme normally had one captain (*trierarchos*), ten hoplite marines (*epibatai*) and one pilot (*kubernetes*; Morrison and Williams 260-67; Jordan 184-94 argues that in large battles marines were much more numerous than ten per ship). Note that the Syracusan marines are treated here and in § 30 as leading men, and therefore presumably of the regular hoplite class. Scholars dispute whether Athenian marines were normally thetes armed at public expense or regular hoplites; see *HCT* 5.56.

they could not revolt against their city: The generals deplore the illegality of their exile, but refuse to act against their government. The scene recalls Sokrates' refusal to break the law in order to avoid death, although he believed his conviction was unjust (Plato, *Kriton*). For other "Sokratic" echoes see § 30, 7.27, 35 and II.4.40-42.

the men must allow him to speak: I follow Calhoun and Hatzfeld in taking λόγον δίδοναι as "allow to speak" rather than "render account" or "defend oneself," its more common meaning. This interpretation of λόγον δίδοναι has parallels in V.2.20 and elsewhere (G. M. Calhoun, "Xenophon, *Hellenica* I, 1.27-29," *Classical Philology* [1912] 479 n. 1; add Men. *Samia* 201). The force of the passage is that Hermokrates and his colleagues feared that the men in the ranks might not be as supportive as the captains, marines and pilots, but found no one present willing to reproach their conduct. Two other treatments of this problematic passage deserve mention: (1) T. Eide, "Xenophon, *Hellenika*, 1,1,28," *Symbolae Osloenses* 54

(1979) 23-26, takes λόγον διδόναι in its more common sense (as in 7.4), but believes that its subject is the Syracusans at home rather than the generals. Thus: "The men, particularly the captains and the marines and the pilots, shouted that the generals should remain in command. But the generals said they could not revolt against their city. If anyone [at Syracuse] had something to accuse them of, the accusers must state their reasons, while remembering . . ." (2) Dindorf and others, including Hude and Delebecque, transpose "keeping in mind . . . on land and sea" to § 27, on the grounds that a reminder of the generals' success is unnecessary here, after the troops' demonstration of support.

"how many battles . . . land and sea.": The switch to direct speech emphasizes the point that the generals had done what generals were supposed to do: keep their soldiers enthusiastic and win.

29. Demarchos the son of Epikydes and Myskon the son of Menekrates and Potamis the son of Gnosias: Thuc. VIII.85.3 names the same three men, without patronymics.

30. care and enthusiasm and accessibility: Qualities of Xenophon's ideal commander. On care and concern for the troops, see IV.5.4 on Agesilaos providing fire for cold and hungry men, *Anab.* IV.5.7-9 on Xenophon finding food for his men in the snow and *Kyr.* I.6.16 for Kambyses' advice to Kyros regarding concern for health. On the importance of enthusiasm, see IV.3.14 on the success of Agesilaos' (false) report of a naval victory, and *Kyr.* I.6.13, 19. The Syracusans will particularly miss Hermokrates' enthusiasm because Kyzikos proved profoundly discouraging, in spite of Pharnabazos' advice (§ 24), while the Athenians were becoming more enthusiastic (§ 34). On openness, compare V.1.14 on Teleutias, *Anab.* IV.3.10 on Xenophon himself, and *Kyr.* VII.5.46 on Kyros.

Note this eulogy's "Sokratic" character: Xenophon praises Hermokrates for practicing a sort of dialectic with his men, never leaving them ignorant of what they ought to know.

31. Astyochos: Lakedaimonian admiral before Mindaros. His lack of success led to the dispatch of eleven "advisers" empowered to replace him, though they did not (Thuc. VIII.39.2). Thucydides reports charges, without vouching for their validity, that Tissaphernes had bribed Astyochos (VIII.50.3, 78.1, 83.3). Perhaps, like Lichas later (VIII.84.5), Astyochos had felt that while the war lasted the Peloponnesians must put up with Tissaphernes, and had therefore not pushed Tissaphernes to fulfill his financial obligations as assertively as others would have liked. But here Xenophon portrays Astyochos as agreeing with Hermokrates'

accusations against the Persian satrap, and it may be that he finally decided the
Spartans should abandon the attempt to collaborate with Tissaphernes.

when he visited Pharnabazos: The chronology of Hermokrates' visit to
Pharnabazos and his return to Sicily is a notorious crux. Diod. XIII.63, under the
year 409/8 (but datable by the context, after the battle of Kyzikos and before
Thrasyllos' Ionian expedition, to 410), refers to his exile and says that he handed
over the Syracusan fleet to his successors in the Peloponnese (an error), received
funds from Pharnabazos, built five triremes at Messene, hired one thousand
mercenaries and returned to Sicily. The story resumes in XIII.75.2-8, under the year
408/7 (datable by the context, after the battle of Notion and Alkibiades' replacement,
to 406), where it ends with Hermokrates' death. But Xenophon says in 3.13 that
Hermokrates accompanied an embassy to the Persian King that departed in 409; it
probably returned in 408 (4.7 n.). Unless Xenophon is mistaken, Hermokrates did
not go back to Sicily until 408 at the earliest.

**began to prepare mercenaries and triremes for his return to
Syracuse:** In spite of the generals' earlier claim that they could not revolt against
their city (§ 28). Xenophon does not recount Hermokrates' actual return to Sicily
and violent death as he attempted to reenter Syracuse, for this story would undercut
Xenophon's point about his obedient acceptance of exile. The anticipatory note here
indicates Hermokrates' standing with Pharnabazos.

32. Thasos: Many scholars have accepted Kahrstedt's emendation to "Iasos," a
city in Tissaphernes' satrapy. A similar emendation is inescapable at Diod.
XIII.104.7, where Lysandros destroys a Karian city, allied to Athens, which the text
calls Thasos. The main objection to Xenophon's text has been "the prominence of
Tissaphernes in the story" (Meiggs 577). Xenophon does not vouch for
Tissaphernes' involvement, however. He merely says that Pasippidas was accused,
along with Tissaphernes, of responsibility. In favor of keeping the text is the fact
that Lysandros sent Eteonikos to the Thraceward region after the battle of
Aigospotamoi (II.2.5), which could be explained by Eteonikos' experience in the
area.

at about this time: This phrase ought to refer to the arrival of the new
Syracusan generals, which Xenophon misplaced from 411 (§ 27 n.). Could this
civil disorder in Thasos also have occurred in 411? This hypothesis would clear up
several oddities: (1) Why was Pasippidas held responsible rather than Agesandridas,
who had ships much closer to Thasos than the allied fleet Pasippidas had collected at
Chios? Agesandridas had forty-two ships at Euboia later in 411 (Thuc. VIII.94-95;
see § 1 n.) and presumably remained in that general area, for he appears in 409
commanding ships in the Thraceward region (3.17). (2) Why was Tissaphernes'

name dragged into the affair? If the incident took place about the time Hermokrates left the Peloponnesian fleet, then it occurred before Agesandridas' mission and at a time when Spartan tempers flared against Tissaphernes.

governor: The term *harmostes* appears only once in Thucydides (VIII.5.2), but frequently in Xenophon (I.2.18, 3.5, 15; II.3.14; III.1.9; IV.8.3, 29; VII.1.43, 3.4, 9). Xenophon uses many special terms avoided by Thucydides in favor of more general vocabulary.

Harmostai could command areas or garrisons or detached forces. See H. W. Parke, "The Development of the Second Spartan Empire 405-371 B.C.," *Journal of Hellenic Studies* 50 (1930) 37-79, and G. Bockisch, "*Harmostai*," *Klio* 46 (1965) 129-239.

Eteonikos: he had served under Astyochos, who gave him command of a detachment of land troops (Thuc. VIII.23.5). For his later career, see 6.26, 35-38; II.1.1-5, 2.5; V.1.1, 13; *Anab.* VII.1.12-20.

Pasippidas the Lakonian: He appears later as an ambassador to the Persian King (3.13) and as having stationed ships at Antandros and the Hellespont (3.17). So either he was recalled from exile quickly, or his exile took place some time later.

who was accused of being responsible, along with Tissaphernes, for what happened: The charge was probably not that Tissaphernes and Pasippidas actually expelled the Lakedaimonian sympathizers and the Spartan governor, but that they failed to prevent their expulsion by the Thasians. The Peloponnesians resented Tissaphernes for failing to support them adequately, not for opposing them.

Kratesippidas: Xenophon does not describe him here as admiral, though he does later (5.1). Diod. XIII.65.3 so terms him in connection with activities at Chios subsequent to Thrasyllos' Ionian expedition. Lysandros did not succeed him as admiral until 407 (5.1 n.), so either Kratesippidas went to Chios as admiral and held the post for more than one year, or he held a lesser office when he first went out. The fact that Klearchos meanwhile collected ships and planned to have new triremes built supports the latter.

33. Agis: The son of Archidamos and Spartan king since his father's death in 427/6 (Diod. XI.48). In the spring of 413 he took and fortified Dekeleia, from which he had caused the Athenians a great deal of trouble ever since (Thuc. VII.19.1, 27.3-5; Diod. XIII.9.2).

Dekeleia: 120 *stadia* (21.3 km.) from Athens, and not much more from the Boiotian border; visible from the city (Thuc. VII.19.2).

up to the walls themselves of Athens: Xenophon brings out the difficulty of withdrawing an army that has advanced close to a city in *Kyr.* VII.5.1-6, where he describes a safe method.

the Lykeion *gymnasion:* East of Athens, outside the gate of Diochares (Strabo IX.1.19, 397). Lynch (9-31) discusses the site. A cult place of Apollo Lykeios, it served as a military exercise ground and had a *gymnasion* for athletes.

34. the light-armed: Normally *psiloi* are archers, javelin-throwers and slingers (for example, in II.4.33); in 2.3 they are distinguished from peltasts.

still more enthusiastic: The comparative implies that they were willing earlier. Diod. XIII.52.1 reports that when the Athenians heard the news of Kyzikos, they sent to "those around Alkibiades" one thousand of the best citizens, one hundred cavalry and thirty triremes. These forces sound like what Diodoros assigns to Thrasyllos at XIII.64.1 (see next n.), and it may be that the Athenians instructed Thrasyllos to take these ships and men on to Alkibiades after his Ionian campaign, as in the event he did.

one thousand hoplites, one hundred cavalry, and fifty triremes: Diod. XIII.64.1 gives the expedition only thirty ships, but has "many" hoplites and agrees with Xenophon on one hundred cavalry. This is the first sure reference to Athenian cavalry in Asia Minor, for Thucydides does not mention cavalry in his account of 412-411. Though this force was small (the Athenian cavalry numbered twelve hundred, including the mounted archers), during the war the Athenians never sent more than three hundred horsemen on a naval expedition, and after the occupation of Dekeleia the need for cavalry in Attika was particularly pressing (Bugh 79-107). The fact that the Athenians found one hundred horsemen to send with Thrasyllos shows they recognized Persian strength in cavalry.

35. Klearchos the son of Ramphias: Thucydides mentions him twice, each time with his patronymic. His father was probably the Ramphias who served as a Spartan ambassador just before the Peloponnesian war (Thuc. I.139.3) and later, with two others, led reinforcements to Brasidas in Thrace (Thuc. V.12). In 412 Klearchos had been named to command the Peloponnesian fleet when it reached the Hellespont (Thuc. VIII.8.2); in 411 he arrived by land himself, while ten of his ships got through and prompted Byzantion's revolt (Thuc. VIII.80.3). In 410 he fought in the battle of Kyzikos (Diod. XIII.51.1). For his later career see 3.15-22, *Anab.* I-II (note especially how Xenophon characterizes him at II.6.1-15); Diod. XIII.98.1, XIV.12.

Xenophon probably has here a doublet of Thuc. VIII.80.3, so that Klearchos had only one mission (P. Krentz, "Had Xenophon Read Thucydides VIII Before He Wrote the 'Continuation' *(Hell.* I-II.3.10)?", *Ancient World* 19 [1989] 16-17). Thucydides' date should is preferable.

proxenos: In a diplomatic world that lacked permanent ambassadors residing in other cities, men who voluntarily represented the interests of another state and its citizens were known as *proxenoi* (from *xenos* = foreigner). The custom goes back to the host-guest friendships Homer portrays so vividly. These private ties evolved into a relationship (*proxenia*) officially granted by the client-city, which might confer benefits and privileges on its *proxenoi* in exchange for their services. Here Klearchos is the Spartan who looks after Byzantion's affairs in Sparta. The institution is best known, however, from Athens: see M. B. Walbank.

36. troop-carriers rather than fast ships: It appears from Thucydides (especially VI.43,VIII.62.2, 74.2) that troop-carriers differed structurally from fighting triremes: They could be (but were not necessarily) rowed by soldiers and could be reconverted into normal triremes. This detail shows the Spartans neglected naval strategy; they should have sent triremes capable of dealing with the nine Athenian ships "that always guarded the merchant ships" in the Hellespont. The Spartans had still not remedied this deficiency, despite Pharnabazos' help, when Byzantion fell in 409 (see 3.17).

Sestos: The manuscript reading can be kept if the story belongs in 411 rather than 410, for in 411 there was a brief period, precisely at the time Thucydides has Klearchos' ships get through, when Sestos was unguarded (see § 7 n.).

37-2.1. One of a series of interpolated passages, including 2.19-3.1, 5.21-6.1, II.1.7-10, 2.24-3.2 and 3.9-10 (D. Lotze, "Die Chronologischen Interpolationem in Xenophons Hellenika," *Philologus* 106 [1962] 1-13, which I here largely resume). Against A. E. Raubitschek's argument that the interpolator was Xenophon himself ("Die sogenannten Interpolationen in den ersten beiden Büchern von Xenophons *Griechische Geschichte*," Akten des VI. Internationales Kongresses für Griechische und Lateinische Epigraphik, Munich, *Vestigia* 17 [1972] 315-25), see Lotze, "War Xenophon selbst der Interpolator seiner Hellenika I-II?" *Philologus* 118 (1974) 215-17. The main points against authenticity are:

(1) The dating by Spartan ephors, Athenian archons, and Olympiads does not fit Xenophon's war-years, which begin in the spring. The interpolator who inserted this information worked backwards from the capitulation of Athens and missed the beginning of at least one war-year ("at the beginning of the spring," 4.1), so that 3.1 and 2.1 are incorrect. (I believe that he missed a second as well at 4.11; see Introduction, pp. 11-14.)

(2) The figures for years elapsed in the war (3.1, 6.1 and II.1.7) are inconsistent with the dating by ephors: In 3.1 Pantakles is ephor and twenty-two years of war have elapsed, in 6.1 Pityas is ephor and twenty-four years of war have elapsed-- though Pityas was ephor directly after Pantakles (II.3.10). Moreover, depending on whether the year left unmarked by Xenophon begins at § 9 or 4.11 or 5.11 (see

Introduction, pp. 11-14), either the last two (as I believe) or all three of these figures are incorrect. This interpolator cannot be the same person who, working in the opposite direction, inserted the ephor dates.

(3) The figure given at II.3.9 for the war's duration war is apparently based on the ephor-list in II.3.9-10 (see n.) and is not only mistaken but also inconsistent with the other figures for elapsed war-years. The ephor-list might have been inserted by the person who added the ephors, archons and Olympic victors. The ephors regularly appear first in these notices.

(4) § 37 describes the fall of Selinos and Himera, but two Selinuntine ships are fighting in the Aegean at 2.8-12 along with twenty-five Syracusan ships that Diod. XIII.61.1 says returned to Sicily before Himera fell in 409/8. This error is therefore consistent with the mistaken interpolation in 2.1. § 37 shares the suspicious introduction "so the year ended" with 5.21 and II.2.24, connecting these three notes on Sicilian history closely to the interpolated ephor- and archon-dates (on these passages see the detailed discussion in Beloch 2.2.254-60). They also provide a clue about this interpolator's source, for the figures in § 37 and 5.21 agree with those given by Timaios (*FGrHist* 566 F 103 [Diod. XIII.54.5] and 25 [Diod. XIII.80.5] respectively). Timaios' chronological work *Olympionikai* combined the various systems of dating, including the lists of ephors, archons, priestesses of Hera at Argos and Olympic victors (*FGrHist* T 10 [Plb. XII.11] and F 164 [Diod. V.9.2]). The discrepancies between the interpolator and Diodoros on Akragas' fall and Dionysios' tyranny suggest, however, that the interpolator did not use Timaios directly. For Diodoros' reliance on Timaios see L. Pearson, "Ephorus and Timaeus in Diodorus," *Historia* 33 (1984) 1-20.

(5) II.1.8-9 purports to give the real reason for Kyros' recall (he executed two nephews of the King), though elsewhere at II.1.13, 15 and *Anab.* I.1.1 Xenophon cites Dareios' illness as sufficient explanation. The incident would be relevant at *Anab.* I.1.1 as evidence that Kyros coveted the crown. Moreover this passage erroneously affirms that Dareios' sister was Xerxes' daughter, it contains curiously inconsistent spellings of Dareios' name and it uses the word *kore* where Xenophon would have written *kandus* (compare *Kyr.* VIII.3.10). "Dareiaios" appears in Ktesias, *FGrHist* 688 F 14-16, but not elsewhere in Xenophon. The other note on Persian affairs, 2.19, cannot be checked for accuracy, but it begins with the "so the year ended" tag (2.18).

I prefer to keep the notices of the beginning of war-years ("in the next year," 2.1; "during the next year," 3.1; "in the next year," 6.1, II.1.10, 3.1), which are closely tied to prodigies and catastrophes (the temple burning in Phokaia, 3.1, the moon's eclipse and the temple burning in Athens, 6.1). The beginnings of years are mentioned several times later (VII.1.1, 2.10, 4.28), and the references to seasons that sometimes accompany these notices have numerous parallels (III.2.6, 30; III.4.16; IV.1.41, 6.12, 7.1, 8.7; V.4.47, 58). Note too that IV.3.10 records another eclipse, and IV.5.4 another temple burning.

2.1-13. *Thrasyllos' expedition to Ionia and the Hellespont*

Despite the enthusiasm of 1.34, Xenophon portrays Thrasyllos' expedition as a failure because Thrasyllos wasted time before assaulting his main objective, Ephesos. Xenophon has something to say about generalship here. Thrasyllos' dilatoriness contrasts with Alkibiades' quick action that led to the victory at Kyzikos.

2.1. [during which . . . at Athens,]: Interpolated (1.37 n.).
the *stadion* race: The shortest Greek sprint, measuring six hundred Greek feet. Though the *stadion* was frequently used as a standard measure of length, it was quite irregular. At the normal 296 mm. per foot it equals 177.6 m. (the figure I use throughout this commentary), but at Olympia the *stadion* measures 192.3 m.
fortified Thorikos: Thorikos, halfway between Peiraieus and Rhamnous, has two harbors. The main, northern one (Frankolimani) is five to twenty m. deep with a gradually inclining beach so that ships could be dragged from the water. Xenophon may mention the fortification to indicate Athens' renewed spunk.

For a report on the remains, see H. F. Mussche, "La forteresse maritime de Thorikos," *Bulletin de correspondance hellénique* 85 (1961) 176-205. Mussche maintains that Thorikos ought to have been built in 412 along with Sounion (Thuc. VIII.4), but Thucydides' silence argues against this suggestion. Without any physical evidence against Xenophon, his date ought to stand (C. A. van Rooy, "Fortifications in South Attica and the Date of Thorikos," *Acta Classica* 12 [1969] 171-80).

Xenophon mentions the Thorikos fort in a very different context at *Poroi* 4.43-48, where he argues that the silver mines could be worked even during a war if the Athenians would add a third fort between their two at Thorikos and Anaphlystos.
the ships that had been voted: See 1.34, where Thrasyllos requested reinforcements for the Hellespont. Why then did he sail for Ionia? Xenophon does not explain Athenian strategy, and he pays little attention to fighting by forces other than the main Athenian fleet. A. Andrewes, "The Generals in the Hellespont, 410-407 B.C.," *Journal of Hellenic Studies* 73 (1953) 2-9, argues that between 410 and 407 the generals in the Hellespont operated independently of the democracy at Athens, which did not dare replace these successful leaders, but sent them neither money nor reinforcements. According to Andrewes, Thrasyllos' expedition to Ionia

aimed at showing that loyal democratic generals could also win; only after, and because of, his failure did Thrasyllos cooperate with Alkibiades. Against this hypothesis see Kagan (265-70) and P. Krentz, "Athenian Politics and Strategy after Kyzikos," *Classical Journal* 84 (1988) 206-215. In these years the Athenians followed a strategy aimed at pressuring both Tissaphernes and Pharnabazos to end the war. Unless both satraps decided that supporting Sparta was not in their best interests, Athenian prospects were bleak. Thrasyllos' campaign was therefore neither strategically eccentric nor misconceived, and inscriptions show that the Athenians followed it with further efforts in Ionia in 409 and 408 (4.8 n.).

peltasts: Javelin-throwers who carried light, crescent-shaped shields (*peltai*). The type originated in Thrace. See Best.

at the beginning of the summer: 410 BC (see Introduction, pp. 11-14). Thucydides' summer included spring and autumn, but Xenophon may not have followed this method.

Samos: A major Athenian base since 412. After the suppression of an oligarchic coup (Thuc. VIII.73), the Samians remained conspicuously loyal until the war's end. See 4.8, II.2.6 nn.

2. for three days: Xenophon uses precise time references throughout this story; see "on the next day" (§ 4), "during the following night" (§ 4), "on the seventeenth day" (§ 7). E. Schwartz believes this precision resulted from Xenophon's own participation in the campaign ("Quellenuntersuchungen zur griechischen Geschichte," *Rheinisches Museum für Philologie* 44 [1889] 164). It may, however, simply be the storyteller's way of emphasizing the time wasted before the assault on the main objective took place.

Pygela: A small town southwest of Ephesos. It may be included among "the cities" which the Chians intended to bring into revolt in 412 (Thuc. VIII.19.1).

the fortifications: This wall had probably been constructed after Pygela's revolt; note Thucydides' general statement about the absence of walls in Ionia at VIII.14.3. The Athenians had a policy of dismantling fortifications in Asia Minor (Meiggs 149-51).

light-armed: Since they are distinguished from the peltasts, they must be the remaining sailors. (Compare "all the others," distinguished from the hoplites, cavalry, peltasts, and marines in § 7.) Their number cannot be calculated, since we cannot be sure how many ships Thrasyllos had--Xenophon says fifty, Diodoros thirty--nor how the horses and hoplites were transported.

3. the peltasts and two divisions of hoplites: Here Thrasyllos' combination of troops works well together.

That the fifth-century Athenian army was split into divisions (*lochoi*) is otherwise known only from an anecdote about the general Lamachos rebuking one of his division commanders (*lochagoi*, Aristoph. *Acharnians* 575; Plut. *Mor.* 186 F). Xenophon uses the word in the *Kyr.* for a unit of twenty-four (VI.3.21), while in the *Anab.* it can include a hundred (III.4.21, IV.8.15). Neither passage describes the Athenian army.

trophy: At the spot where they first routed the enemy, victors erected a trophy consisting partly of captured arms (see Pritchett 2.246-75).

4. Notion: The harbor of Kolophon, northwest of Ephesos, to which the Kolophonians had moved after the Persians captured Kolophon in 430. The Athenians sent out settlers to Notion after they intervened in an internal dispute in 427 (Thuc. III.34). Xenophon does not say whether Notion had revolted; a possible occasion is Pedaritos' advance by land from Chios to Erythrai in 412 (Thuc. VIII.28.5, with *HCT* 5.69). Apparently the Athenians landed uneventfully now.

Kolophon: That is, the old Kolophon, some thirteen km. inland from Notion.

at the time when the grain was ripening: May-June. For the Greek agricultural calendar, see Brumfield 11-53.

5. Stages, the Persian: Thuc. VIII.16.3 calls him "Tissaphernes' *hyparchos*." *Hyparchoi*, like mediaeval vassals, seem to have been large fief-holders who could, as after the Ionian raid in 499, put large forces into the field (Cook 178).

in search of private booty: Xenophon disapproved (compare *Anab.* V.8.13).

6. Ephesos: Ephesos had been in Athenian hands as recently as spring 414, when the treasurers of Athena made payments to an Athenian general ἐν Ἐφ[έσοι] (*IG* 1³.370 line 79) and the Ephesians were still paying tribute (*IG* 1³.290 col. I line 26). In the summer of 412 it served as a refuge for a Chian ship (Thuc. VIII.19.3), which may imply defection. Noting that "Thucydides is curiously silent about events at Ephesos," Lewis assumes that its revolt was "early and spontaneous" (90 n. 39). It may, however, have been prompted by Tissaphernes. Ephesos had always been an eastward-looking city. Plutarch says that when Lysandros arrived, he found the city in danger of becoming barbarized, in part because "the King's generals were spending a great deal of time there" (*Lys.* 3.3).

Artemis: This proclamation may mean that the satrap of Sardis claimed some special relationship with the deity (*HCT* 5.358). Like other Persians, Tissaphernes could venerate Artemis (compare *Anab.* I.6.7), probably equating her with the Persian goddess Anahita. He had visited Ephesos to sacrifice to Artemis in 411 (Thuc. VIII.109.1).

7. He disembarked the hoplites near Koressos: The *Hell. Oxy.* shows that Thrasyllos commanded the hoplites himself (Cairo fragment, line 10). It identifies Koressos as a harbor (line 12), presumably near the later city gate of the same name, north of the Panajir Dagh and southwest of the Artemision. The river mouth continued to silt up, so that Ephesian harbors--and the location of the city itself--changed over time. The impressive ruins visible today are not those of the classical city, but post-date Lysimachos' refounding in 286. For Ephesian topography see W. Alzinger, "Ephesos," *Real-Encyclopädie der classischen Altertumswissenschaft* Suppl. 12 (1970) 1592-1686.

the cavalry, peltasts, marines and all the others: The *Hell. Oxy.* identifies their leader as the Athenian Pasion (Cairo fragment, line 7), which McKechnie and Kern favor emending to "Pasiphon," an Athenian general at Samos in 410/9 (Dittenberger no. 109 lines 34-36) who died while serving as "commander of the navy" (ἄρχων τοῦ ναυτικοῦ) in an uncertain year, perhaps 409 (Bradeen no. 23).

near the marsh on the opposite side of the city: Farther away than the hoplites, according to the *Hell. Oxy.*, so that when the attack began they were unseen (Cairo fragment, lines 8-9). The marsh should be north of the Artemision near what was then the mouth of the Kaystros River.

8. The Ephesians: Other possible corrections for the manuscripts' σφίσιν cannot be ruled out, but Diod. XIII.64.1 says the Ephesians fought "with all their forces" (πανδημεί), while the *Hell. Oxy.* gives them a prominent place in the fighting and supplies the names of two Ephesian commanders, Timarchos and Possikrates (Cairo fragment, lines 23-24 and 46-47).

the allies whom Tissaphernes led: These must be troops raised by the Persians. The *Hell. Oxy.* apparently indicates that Lakedaimonians were present ([Λακε]δαιμονίων, Cairo fragment, lines 5-6), but surely Tissaphernes did not command them. Omitting the Lakedaimonians adds to Xenophon's negative portrayal of Thrasyllos by minimizing the opposing forces' strength.

the Syracusans from the previous twenty ships: That is, from the twenty ships that arrived in 412 (Thuc. VIII.26.1), were burnt at Kyzikos (1.18) and replaced at Antandros (1.26).

Eukles, the son of Hippon, and Herakleides, the son of Aristogenos: Probably the Eukles and Herakleides elected generals, along with Tellias, in 414 (Thuc. VI.103.4).

the crews of two ships from Selinos: They had arrived with the Syracusan twenty in 412 (Thuc. VIII.26.1).

9. first: The *Hell. Oxy.* also has the battle begin with the hoplite struggle, but it adds numerous details and would add still more if the text were better preserved. Victorious in the first contact near the harbor. Thrasyllos divided his hoplites, leaving some to attack and leading others to a high and inaccessible hill (Cairo fragment, lines 17-21). He probably sent some to attack Ephesos from the southwest and others to seize Panajir Dagh as a potential base. Pasion landed at a different location (§ 7 n.) and attacked Ephesos from the north. His men drove back their opponents and pursued them eagerly, "with the intention of taking the city by assault" (lines 45-46). But Timarchos and Possikrates, the Ephesian commanders, summoned their hoplites (who must by now have defeated both groups of Athenian hoplites) and overcame Pasion. This version supplements rather than contradicts Xenophon. Though the papyrus has a flight to the sea in the second part of the battle while Xenophon has one in the first part, the damaged section following line 23 may have described an earlier flight. The impression given of Thrasyllos' generalship, however, differs considerably: He very nearly captured the city. Kagan's (272-73) assessment of the campaign spells out Xenophon's implied criticisms of Thrasyllos and illustrates how effective Xenophon's style can be.
killing about one hundred . . . about three hundred of them died: Diod. XIII.64.1 is less specific, but agrees with these figures by giving a total of four hundred Athenian dead. None of our sources lists casualties for the other side.

10. one trophy there and another at Koressos: The two trophies, plus the Athenians' recovery of their dead under a truce (§ 11), indicate that the Ephesians controlled the battlefields. Plut. *Alk.* 29.2 mentions only one trophy, made of bronze and presumably a permanent replacement for one of the temporary trophies.
prizes for valor: On these prizes (*aristeia*) see Pritchett 2.276-90.
since their city had been destroyed: See 1.37

11. After taking up their dead under a truce: Greek custom required victors to allow burial of the vanquished (Pritchett 4.94-259). This note here stresses again that the Athenians had lost.
burying: Pritchett (4.202-203) maintains that θάπτειν means "dispose of the dead," and that the Athenians cremated the corpses with funeral rites at Notion, then sent the ashes to Athens according to their custom.

12. in Methymna on Lesbos: Methymna, the second-largest city of Lesbos, was the only one that did not revolt in 428. Athens quickly suppressed its revolt in 412 (Thuc. VIII.22.2-23.6). The Athenian garrison in Mytilene repelled an attack by Methymnian exiles in 411; thereafter Methymna served as a stopping point for

Thrasyllos and supplied (probably five) ships for his fleet (Thuc. VIII.100.3-5).

Plut. *Mor.* 345D implies that this victory was greater than Xenophon indicates, for Plutarch includes Thrasyllos' "spirited actions" (*neanieumata*) near Lesbos among the indispensable items in Kratippos (the others: Alkibiades' exploits in the Hellespont, Theramenes' overthrow of the Four Hundred, Thrasyboulos' and Archinos' revolt from Phyle against the Spartan hegemony and Konon's restoration of Athens' naval power). The *Hell. Oxy.* may have dealt with this incident, but the third column of the Cairo fragment is too badly damaged to help.

13. **Alkibiades the Athenian, the cousin and fellow exile of Alkibiades:** This cousin is "beyond any serious doubt" (Davies 17) the Alkibiades of Phegous who went into exile after instigating Diokleides' false accusation in the Herms affair (Andok. I.65-66). He had chosen not to return with his cousin to Athens' side.

stoned to death: Some editors have found it incredible that Thrasyllos would kill Alkibiades' cousin immediately before joining Alkibiades. But the cousin could now be considered a traitor. Alkibiades the general may have been embarrassed by his cousin's behavior and not sorry to see him killed.

Stoning was an unusual form of execution for Athenians. In fact the only other certain stoning victim is the Lykides who advocated surrendering to the Persians in 479 (Hdt. IX.5; see V. J. Rosivach, "Execution by Stoning in Athens," *Classical Antiquity* 6 [1987] 232-48).

This incident fits into Xenophon's theme of the value of clemency, a virtue Thrasyllos lacks. The point becomes clear from other examples of more generous behavior (see 1.20 n.) and from other negative examples such as Athenian treatment of prisoners (§ 14, II.1.31-32). Ironically, Thrasyllos himself falls victim to Athenian vindictiveness after Arginousai (I.7). For Xenophon's attitude toward Thrasyllos see 1.8 n.

Lampsakos: After its revolt in 411, Strombichides defeated the rebels in a battle and recaptured the unfortified city almost immediately. He confiscated slaves and property, but resettled the free men (Thuc. VIII.62.1-2). Lampsakos then remained loyal until captured by Lysandros in 405 (II.1.18-19).

14-19. *The Syracusan prisoners' escape. Unification of Thrasyllos' and Alkibiades' men. Notes on the Spartan treaty with the helots and the betrayal of the Spartan harmost in Herakleia Trachinia*

Several themes return in these brief notes: the parallel between Syracuse and

Athens, Thrasyllos' failure and Spartan difficulties in governing an empire.

14. in the stone quarries of Peiraieus: The limestone quarries on the Akte peninsula.

Xenophon continues to draw a parallel between Athens and Syracuse (see 1.27 n.). The Syracusans had confined many Athenian prisoners in stone quarries in 413, under pathetic conditions (Thuc. VII.86.2-87.6). The Athenians show a similar lack of compassion here.

15. This anecdote emphasizes Thrasyllos' humiliation. Plutarch presents a slightly more detailed version, saying that Alkibiades' men wanted to share "neither exercises nor quarters in camp" (*Alk.* 29.3). Behind these stories may lie only the fact that Alkibiades and Thrasyllos operated separately for a time, as Diod. XIII.64.4 probably indicates ("Alkibiades, after giving Thrasyboulos a separate command [ἀπολύσας], sailed to the territory held by Pharnabazos, and by ravaging a great deal of it jointly [κοινῇ] . . .").
fortifying Lampsakos: Wall remnants could still be seen in the seventeenth century (Leaf 94), but they did not prevent Lysandros from taking the city by assault in 405 (II.1.18-19).

16. an expedition against Abydos: See also Diod. XIII.64.4 and Plut. *Alk.* 29.4-5. The expedition failed to capture the Spartan base, but Xenophon puts it in a positive light.
Menandros: Probably the man who had commanded in Sicily (Thuc. VII.16.1, 43.2, 69.4; Plut. *Nik.* 20), and served again as general in 405 (II.1.16, 26). Plutarch describes him as ambitious and jealous.

17. ravaged the King's land: Thus continuing the strategy of attacking the King's territory that Thrasyllos had begun in Ionia. It aimed at damaging both Pharnabazos and Tissaphernes enough that they would advocate switching sides or reaching a settlement with Athens. Diod. XIII.64.4 confirms that the Athenians ravaged Pharnabazos' territory.

18. During this time the Lakedaimonians let go under a treaty the helots who had revolted and fled from Malea to Koryphasion: A remarkably brief statement of Sparta's recovery of the site of Demosthenes' famous victory in 425 (Koryphasion was the Lakedaimonian name for Pylos, as Thuc. IV.3.2 explains). Despite the stipulation in the Peace of Nikias that it be returned to Sparta (Thuc. V.18.7), the Athenians had kept control. Diod. XIII.64.5-7 gives a much fuller account: The Spartans, thinking that all the Athenian forces were at the Hellespont (confirming roughly Xenophon's chronological pointer), sent eleven ships (five Sicilian ships and six of their own) plus a land force against the Messenian garrison. The Athenians sent Anytos son of Anthemion with thirty ships to its relief, but storms prevented him from rounding Cape Malea (which again confirms Xenophon's indication of the season). The Messenians resisted for some time, but finally surrendered under a truce. Xenophon's much simpler statement reminds the reader of the great internal threat to Spartan society. Sparta recovered Pylos, but the helots won their freedom.

the Achaians: Since the Peloponnesian Achaians had originally been excluded from the colony (Thuc. III.92.5), these are the Phthiotian Achaians, whom Agis had compelled to give hostages and money (Thuc. VIII.3.1). Alternatively but less likely the Peloponnesian Achaians had been admitted to the colony later.

Herakleia Trachinia: The Lakedaimonians had colonized and fortified Herakleia Trachinia in 426; Thucydides says the colony never much threatened the Athenians, as they had feared it would, since its neighbors opposed it strongly (Thuc. III.92-93; Diod. XII.59.3-5). They won a victory in 420/19, killing the Lakedaimonian commander, and as a result the Thebans took over the place in the summer of 419 (Thuc. V.51-52.1; Diod. XII.77.4). Herakleia had returned to Spartan control during Agis' campaign against the Oitaioi in 413 (Thuc. VIII.3.1), if not earlier.

Thuc. III.92.6 locates Herakleia about forty *stadia* (7.1 km.) from Thermopylai and twenty *stadia* (3.6 km.) from the sea, perhaps mistakenly (see *HCT* 2.396).

their enemies the Oitaians: The enmity goes back at least to 426 (Thuc. III.92.2).

Labotas: Otherwise unknown.

19. Probably interpolated. See 1.37 n.

3.1-22. *Recovery of Kalchedon. Capture of Byzantion*

Here Xenophon again portrays Alkibiades as the successful leader, to the extent that Pharnabazos insists on swearing an oath with Alkibiades personally and is persuaded to negotiate.

3.1. the temple of Athena in Phokaia burned: For Xenophon, such prodigies revealed the future. In the year the old temple of Athena in Athens burned (6.1), victory at Arginousai turned into tragedy. When the temple of Poseidon burned (IV.5.4), disaster at Lechaion soon followed. What this Athena temple burning portends is not at first clear. It must be something ill for Athens, whose patron deity Athena was. Xenophon's narrative for this year, however, has nothing but successes for the Athenians. Not until the narrative of the following year (4.2-3) do we learn what else happened in the year Athena's temple burned: The King made up his mind to support the Peloponnesians wholeheartedly, and appointed his son Kyros to a command overriding the satraps' authority. This decision spelled defeat for Athens.

When the winter ended . . . at the beginning of the spring: 409 BC (see Introduction, pp. 11-14).

[Pantakles . . . archon,] . . . [after . . . elapsed,]: See 1.37 n.

with their entire force: From Lampsakos (2.15) Alkibiades and Thrasyllos joined Theramenes, who now had seventy ships according to Diod. XIII.66.1. The phrase ought to include Thrasyboulos' fleet from the Thraceward region (Diod. XIII.64.3), but since Thrasyboulos is not mentioned in what follows he probably stayed in the north.

2. movable goods: Whatever the enemy could pillage, expressed in § 3 as τὰ χρήματα.

the Bithynian Thracians: in Pharnabazos' satrapy (Hdt. III.90.2, VII.75), though Xenophon says later that they often fought against the satrap (3.2.2).

4. as much of the river as possible: Xenophon writes as if the reader knows the topography. The city was on a peninsula above a river, with harbors both east and west (Diony. Byz. 34.11-35.2 Güngerich). G. E. Bean identifies the river with the stream that flows into Moda Bay, and places the city between the Kadiköy boat station and Moda Point (Stillwell 216). The stockade was built on the north and followed the river where possible; it appears from § 7 that the river bisected the wall at some point. Thus the palisade prevented Pharnabazos from offering effective support to Hippokrates.

6. Thrasyllos: See 1.8 for Xenophon's attitude toward Thrasyllos. Here Thrasyllos cannot win without help.

Alkibiades: Again Alkibiades' intervention led to Athenian victory. He presumably had been fighting Pharnabazos with the Athenian cavalry (compare Plut. *Alk*. 30.2).

7. the Herakleion of the Kalchedonians: Presumably near the city. Pharnabazos therefore still threatened the Athenians, which helps to explain why the Athenians negotiated a treaty.

8. to raise money: According to Diodoros, Alkibiades collected money, persuaded many Thracians to campaign with him, and added to his army the inhabitants of the Cherronesos in full force (πανδημεί, XIII.66.3-4).

Hatzfeld (1940: 320) plausibly dates to this period the forts mentioned but not named by Xenophon at 5.17, II.1.25. They included Ornoi (Lys. 14.26; Nepos *Alc*. 7.4), Neon Teichos (Nepos *Alc.* 7.4; for the site compare *Anab.* VII.2.38), Paktye in the Thracian Cherronesos (Diod. XIII.74.2; for the location compare 5.17) and a place near Bisanthe on the Propontis (Plut. *Alk*. 36.3; Nepos *Alc*. 7.4).

the other generals agreed with Pharnabazos: According to Diod. XIII.66.3, "those around Theramenes made an agreement with the Kalchedonians"; Plut. *Alk*. 31.1 agrees with Xenophon. The presence of this clause in Diodoros argues against V. J. Gray's view that he depends ultimately on Xenophon for this episode ("The value of Diodorus Siculus for the years 411-386 BC," *Hermes* 115 [1987] 75-77) . There may have been two treaties, one between the Athenians and Pharnabazos, the other between the Athenians and the Kalchedonians.

on the subject of Kalchedon: Pharnabazos was to pay twenty talents to the Athenians: Taking ὑπὲρ Καλχηδόνος with συνεχώρησαν; alternatively, taking ὑπὲρ Καλχηδόνος with δοῦναι, "the other generals agreed with Pharnabazos: Pharnabazos was to pay twenty talents to the Athenians for Kalchedon." M. Amit prefers the latter, on the grounds that the former would be odd coming before a treaty that went beyond the status of Kalchedon ("Le traité de Chalcédoine entre Pharnabaze et les stratèges athéniens," *L'Antiquité classique* 42 [1973] 450) . The only clause not directly relevant to Kalchedon, however, is that providing for an embassy to the King, and if the Athenians did not recover Kalchedon now, Xenophon has failed to tell us when they did (at II.2.1 the Athenian garrison in Kalchedon surrenders to Lysandros).

to conduct Athenian ambassadors to the King: See § 13-14, 4.1-7. Xenophon does not say what proposals the Athenians had in mind. Amit (see previous n.) argues that they envisioned a deal that would leave the Greeks in Asia in the Persian empire but obligate them to pay tribute to Athens.

9. they exchanged oaths: Oddly the agreement about the embassy to the king is not included here in the oaths. Later Xenophon says Pharnabazos told Kyros that he had sworn to bring the Athenian ambassadors back to the sea (4.7).

that the Kalchedonians would pay their customary tribute to the Athenians: A fixed tribute, not the ten per cent tax collected at Chrysopolis (1.22) or the five per cent (*eikoste*) on goods travelling by sea substituted for the tribute in 413 (Thuc. VII.28.4). Kalchedon had regularly paid nine talents, later six, still later somewhat less (Meiggs 544-45). This passage supports the thesis that tribute was restored and that the last tribute assessment list (*IG* 1³.100) belongs to 410. Mattingly has argued against this view, relying on the mention of a "twentieth-collector" (*eikostologos*) in Aristoph. *Frogs* 363 (produced in 405) to support his belief that Athens never restored the tribute. (Kalchedon may have been an exception.) See Meiggs (438-39) for a summary of the debate, with references.

Plut. *Alk.* 31.1 lacks this clause but has instead "the Kalchedonians again to be subjects (ὑπήκοοι) of the Athenians," which may be an erroneous deduction from Xenophon.

and would repay the amount they owed: This implies that the tribute had been restored some time earlier. See previous n.

the Kalchedonians: Hatzfeld's emendation (1940: 285 n. 2) to "Pharnabazos" makes Xenophon agree with Plut. *Alk.* 31.1, where the Athenians promised "not to harm Pharnabazos' territory." But there is no textual justification for emending Xenophon. Perhaps the Athenians promised not to attack either Kalchedon or Pharnabazos.

10. Alkibiades was not present for the oaths, but was at Selymbria. After capturing that city: On Selymbria see 1.21, where the city refused to admit Alkibiades, though it gave him money.

Plut. *Alk.* 30.3-10 tells a colorful story: The betrayers agreed to signal with a torch at midnight, but when one of them changed his mind the others signalled before Alkibiades' army was ready. Nevertheless he ran into the city with thirty men (hoplites?) and twenty peltasts. When he saw the enemy drawn up for battle, he had a proclamation made that the Selymbrians must not carry arms against the Athenians. While discussions were under way, Alkibiades' army arrived; he sent his Thracians out of the city so that they would not plunder it, then agreed not to harm the city. He did take money and left a garrison. Diod. XIII.66.4 agrees that Selymbria fell through treachery, that Alkibiades took much money and that he left a garrison.

IG 1³.118 (= Meiggs and Lewis no. 87) contains the last part of the settlement and a decree moved by Alkibiades ratifying it. The conciliatory agreement restored hostages, guaranteed Selymbrian autonomy, perhaps cancelled debts to Athens, and abandoned Athenian and allied claims to property lost in the war or owed by Selymbrians, except for real property.

he came to Byzantion: Diod. XIII.66.3-4 says that Alkibiades joined Theramenes, who had already begun to wall off the city. Xenophon's reader would suppose that Alkibiades deserved credit for beginning the siege.

with the Cherronesians in full force and soldiers and more than three hundred cavalry from Thrace: Xenophon does not explore Alkibiades'

Thracian activities in detail, but even this brief passage lends credibility to Diodoros' story that Alkibiades later offered to bring Thracian infantry to help the Athenians at Aigospotamoi (XIII.105.3).

12. Euryptolemos: Almost certainly the son of Peisianax, Alkibiades' cousin, who greeted Alkibiades on his return to Athens in 407 (4.19) and later defended the generals at the Arginousai trial (7.12, 16, 34). A difficulty is that he was a member of the Athenian embassy escorted by Pharnabazos (§ 13), which according to 4.7 did not return for three years. Emendation is probably in order. See 4.7 n.

the common oath: That is, the oath sworn by the others in § 9.

gave assurances to each other personally: Yet a few years later Pharnabazos arranged Alkibiades' murder (Diod. XIV.11, Plut. *Alk.* 39.1-8).

13. in Kyzikos: This shows that the ambassadors went from the fleet, not from Athens.

Dorotheos: Otherwise unknown, unless he was the Dorotheo[s] who was secretary to the treasurers of the other gods in 408/7 (*IG* 1².313 line 175).

Philokydes: Otherwise unknown.

Theogenes: Possibly the member of the Thirty in 404/3 (II.3.2).

the Argives Kleostratos and Pyrrolochos: This implies that Argives were among the Athenian army. In 412 1,500 Argives lost heavily at Miletos and went home (Thuc. VIII.25.1, 3; 27.6). Since then nothing is known about Argives fighting, though Argos sent ambassadors offering aid to the democratic fleet at Samos in 411 (Thuc. VIII.86.8). Alkibiades declined the offer, at least at that time.

ambassadors of the Lakedaimonians, Pasippidas and others: Contrasted to ἐπέμφθησαν, the verb ἐπορεύοντο might mean "they went (on their own)," and since Pasippidas had been exiled (1.32) some scholars have maintained that this was not an official embassy of the Lakedaimonians. If this view is correct "ambassadors" (πρέσβεις) cannot stand. But then who are the "others"? I prefer the less drastic step of assuming that Pasippidas had been recalled. Compare Thibron, exiled at III.1.8 but in command again, without explanation, at IV.8.17. See also § 17 n.

Hermokrates: See 1.31 n.

14. building a stockade: See § 10 n.

15. some *perioikoi*: The *perioikoi*, free men but not Spartan citizens, inhabited towns in Lakonia and Messenia (other than Sparta and Amyklai; Cartledge [178-91] examines their status and sites). Though they did not go through the *agoge*, they fought in the Spartan phalanx behind the Spartans. By the last quarter of the fifth century some *perioikoi* probably found themselves as far forward as the third rank (T. J. Figueira, "Population Patterns in Late Archaic and Classical Sparta," *Transactions of the American Philological Association* 116 [1986] 199).

a few neodamodeis: The *neodamodeis*, first mentioned at Thuc. V.34.1, were probably helots freed before they enrolled in the army (unlike the "Brasideioi" and the helots sent to Sicily in 413). In effect they became *perioikoi*.

H. D. Westlake cites this passage as evidence that the land troops the Spartans sent to Asia were "meagre in size and perhaps deficient in quality" ("Ionians in the Ionian War," *Classical Quarterly* 29 [1979] 31). But note the presence of Megarians, Boiotians, and--according to Diod. XIII.66.5--mercenaries. Byzantion did not topple easily.

under the command of Helixos the Megarian: As general in 411 he had reached Byzantion with ten ships and brought the city into revolt (Thuc. VIII.80.3). The Megarian origin of Byzantion may help explain his presence.

Koiratadas: Xenophon knew him (*Anab.* VII.1.33-41) and may have relied on him for the account given here (see §§ 21-22).

17. Some ships had been left as guards in various places in the Hellespont by Pasippidas: This passage supports the view (§ 13 n.) that Pasippidas had been recalled from exile, for earlier we hear of him in association with Tissaphernes (1.32 n.). His first connection with Pharnabazos is at § 13, where he appears as a Lakedaimonian ambassador *en route* to the King. It makes sense that he had brought reinforcements to the Hellespont before proceeding into Asia.

Agesandridas (Mindaros' lieutenant) had some in the Thraceward region: A lieutenant (*epibates*) is mentioned elsewhere only at Thuc. VIII.61.1 (where Antisthenes' lieutenant, Leon, commands a detachment of 12 ships) and *Hell. Oxy.* XXII (XVII).4 (where the admiral Cheirikates' lieutenant, Pankalos, commands five ships). Perhaps a lieutenant held an official but irregular position, appointed when necessary to command a detachment of ships, but outside the normal chain of command.

at Antandros: For ship-building at Antandros see 1.25-26.

to draw the enemy away from Byzantion by attacking Athens' allies with his combined fleet: A bold and intelligent plan that might have worked, had Pharnabazos been supportive and Byzantion held out. Xenophon admired Klearchos, with reservations (*Anab.*II.6.1-15); his admiration shows here in the way he credits Klearchos with initiating an aggressive plan for saving Byzantion, after taking the best measures he could for its defence in his absence.

19. **(who . . . Lakedaimonians):** Xenophon makes this extraordinary parenthetical statement because Anaxilaos' acquittal exemplifies Spartan clemency, of which the most remarkable instance comes at the end of the war (II.2.20). The Athenians, though they can show mercy (1.20, 5.19), more typically do not (2.13-14, 7.34, II.2.31-32, as well as the earlier actions the Athenians remember at II.2.3). Xenophon's interest in loyalty and treachery is also relevant here; see Theramenes' trial (II.3.9-56) for his fullest exploration of this theme in the *Hellenika*.

This statement supplies the immediate reason for the betrayal of the city. Anaxilaos does not deny that he hated the Lakedaimonians; he only says that hatred was not his motive for admitting the Athenians. It is striking, however, that of the four governors Xenophon has mentioned, the local inhabitants have turned against Eteonikos (1.32), Labotas (2.18) and now Klearchos. The system of governors has not been working well.

In his story about Anaxilaos' fate (*Alk.* 31.6-8), Plutarch adds that the betrayers agreed with the Athenians that no Byzantine was to be exiled or executed. Diodoros does not mention Anaxilaos, but describes the betrayers as: "hating the oppressiveness of his administration, for Klearchos was a harsh man" (XIII.66.6). In *Anab.* II.6.13 Xenophon describes Klearchos as one who "never had men following him out of friendship and good will," and as "consistently harsh and savage."

20. **Alkibiades:** As often, Xenophon names only Alkibiades among the Athenians. He says nothing about the Athenian stratagem, involving the fleet's pretended withdrawal to create a diversion at the harbor and give the Athenians the chance to enter the city safely (Plut. *Alk.* 31.3-4; Diod. XIII.67.1-2; Frontin. *Strat.* III.11.3; Polyain. I.40.2 [not specifically located at Byzantion] and 47.2 [attributed to Thrasyllos]. Nor does he mention Theramenes' command of the left wing during the battle that followed (Plut. *Alk.* 31.5). See H. D. Westlake for a defense of the non-Xenophontic tradition, which probably goes back to the Oxyrhynchos historian ("Abydos and Byzantium," *Museum Helveticum* 42 [1985] 322-27) . For the view that Diodoros has a conventionalised and amplified account see V. J. Gray, "The value of Diodorus Siculus for the years 411-386 BC," *Hermes* 115 (1987) 87-89.

Some scholars believe that *Hell. Oxy.* V refers to the siege of Byzantion. The passage describes a secret communication by letters attached to a rope between one Myndos (or, reading *Mynd<i>os*, a man from Myndos in Karia), who apparently hid in a wood around the temple of Demeter and Kore close to the city wall, and the betrayer Athenaios (or, if Athenaios is a proper name, an Athenian deserter) on guard duty. Diony. Byz. 13 mentions a temple of Demeter and Kore at Byzantion. But the episode does not appear in Diod. XIII.67, and it might be part of one of several other known incidents or of an incident otherwise unrecorded. For discussion and references see McKechnie and Kern 130.

by opening the gates: According to Diod. XIII.67.3, Alkibiades' men used ladders to enter the city.

the so-called Thrakion: A large flat area, according to *Anab.* VII.1.24, where τὸ Θρᾴκιον καλούμενον confirms Dindorf's emendation here.

21. who knew nothing of what was going on: Henry (7) misses the point when he cites this passage as an example of Xenophon's disjointed style, wondering why the garrison hurried to the rescue if its commanders "knew nothing of the introduction of the Athenians." Xenophon is defending Helixos and Koiratadas against the suspicion of treachery: They knew nothing of the treason, but realized the city was under attack. See § 15 n. for the possibility that Koiratadas was Xenophon's source.

came with all their forces to the agora: According to Diod. XIII.67.4, half of the Peloponnesian troops remained at the harbor.

they had no choice but to surrender themselves: According to Diod. XIII.67.5-7 they fought long and hard until Alkibiades proclaimed that the Athenians would not harm the Byzantines.

22. They were sent: The Athenians captured about three hundred prisoners, according to Plut. *Alk.* 31.5, or about five hundred, according to Diod. XIII.67.6.

Koiratadas slipped into the crowd and escaped: A remarkable escape; Chaireas managed something similar in 411 (Thuc. VIII.74.3), but he was an Athenian.

4.1-7. *Arrival of Kyros*

4.1. the ambassadors: See 3.13.

at Gordion in Phrygia: On the Sangarios River, on the borders of Greater and Hellespontine Phrygia (Arrian *Anab.* I.29.5, Justin XI.7.3). Pharnabazos, satrap of Hellespontine Phrygia, appears to control it here.

Excavators have uncovered a 6.25 m. wide packed gravel road running eastward from Gordion, on the line of the King's Road from Sardis to Susa (Hdt. V.52-53; R. S. Young, "Gordion on the Royal Road," *Proceedings of the American Philosophical Society* 107.4 [1963] 348-64). Up to this point, then, Pharnabazos was fulfilling his agreement to take the Athenian ambassadors to the King.

2. At the beginning of the spring: 408 BC (see Introduction, pp. 11-14).

the Lakedaimonian ambassadors, Boiotios and his colleagues: Some scholars, including recently Bommelaer (62-65), have maintained that Xenophon refers here to the Lakedaimonian embassy of 3.13, which had (in their view) proceeded to the King while the Athenians wintered at Gordion. But the leader of that embassy was Pasippidas, while here Xenophon names Boiotios: a most confusing presentation, if the same group is meant. Boiotios' group probably went earlier, perhaps after the battle of Kyzikos in 410. The Peloponnesians would have wanted to send fresh representatives along with the Athenians, since they did not yet know what Boiotios had achieved.

the Lakedaimonians had gained everything they asked for from the King: Xenophon later has Kyros refer to an agreement to provide three thousand drachmai a month for each ship, with no limit on the number of ships (5.5). This clause does not appear in the 412/11 treaties (Thuc. VIII.18, 37, 58) and can safely be assigned to this "Treaty of Boiotios" (Lewis 124). The daily pay, three obols (or half a drachma) per man, matches the current rate for Athenian sailors (Thuc. VIII.45.2), though before the Sicilian disaster the Athenians had probably paid twice as much (see HCT 5.97-99 against Pritchett 1.24-29).

Lewis (124-25) maintained that Xenophon's strong language here requires more than an agreement about pay, and suggested that a territorial clause "provided for the autonomy of the Greek cities of Asia Minor, possibly with more explicit assurances as well, on condition that they paid the ancient tribute to the King." For objections to Lewis, see Cartledge 266 and R. Seager and C. J. Tuplin, "The Freedom of the Greeks of Asia," *Journal of Hellenic Studies* 100 (1980) 144 n. 36.

3. Kyros: Curiously he gets no introduction, perhaps because he was such a familiar figure or because Xenophon introduced him in his *Anabasis*. Kyros was the second son of Parysatis and the Persian King Dareios. He was born after his father became king (Ktesias, *FGrHist* 688 F 15, where Photios says Ktesias claimed his source was Parysatis herself; Plut. *Art*. 2.4), that is after 16 August 424 (Lewis 72). At the time of his appointment in 408 he was no more than 15 years old: as our sources describe him, a "youth" (*neaniskos*, Diod. XIII.70.3) and a "lad" (*meirakion*, Plut. *Lys*. 4.3).

the royal seal: For other instances of the King's seal attesting the authenticity of documents see V.1.30 and VII.1.39. Schol. Thuc. I.129 says: "According to some the seal of the Persian King has the image of the king, according to others the image of Kyros their first king, and according to others the image of Dareios' horse, on account of whose neighing he became king."

karanon . . . "lord.": In the *Anabasis*, Xenophon details Kyros' position: "satrap . . . and general of all those who marshal in the plain of Kastolos" (I.1.2) and "satrap of Lydia and Greater Phrygia and Kappadokia, and general of all those who marshaled in the plain of Kastolos" (I.9.7). Exactly what these expressions mean is not clear. Ionia is not mentioned, though "on the coast" just above ought to include it. The explanation may be that Kyros personally controlled the tribute from the Ionian cities, though they remained outside the satrapal system (see II.1.14 n.). Kyros' authority extended over Pharnabazos (§ 5), and Tissaphernes became one of his advisers (5.8-9, *Anab.* I.1.2, with S. Ruzicka, "Cyrus and Tissaphernes, 407-401 B.C.," *Classical Journal* 80 [1985] 204-211).

The plain of Kastolos, in Lydia east of Sardis, was a marshaling or gathering point (*syllogos*). According to *Oik.* 4.6, the King held an annual inspection of his mercenaries and other troops (except garrison troops) at these gathering points. The only other one named is Thymbrara (*Kyr.* VI.2.11).

Some have supposed κάρανον Doric Greek for κάρηνον, "chief," and have deleted the explanatory sentence as a gloss. Others think it a Persian term. For a recent discussion see P. Petit, "Étude d'une fonction militaire sous la dynastie perse Achéménide," *Études Classiques* 51 (1983) 35-45.

4. saw Kyros: By spring 408, then, Kyros was somewhere east of Gordion.

5. since he wanted . . . going on: This wish implies that Kyros will not proceed directly to Sardis. But nothing known about Kyros' plans or actions suggests he needed secrecy. Perhaps Pharnabazos wanted to conceal what had happened to prevent further raids on his territory, and represented Kyros as responsible in his excuses to the Athenians. Or the desire for secrecy might have come from the Lakedaimonians, who needed a conducive environment for the 408/7 embassy that arranged an exchange of prisoners and fixed a ransom for the remaining prisoners (Androtion, *FGrHist* 324 F 44). In any event, Xenophon's phrase conveys the impression of a commander who will prove a difficult foe.

7. when three years had passed: Amit's emendation "months" for "years" is very attractive. Only by changing the text can we have Mantitheos back in the Hellespont by 408 (1.10 n.) and Euryptolemos back in Athens by 407 (3.12 n.).
Ariobarzanes: Probably the Ariobarzanes who succeeded Pharnabazos as satrap, V.1.28.
Kios in Mysia: On the Propontis, about two hundred km. east of Kyzikos.
they sailed to rejoin the rest of the army: To Samos, where the Hellespontine fleet moved in the summer of 408 (§ 8). Alkibiades spent at least part of the 408 campaigning season in Karia (see next n.), but the remaining fleet operated from Samos. See § 10 n.

8-10. *Alkibiades in Karia. Thrasyllos' capture of Thasos.*
Election of generals

8. Samos: See 2.1 n. Though Xenophon has not mentioned Samos since Thrasyllos' Ionian expedition, we know from *IG* 1³.375 lines 35-36 that four Athenian generals operated at Samos in 409. In the same year the Athenians thanked the Halikarnassians for helping [ἔς τε τὴν στρατιὰ]ν καὶ τὴν πόλιν [τὴν Ἀθηναίων], (*IG* 1³.103 lines 7-8). Further evidence for campaigning in Ionia comes from Bradeen's restoration of a funerary monument dating to 409 or 408, providing space for 900-1400 casualties, far more than we would suspect in the Hellespont and therefore probably from Ionia and Karia (Bradeen no. 23). Thus Samos may have served continuously as the Athenian base in the south.
one hundred talents: In his study of Karia, Hornblower (5-8) calls this levy "astounding" and confesses his inability to identify the assets that made it possible in (on the chronology he accepts) such a short time. Kagan (310 n. 69) finds the figure so implausible that he suggests emending the text. At the height of Athenian control the Karian region paid less than fifty talents in annual tribute. Its payment record shows frequent absenteeism, and efforts to collect tribute by force during the Archidamian War failed (Thuc. II.69, III. 19). All this supports Robertson's contention that Alkibiades might have spent the entire 408 campaign in Karia (Introduction, pp. 11-14). A comparison with the Peloponnesian collection on Rhodes in 411 may help. In mid-century Rhodes had contributed eighteen talents of the Karian annual tribute; its wartime contributions increased to nearly forty talents (*HCT* 5.92). Yet a Peloponnesian fleet of ninety-four ships, having just prompted the Rhodians to revolt from Athens, collected only thirty-two talents in eighty days. Even if the figure be emended to forty or fifty days (for references see *HCT* 5.147), it suggests that Alkibiades with only twenty ships would have required months to raise one hundred talents from Karia excluding Rhodes.

9. Thrasyboulos: He had been in the Thraceward region before Kyzikos (1.12, Diod. XIII.49.1). Xenophon has not mentioned him since that battle, but according to Diodoros he returned to Thrace, where he brought over "the cities in this area" (XIII.64.3), including Thasos and Abdera at the time of the battle of Notion (XIII.72.1-2). This last date conflicts with 5.11, but Thrasyboulos was probably in the Thraceward area continuously between 410 and 407, and he may have been, like Dieitrephes earlier (Thuc. VIII.64.2), elected to govern the Thraceward region. Xenophon's phrase here refers back several years--not something we would have guessed without Diodoros' testimony.

Xenophon gives Thrasyboulos thirty ships. This figure is not confirmed by

Diod. XIII.64.4, where "Thrasyboulos" is a mistake for "Thrasyllos." Diod. XIII.72.1, which gives Thrasyboulos only fifteen ships for his assault on Thasos, can be reconciled with Xenophon by supposing that Thrasyboulos operated in the area with thirty ships for several years, but used only fifteen for his final attack on Thasos (Meiggs 575, though Meiggs concludes by preferring Xenophon's figure).

Thasos: For the previous history of Thasos, see 1.12, 32 nn. The "fighting" mentioned here was against Thrasyboulos, perhaps against other Athenian generals (Oinobios is known from *IG* 1³.101 [= Meiggs and Lewis no. 89] line 47 to have acted in the region, probably in 410/409 [compare *IG* 1³.375 line 28]), and against the Thasian colony Neapolis (honored in two separate decrees on *IG* 1³.101).

Evidence for civil disorder in Thasos is limited to 1.32 and an inscription that records two decrees offering rewards for informers about plots (Meiggs and Lewis no. 83).

Diod. XIII.72.1 says that Thrasyboulos killed two hundred Thasians and besieged the survivors. He forced them to recall their pro-Athenian exiles, accept a garrison and become allies of Athens.

10. Thrasyllos sailed to Athens: Robertson argues that Thrasyllos returned in 408, a year before Alkibiades (see Introduction, pp. 11-14). He cites Diod. XIII.69.3 and Plut. *Alk.* 35.1 to show that the Athenians elected generals for 407/6 when Alkibiades was present. However, Xenophon would then have no reason to specify that Alkibiades sailed from Samos to Paros with twenty ships (§ 11), for that was all he had (§ 8). I prefer to believe that Alkibiades operated in Karia with twenty ships while the main fleet stayed in Ionia during 408. The passages in Diodoros and Plutarch need not be rejected: They may mean that the Athenians selected, from the board already chosen, the commanders for Alkibiades' 407 campaign whom he wished. Not all the generals would have gone with Alkibiades. (Thrasyboulos in Diod. XIII.69.3 may be a mistake, as at XIII.64.1, 66.1 and elsewhere, for Thrasyllos.)

Before he arrived: Xenophon emphasizes Alkibiades' popularity by noting that the Athenians elected him general without his sailors' votes.

the Athenians chose as generals: Presumably at the regular election (1.2 n.). Though Xenophon names only three elected generals, there were probably ten as usual. See § 21 for Aristokrates and Adeimantos as generals on land; another whose name began with P, perhaps Perikles son of Perikles of Cholargeus, is known from *IG* 1³.117 lines 5-6. The election reported here may have been only the choice of the chief commanders out of the previously-chosen board. If this was the regular election, we can suppose that Xenophon chose to name only the fleet commanders-- perhaps those assigned to Ionia, the Thraceward region, and the west respectively.

Alkibiades, who was in exile: This statement is not literally correct, for Alkibiades had been condemned to death, not exiled (Thuc. VI.61.7), and the Five Thousand had recalled him in 411 (see 1.5 n.). Unless the restored democracy refused to recognize the recall's validity--and no other evidence indicates that the restored democracy overturned the Five Thousand's acts--Alkibiades was only a voluntary exile in 408. Perhaps Xenophon used "exile" (φεύγων) because Alkibiades had not yet returned to Athens, had not yet regained his property, and still faced the curses of the Eumolpidai and Kerykes (Plut. *Alk.* 33.3; Diod. XIII.69.2; Nepos *Alc.* 6.5). Xenophon may also be playing on the sense of φεύγων as "defendant." The word helps Xenophon paint Alkibiades as timorous rather than haughty.

Konon: The son of Timotheos of Anaphlystia. On the family see Davies no. 13700. He first appears commanding eighteen ships at Naupaktos in 414/13, but Thucydides does not call him "general" and he may have held a lesser office (Thuc. VIII.31.4; *HCT* 5.32-33). Diod. XIII.48.6 has him commanding in the same area again, this time specifically as "general" and intervening in a civil disorder in Kerkyra put in 410/9 but datable by context to late 411. Between his generalship in 411/10 and his election for 407/6 our sources do not mention Konon. He may nevertheless have been active in the Thraceward region, Ionia or (most likely) the west. He next appears at 5.16.

11-23. *Alkibiades' return to Athens. His election as commander-in-chief and departure for Ionia*

11. Gytheion: "Where the Lakedaimonian dockyards were" (VI.5.32), on the Lakonian Gulf about fifty km. south of Sparta.

the thirty triremes . . . there: Alkibiades knew that the war was not yet won. The embassy sent with Pharnabazos had returned empty-handed (§ 7), and now he saw the Lakedaimonians preparing new ships.

12. he sailed into the Peiraieus: Xenophon's account portrays Alkibiades as diffident; other sources describe a grander scene. According to Diod. XIII.68.1-69.1 and Nepos *Alc.* 6.5-7.3, the generals (Nepos names Alkibiades, Thrasyboulos [a mistake for Thrasyllos?] and Theramenes) returned together and brought not less than two hundred captured ships. They decorated their own triremes with gilded armor, wreaths, and other spoils. Plut. *Alk.* 32.1 also says that the Athenian triremes, decorated with shields and spoils, towed many captured ships; they brought not less than two hundred ship-ornaments (*akrostolia*). Here the garlands are given to Alkibiades after he landed (33.3). Plutarch goes on to summarize Douris of Samos' story that Alkibiades had Chrysogonos, a flute-player who had won a victory at the

Pythian games, and Kallippides, a tragic actor, keep time for the rowers, and that his own ship had purple sails. Plutarch rejects Douris' version because he did not find it in Theopompos, Ephoros or Xenophon. Chrysogonos and Kallippides also appear in Athenaios 12.535d.

The most serious discrepancy here is whether Alkibiades came home separately with only twenty ships (Xenophon), or whether the fleet returned together (Plutarch, Diodoros, and Nepos). Xenophon was probably an eyewitness. But the way Xenophon divides the fleet helps him portray Alkibiades as cautious, a portrayal that culminates in the dramatic image of Alkibiades hesitating on board ship until he saw his cousin welcoming him home (§ 19). Xenophon's attitude raises concern about his reliability.

on the day when the city was celebrating the Plynteria: "The Praxiergidai carry out these secret rites on Thargelion 25, removing the clothing [from Athena's statue] and covering the image. Therefore the Athenians regard this day as the most inauspicious of the days forbidden for business. The goddess seemed to veil herself and drive Alkibiades away from herself rather than to receive him with friendly good will" (Plut. *Alk.* 34.1-2). Other sources indicate that on this day the cult statue of Athena Polias was enshrouded, escorted by mounted ephebes down to the sea near Phaleron, and washed. Simon (46-48) suggests that the day was considered inauspicious because the goddess left the city; sanctuaries were closed by ropes.

The date remains uncertain. Phot. "Plynteria" gives the penultimate day of Thargelion (May/June), and according to the Nikomachos calendar a cloth was presented to Athena on Thargelion 29. But the assembly met on that date several times, and the Thorikos calendar lists Plynteria in Skirophorion (June/July; Burkert 439 n. 5).

which some people considered to be inauspicious: This detail lends an ominous note to the entire scene.

13. the city: The *asty* is the city proper, seven or eight km. northeast of the port. See also § 19.

Some people said that he was the best . . . : Xenophon presents the positive (§§ 13-16) and negative (§ 17) views of Alkibiades, without taking a side explicitly. Like Tacitus summing up opinions on Augustus (*Ann.* I.9.3-10.8), however, he does not give equal space to the two sides. For Xenophon's favorable attitude toward Alkibiades, see 1.7 n.

men less powerful than he, scoundrels who acted politically for their own private gain: Thucydides describes Alkibiades' opponents similarly, if not quite as pejoratively: "those who resented Alkibiades for standing in the way of their secure leadership of the people and thought that, if they could drive him out, they would be the leading citizens" (VI.28.2). Of the three known opponents, Androkles was murdered by young revolutionaries in 411 (Thuc. VIII.65.2), Peisandros had fled to Dekeleia when the revolution failed (Thuc. VIII.98.1) and Thessalos son of Kimon has not been heard of since 415.

14. At the time he had wanted to be tried immediately . . . absent: See Thuc. VI.28-29, 61.

15. the enemy: The Spartans and the Persians.
in daily danger of losing his life: The Spartans had condemned him to death in 412 (Thuc. VIII.45.2-5).

16. It was not the character . . . of men like Alkibiades: This defense against the charge of being a revolutionary might hold for 415 (see Thuc. VI.27.3-28.2), but not for 411 (see Thuc. VIII.48.1). Even if Alkibiades did not care what constitution Athens had so long as it accepted Alkibiades, as Thuc. VIII.48.4 and Alkibiades' later behavior suggest, he must still bear responsibility for starting the oligarchic revolution.
they destroyed the best persons during the oligarchical government: In 411. Xenophon uses *beltistoi* in a political sense to designate the aristocrats (V.2.6; *Kyr.* VIII.1.16), but he can use it to refer to as many as three thousand (II.3.19) and he once says "the majority and best" (οἱ πλεῖστοι καὶ βέλτιστοι, IV.4.1).

17. he alone was responsible . . . in the future: These sweeping charges, while damning enough, lack detail and therefore conviction.

18. Like a modern public relations specialist working for a political candidate, Xenophon puts considerable "spin" on the story of Alkibiades' homecoming here. Xenophon's interpretation of Alkibiades' action is not the only possible interpretation: Alkibiades may have stood on deck for a moment to enjoy the crowd's adulation as well as to look for protectors.

19. Euryptolemos the son of Peisianax, his cousin: See 3.12 n. Davies (378) argues that Xenophon used *anepsios* loosely for "third cousin." This conclusion can be avoided by either (1) identifying Euryptolemos' father as a brother of Alkibiades' mother Deinomache (P. J. Bicknell, "Diomedon Cholargeus?" *Athenaeum* 53 [1975] 177), or (2) identifying the father as the son of Kimon (Schol.

Aristeid. *Hypothesis to Kimon* in *On the Four* [Dindorf 3.515]) and a sister of Deinomache (W. E. Thompson, "Euryptolemos," *Transactions of the American Philological Association* 100 [1969] 583-86).

20. he defended himself . . . .   Though the Athenians had already recalled Alkibiades and elected him general, the curses against him had not yet been revoked (Plut. *Alk.* 33.3).

that he had been treated unjustly: According to Diod. XIII.69.1, he made everyone agree that the city had been at fault. But according to Plut. *Alk.* 33.2 he blamed the people only a little, while ascribing the fault "to his own ill fortune and an envious divine power."

commander-in-chief: Compare Diod. XIII.69.3, "establishing him as commander-in-chief (*strategos autokrator*) both on land and sea, they handed over all forces to him," and Plut. *Alk.* 33.2, "commander-in-chief (*autokrator strategos*) on land and sea."   At *Anab.* VI.1.21 Xenophon uses *autokrator* to mean, as VI.1.18 shows, a single general who did not have to consult with other generals.   This occasion is the first and only time the Athenians named a single general *autokrator*. Contrast Thuc. VI.8.2, where Nikias, Alkibiades and Lamachos are all *autokratores* for the Sicilian expedition; they have to consult and agree on strategy.

the Athenians had previously been making the procession of the Mysteries by sea because of the war: That is, since the Lakedaimonians had fortified Dekeleia (as stated explicitly by Plut. *Alk.* 34.4), in 413.

he conducted it by land, leading out all the soldiers: Alkibiades no doubt intended to deflect any remaining suspicions about his piety.   According to Plut. *Alk.* 34.6-7, he informed the Eumolpidai and Kerykes (the two families which supervised the mysteries) of his intentions, stationed lookouts on the hilltops, dispatched an advance force, and accompanied the silent procession with an armed force--all without incident.   Plutarch goes on to say that his supporters called him *hierophantes* (normally a member of the Eumolpidai family) and *mystagogos* (each *mystes* had a *mystagogos* to lead him or her into the sanctuary), and the poor even hoped he would become tyrant.

The procession of the *mystai* to Eleusis, more than thirty km. along the "Sacred Way," took place on 19 Boedromion (September/October; Mikalson 58-59).

21. one hundred ships: Diod. XIII.69.4 and Plut. *Alk.* 35.2 have the same figure.

In the third month: Given the dates of the Plynteria (§ 12 n.) and the Eleusinian mysteries (§ 20 n.), the manuscript figure must be wrong, unless the Plynteria were postponed.   Since the Plynteria's exact date is uncertain, either "fourth" or "fifth" is possible. Alkibiades left Athens in September at the earliest. The need to repair and dry out ships, the troops' desire for some rest at home, and Alkibiades' wish to conduct the procession to Eleusis explain the delay.

Andros, which had revolted: The revolt's date is unknown. Andrians had fought on Athens' side (Thuc. IV.42.1, VII.57.4), and Andrian troops helped establish the Four Hundred in 411 (Thuc. VIII.69.3).

Aristokrates: Probably the son of Skellias who (on the likely assumption that all the contemporary generals named Aristokrates are the same man) swore to the peace and the alliance in 421 (Thuc. V.19.2, 24.1), was general in 412 (Thuc. VIII.9.2), took part in the Four Hundred (Thuc. VIII.89.2, 92.2, 4), then helped Theramenes overthrow the oligarchy (Lys. 12.66; Aristot. *Ath. Pol.* 33.2), and served as general in 410/9 (*IG* 1³.375 [= Meiggs and Lewis no. 84] line 35).

Adeimantos the son of Leukolophides: Probably given his patronymic to distinguish him from Plato's brother, the son of Ariston (Plato *Apol.* 34a). After being denounced for profaning the mysteries in 415 (Andok. 1.16), he went into exile and his property was sold (*SEG* XIII.17 lines 17, 53, 116, 131, 174, 178, part of which is reproduced as Meiggs and Lewis no. 79).

22. in the city: That is, the city of Andros.

killing some but not many: Diod. XIII.69.4 says that many were killed, but Diodoros' rhetorical battle descriptions regularly contain such claims.

the Lakonians who were there. Diod. XIII.69.4 mentions Peloponnesians (a more general term), Plut. *Alk.* 35.2 Lakedaimonians (equivalent to Lakonians, including both Spartiates and *perioikoi*).

23. Alkibiades erected a trophy: Xenophon has Alkibiades set up the symbol of victory, but omits his unsuccessful assaults on the city (Diod. XIII.69.5, Plut. *Alk.* 35.2). Plutarch says Alkibiades' enemies made this failure the first of the new charges against him. Pro-Alkibiades as always, Xenophon leaves a different impression.

Xenophon does not mention any forces left behind. Diod. XIII.69.5 has Alkibiades leave an "adequate garrison" under the command of Thrasyboulos, probably a mistake for Thrasyllos (see § 10 n.). On whether ships were left behind, see 5.18 n.

and carried on the war from there: Diod. XIII.69.5 has Alkibiades plunder Kos and Rhodes. These operations probably belong to winter 407/6.

5.1-7. *Lysandros and Kyros*

This first story about Lysandros shows him to be a good leader, concerned about his men. Direct speech highlights Lysandros' cleverness in getting Kyros to concede an increase in the troops' pay.

Noting parallels in Herodotos to the story's form (the offer of a favor leading to an unexpected request that must be granted), Gray (14-22) questioned the episode's historicity. However, Lysandros might have known his Herodotos too and waited patiently for his opportunity. Xenophon elsewhere claims he heard about a conversation between Lysandros and Kyros from an unnamed host in Megara (perhaps Hermon, Lysandros' pilot) who heard it from Lysandros himself (*Oik.* 4.20-25, from a later occasion, since Kyros has had time to design a garden). The same source might have related this conversation as well. This is not to say that Xenophon was unaware of the parallel between his story and Herodotos'.

5.1. Not long before these events: That is, not long before Alkibiades' return to Athens. See next n.

Lysandros: His father's name was Aristokritos (*IG* 2².1385 line 20 [partially restored], 1388 line 32, 1400 line 15; Paus. 6.3.14), not Aristokleitos as in the manuscripts of Plut. *Lys.* 2.1. Plutarch says his family, though impoverished at the time of his birth, was descended from Herakles (as, according to Greek tradition, were the two Spartan royal families). Later sources say he was a *mothax* (Phylarchos, *FGrHist* 81 F 43; Aelianus *VH* 12.43), that is, a man who had needed help from a Spartiate to receive Spartan training (see D. Lotze, "*Mothakes*," *Historia* 11 [1962] 427-35.). This claim need not be inconsistent with Plutarch: A wealthy friend may have subsidized Lysandros' education. Detractors could have held this fact against him (note III.5.12 and Isok. 4.111), since other *mothakes* had humbler origins. Plutarch's claim that Lysandros had been Agesilaos' *erastes* (*Lys.* 22.6, *Ages.* 2.1) suggests a birthdate of about 454. His earlier career is a blank.

since Kratesippidas' admiralship had expired: Recently several scholars have recognized that Beloch's view (2.2.269-89) that the Spartan admiral (*nauarchos*) always held office for one year, beginning in the autumn, will not work for the Ionian war. R. Sealey, "Die spartanische Nauarchie," *Klio* 58 (1976) 335-58, argues that until the Ionian War the *nauarchos* commanded a particular fleet for a particular task, without a time limit. The new conditions of the Ionian war--a large fleet operating far from home for years--prompted a new law instituting annual tenure beginning in the spring and prohibiting a man from holding the office twice (see II.1.7). Bommelaer (75-79), on the other hand, believes Beloch's view correct until Lysandros and his friends arranged to coordinate the command year with the military year. On this hypothesis the change benefitted Lysandros. I doubt whether Lysandros had such influence so early, and prefer Sealey's theory.

Rhodes: The island had revolted from Athens in winter 412/11, and the Rhodians had then contributed thirty-two talents to the Lakedaimonian fleet (Thuc. VIII.44.2-4; see 4.9 n.). In late summer Mindaros sent Dorieus with thirteen ships to quell a possible revolution at Rhodes (Diod. XIII.38.5), which Dorieus did (Diod. XIII.45.1) before sailing to the Hellespont (see 1.2 with n.). Xenophon omits the unification of Ialysos, Lindos and Kameiros into the single city of Rhodes, an event Diodoros places in 408/7 (XIII.75.1).

Kos: The visit was apparently uneventful, which suggests that Kos had gone over to the Peloponnesians or at least expelled the Athenian archon or archons left by Alkibiades after he fortified Kos in the summer of 411 (Thuc. VIII.108.2). Diodoros' story about Alkibiades plundering Kos and Rhodes to secure provisions for his troops (XIII.69.5) should be placed shortly after Lysandros' visit.

Ephesos: Xenophon does not explain why Lysandros chose Ephesos for his base. H. Schaefer, "Alkibiades und Lysander in Ionien," *Würzburger Jahrbücher für die Altertumswissenschaft* 4 (1949/50) 301-302, argues on the basis of Plut. *Lys.* 3.3 (which says that the city was impoverished and in danger of being completely barbarized by Persian customs when Lysandros arrived) that he wanted to draw the city away from Persian influence. Lotze (15, 25) holds that, on the contrary, Lysandros went to Ephesos precisely because he sought close ties with the Persians, especially Kyros. Kallikratidas, who did not want such close Persian collaboration, returned to Miletos (6.7). Furthermore, Ephesos is much closer to Sardis than Miletos is, and the Athenians at Samos could no longer interrupt Peloponnesian communications with Chios.

with seventy ships: Diod. XIII.70.2 says that Lysandros gathered nearly seventy ships, including contingents from Rhodes, Ephesos, Miletos and Chios.

2. Lysandros went inland to visit him with the Lakedaimonian ambassadors: And, according to *Oik.* 4.20, with presents from the allies. The ambassadors apparently are those of 4.2, who had probably seen Kyros already.

what he had done: For Tissaphernes' lukewarm support for the Peloponnesians, see 1.9 n.

3. five hundred talents: One talent = sixty mnai = six thousand drachmai = thirty-six thousand obols. At the expected rate of thirty mnai for each ship each month (§ 5), five hundred talents (= thirty thousand mnai) would support Lysandros' seventy ships for more than fourteen months.

he would coin into money the silver and gold throne on which he sat: Kyros' fine words recall Tissaphernes' promise, reported by Alkibiades at Thuc. VIII.81.3, to sell his own bed if necessary to keep the Athenians supplied.

Lysandros presses for an immediate and tangible proof of the new Persian attitude.

4. urged him to fix the pay at one Attic drachma for each sailor:
That is, one Attic drachma (six obols) per day, or twice the current rate of pay in the Athenian navy (Plut. *Alk.* 35.5; see also Thuc. VIII.45.2, with *HCT* 5.97-99). At this rate five hundred talents (= three million drachmai) would last little more than seven months for seventy ships with two hundred men per ship (§ 5 n.).
the sailors of the Athenians would desert: According to Plut. *Lys.* 4.7, after the battle of Notion the pay increase Lysandros secured persuaded the majority of the sailors to leave the Athenian ships, while those who remained were dispirited and seditious. Kagan (311) accepts Plutarch's testimony (though he alters Plutarch's chronology) on the grounds that Konon could only find crews for seventy triremes instead of the previous one hundred plus (§ 20), while the Peloponnesian fleet doubled from seventy to 140 by the end of Lysandros' year in command (6.3). But this argument contradicts Xenophon, who says in 6.16 that Konon picked "the best rowers from many crews" and as a result had seventy fast ships. No doubt some Athenian sailors deserted, but Plutarch exaggerates wildly.
he would spend less money: Because the war would end sooner.

5. the agreement: Presumably the "Treaty of Boiotios" (4.2 with n.).
thirty mnai for each ship each month: Since each sailor had been receiving three obols per day (§ 7), this passage agrees with others (Hdt. VII.184.1, VIII.17; Thuc. VI.8.1) that a trireme carried a crew of two hundred.

6. what favor . . . would please Lysandros most: No doubt Kyros expected Lysandros to ask for something personal. By asking for increased troop pay, Lysandros demonstrates that his concern for his men outweighs his desire for personal profit. At *Ages.* 4.6 Xenophon records as praiseworthy Agesilaos' rejection of Persian gifts on the grounds that a leader ought to enrich his army rather than himself.

7. the wage was four obols: At this rate, five hundred talents would pay the sailors on seventy triremes for almost eleven months. Of course, Lysandros planned to expand his fleet.
what was owed and a month's wage in advance: Diod. XIII.70.3 and Plut. *Lys.* 4.6 say that Kyros handed over ten thousand darics, or (at one daric = twenty drachmai) 33 1/3 talents, significantly less than the 46 2/3 talents needed to pay the crews of seventy triremes for a month at the new rate. Xenophon may exaggerate Kyros' generosity.

with the result that the army became much more enthusiastic: On the importance of pay and provisions for the soldiers' morale, and on the general's responsibility to provide them, see II.1.5, 5.1.13; *Hipparch.* 6.2; *Anab.* II.6.8, IV.5.7-9; *Mem.* 3.1-2, 4.

8-9. *Failure of Athenian attempt to negotiate with Kyros*

8. the Athenians: I suspect that Alkibiades played the leading role; this general expression conceals his failure in these negotiations.

through Tissaphernes: When last mentioned Tissaphernes had successfully defended Ephesos against Thrasyllos' assault in 410 (2.6-9); previously he claimed the King had instructed him to fight Athens (1.9), though Alkibiades' escape from his custody suggests they colluded (1.10 n.). Xenophon has not indicated what led Tissaphernes to discourage Kyros from decisive intervention, but Athenian campaigns against Tissaphernes since 410 (4.8 n.) might have convinced him that the Persians needed immense Peloponnesian help to defeat Athens. Victory therefore might also mean the loss of Ionia to the Peloponnesians, should they choose to defend it (as they did in the 390s). If the Athenians were willing to concede the mainland, Tissaphernes might have concluded the time was ripe for negotiating.

9. (as he himself was doing, on Alkibiades' advice): See 1.9 n.

10-21. *The Battle of Notion. Alkibiades' deposition and departure. Konon's assumption of the command*

10. ninety ships: Xenophon does not explain the increase from the seventy previously mentioned (§ 1). The new ships may have been built at Ephesos, or they may have come from the allies, either because of the increased pay or because of Lysandros' political machinations. Diod. XIII.70.4 and Plut. *Lys.* 5.5-6 agree that Lysandros called the most powerful, daring men from the cities to Ephesos, where he urged them to support his efforts and promised to establish them in control of their cities if he succeeded. They responded positively, and may therefore have been responsible for the twenty additional ships or their equipment. Unfortunately the chronology is uncertain: Diodoros places the plot before the battle of Notion, Plutarch after.

while he repaired and dried them out: Unless triremes were periodically dried out and repaired, they lost perhaps ten per cent of their top speed, while the time taken to ram an enemy ship from rest might increase by more than fifteen per cent. For top performance triremes needed to have marine growths scraped and pitch reapplied (Morrison and Coates 230-32).

11.   In the lacuna he posits between §§ 10 and 11, Delebecque (77) suggests
Xenophon would have indicated Alkibiades' movement from Samos (4.23) to Notion
(§ 12) "in the following year" or "at the beginning of the spring"; Delebecque thinks
Xenophon may also have said something about Thrasyboulos, last mentioned at
Thasos (4.9). Xenophon's narrative, however, has a rough quality elsewhere as well,
and I would not put a year-marker here (see Introduction, pp. 11-14).
his pilot Antiochos: An exceptional appointment.   Plutarch tells a charming
story about the young Alkibiades befriending Antiochos after Antiochos recaptured a
quail that escaped from under Alkibiades' coat during an assembly meeting (*Alk.*
10.1-2).   Plut. *Alk.* 35.6 describes Antiochos as "brave but foolish and vulgar,"
Diod. XIII.71.2 as "by nature impetuous and eager to do something brilliant by
himself."   Pilots were veteran sailors, and apparently no one objected to Antiochos'
promotion.   No generals were available, for Konon had remained on Andros (§ 18),
while Aristokrates and Adeimantos, whom Xenophon describes as "generals on land"
(4.21), presumably accompanied the land troops north.
with orders not to attack Lysandros' ships: Thus Alkibiades bore no
direct responsibility for what happened. Plut. *Alk.* 35.6 and Diod. XIII.71.1 have
slightly different orders ("do not fight a naval battle even if the enemy attacks" and
"do not fight a naval battle until I am present," respectively).
sailed across: An ill-chosen verb to describe a voyage from Notion to Phokaia,
but appropriate for a trip across the Gulf of Smyrna from Klazomenai, to which
Diod. XIII.71.1 says Alkibiades had sailed from Notion (*Hell. Oxy.* III.22 has ταῖς
Κλα[ζομεναῖς], so this detail probably came from the Oxyrhynchos historian).
Xenophon has compressed events. Plut. *Lys.* 5.1 has Alkibiades sail directly to
Phokaia, as in Xenophon, but in *Alk.* 35.5 he goes to Karia to collect money.   In
this last passage Plutarch evidently misdates an earlier visit to Karia, perhaps that in
4.8.

Xenophon indicates neither Alkibiades' purpose nor how many ships he took.
According to Diod. XIII.71.1, Alkibiades took the troop-ships (number unspecified)
and went to defend Klazomenai from attacks by its exiles. M. Amit, "La campagne
d'Ionie de 407/6 et la bataille de Notion," *Gräzer Beiträge* 3 (1975) 8-11, plausibly
reconstructs Alkibiades' strategy as follows: The fleet at Notion was to watch
Lysandros and prevent him from moving north, while Alkibiades would secure the
Gulf of Smyrna, operating primarily with land forces. The Athenians would then
control both sides of the Erythrian peninsula and could hope to capture Erythrai.
From Erythrai they could assault Chios.
Thrasyboulos, who he heard had come out of the Hellespont: At 4.9,

Thrasyboulos was operating in the Thraceward region, where he captured Thasos (and, Diod. XIII.72.2 adds, Abdera, though he places the notice of Thasos' and Abdera's capture after the battle of Notion). Perhaps he had moved then to the Hellespont.

to fortify Phokaia: The text need not be emended. Phokaia had received Astyochos' fleet in early winter 412 (Thuc. VIII.31.3-4) and may have revolted earlier that year (Thuc. VIII.22.1). But it is not known to have played an active role in hostilities, and the Athenians may not have regarded it as rebellious. Thrasyboulos may have decided to fortify a convenient port between Samos and Lampsakos, the main Athenian bases, to serve as a base for assaults on Peloponnesian allies in northern Ionia. The Athenians apparently did not leave a sizeable garrison, since most of the Peloponnesian survivors of the battle of Arginousai fled to Phokaia (6.33).

12. But having sailed from Notion into the harbor of Ephesos with his own ship and one other: Diod. XIII.71.1 makes explicit that Alkibiades had moved his fleet to Notion (see § 11 n. for the possibility of a lacuna in Xenophon).

Diod. XIII.71.2 has Antiochos set out with ten ships, a figure that goes back to *Hell. Oxy.* IV.1, 3. Diodoros does not explain Antiochos' intentions any better than Xenophon does, but it appears from the Oxyrhynchos historian that Antiochos meant to set an ambush with ten ships for a part of Lysandros' fleet. He himself sailed ahead with an unknown number of ships (possibly two as in Xenophon), ordering the rest of the ten to wait until they drew the enemy ships far from land (that is, lured them from the Bay of Ephesos). Diodoros evidently misunderstood his source here; he has Antiochos order the fleet at Notion to remain ready in case a naval battle became necessary.

Xenophon's failure to explain Antiochos' thinking shows nothing about his sources, for he is interested only in Antiochos' disobedience and its result.

sailed past the very prows of Lysandros' ships: Thus exposing his ships to enemy rams. Plut. *Alk.* 35.6-7 has an embellished version of Xenophon's story in which Antiochos made rude gestures and shouted insults; Diod. XIII.72.2 has Antiochos (with ten ships) challenge Lysandros to battle. Xenophon describes Antiochos' actions in terms that would suit either an insult or a lure (but not the observation mission that Delebecque [78] suggests was Antiochos' aim).

13. Lysandros launched a few ships and pursued him: Xenophon describes Lysandros simply as responding to Antiochos. Paus. IX.32.6 says that Lysandros waited until Alkibiades was away and then enticed (ἐπηγάγετο)

Antiochos into thinking he could fight a naval battle with the Lakedaimonians. A. Andrewes, "Notion and Kyzikos," *Journal of Hellenic Studies* 102 (1982) 16-18, points out that an ambush of only ten ships requires a still smaller victim, and found hints in poorly preserved parts of the *Hell. Oxy.* that suggest Lysandros had been in the habit of sending out three triremes for an unknown purpose. He guessed that these three ships were part of Lysandros' plan. Lysandros' three ships could not have routed Antiochos' ten, so he must have had others ready for action (Bommelaer [94] speculates in addition that Pausanias' source was Ktesias and entertains the possibility that Lysandros used fake deserters to transmit false information).

Xenophon may have omitted the enticement, if there was one, because of disinterest rather than ignorance. We cannot safely conclude, as Andrewes (18) does, that Xenophon's source was a Spartan unaware of Lysandros' plans.

Hell. Oxy. IV.2 agrees with Xenophon against Diodoros that Lysandros committed only a few ships during a stage of the battle.

the Athenians came to Antiochos' aid: According to Diod. XIII.71.3 and *Hell. Oxy.* IV.2, Antiochos' own ship was wrecked.

Lysandros arranged all his ships in formation and attacked: Whether or not Lysandros had planned the battle in any way, he gains credit for managing to get his ships into formation, unlike the Athenians. Xenophon repeatedly spotlights the importance of fighting in order, both on land and on sea.

as each got clear of the land: On this verb see 1.2 n.

14. the Peloponnesians in formation, the Athenians with their ships scattered: *Hell. Oxy.* IV.3 and Diod. XIII.71.4 agree that the Athenians lost due to disorderliness.

fifteen triremes: Diodoros XIII.71.4 says twenty-two, following *Hell. Oxy.* IV.3. Plut. *Lys.* 5.2 follows Xenophon. H. R. Breitenbach, "Die Seeschlacht bei Notion (407/06)," *Historia* 20 (1971) 168-71, argues that Xenophon's lower figure indicates that he followed an official Athenian source dependant on Alkibiades' report while the *Hell. Oxy.* has the Spartan version, which exaggerated Athenian losses. But the Oxyrhynchos historian could just as well be following an Athenian hostile to Alkibiades and Xenophon an honest Spartan. I see no way to determine the correct figure.

Most of the men escaped, but some were captured: The extant *Hell. Oxy.* fragments lack this detail, and it is unlikely to have been included in a parenthetical remark following the preserved text, but it appears in Diod. XIII.71.4. Ephoros may have taken it from Xenophon.

to Samos: Diod. XIII.71.4 has the Athenians return to Notion, where Alkibiades rejoined the fleet and transferred it to Samos after Lysandros refused battle. *Hell.*

Oxy. IV.4 specifies that the Athenians remained at Notion for three days. It seems more probable that they would have waited for Alkibiades and his ships before venturing to cross back to Samos.

15. He drew them up in formation in front of the harbor mouth: That is, he did not enter the bay as Antiochos had (§ 12).

because he was outnumbered by many ships: On Xenophon's figures, the Athenians have lost fifteen of their one hundred (4.21) ships; they have presumably been joined by Thrasyboulos' thirty (4.9, § 11), for a total of 115. Lysandros had ninety before the battle of Notion (§ 10), in which no Peloponnesian losses are mentioned. Therefore by Xenophon's count the Athenians now outnumber the Peloponnesians 115 to ninety. In Diodoros the Athenians have lost twenty-two (XIII.71.4) out of their one hundred (XIII.69.4); Thrasyboulos has only fifteen (XIII.72.1), though these are not said to have joined Alkibiades. Diodoros mentions no figure higher than "nearly seventy" for Lysandros' fleet (XIII.70.2). By his count, then, the Athenians outnumbered the Peloponnesians probably ninety-three to "nearly seventy." Thus Xenophon and Diodoros agree that the Athenians had about twenty-five more ships than the Peloponnesians. (These calculations do not take into account the possibilities that unmentioned reinforcements arrived from Ionian allies or that Alkibiades left twenty triremes behind at Andros. For the latter possibility see § 18 n.)

Delphinion and Eion: In 412 the Athenians fortified Delphinion, a strong position with harbors fifteen km. north of Chios town (Thuc. VIII.38.2). Eion, Amphipolis' port, was on the Strymon River in Thrace, so Schneider proposed an attractive emendation to "Teos" on the basis of Diod. XIII.76.3-4, which ascribes the capture of Delphinion and Teos to Kallikratidas. Since Xenophon credits these successes to the Lakedaimonians generally and says they occurred "a little later," Diodoros may be correct that they belong to Kallikratidas. They show that the Athenians are not keeping the Peloponnesians bottled up in Ephesos, but note that they do not campaign in the south past the Athenians at Samos.

16. thinking that he had lost the ships through carelessness and dissolute behavior: A sharp reversal in the public perception of Alkibiades; contrast 4.13. Xenophon's narrative, though it does not explain Alkibiades' reason for leaving the fleet, makes this accusation appear unfair. Alkibiades had given explicit instructions not to fight in his absence, and after the battle he demonstrated that he controlled the situation by challenging Lysandros.

Xenophon omits other charges known from Diod. XIII.73.3-74.1, Justin 5.5, Nepos *Alc.* 7 and Plut. *Alk.* 36.1-3: that he had plundered Kyme, an ally; that he handed over his generalship to his drinking companions so that he could sail about collecting money, drinking and enjoying the prostitutes of Abydos (!) and Ionia; that he had built a private fort in Thrace; that he favored the Lakedaimonians and befriended Pharnabazos so he could rule post-war Athens. No doubt his enemies accused him of such things--Xenophon did not intend to repeat what blackened Alkibiades' reputation--but their reliability is another matter. I take it that Alkibiades had been compelled, as he had in the past, to raise money by force. He may also have been blamed for the failed attempt to negotiate with the Persians (§§ 8-9); certainly Lysandros' success with Kyros would have reminded people that Alkibiades failed to produce the Persian aid he had promised in 411. Alkibiades was a serious source of divisiveness in Athens at a time when the Athenians needed unity.

We have only two names for Alkibiades' opponents on this occasion: Thrasyboulos the son of Thrason of Kollytos, who sailed to Athens to denounce the general (Plut. *Alk.* 36.1), and possibly Kleophon (6.35 n.), for a late source says "Kleophon indicted Alkibiades" without giving any details (Himerios 36.16 [Phot. *Bibl.* 377]). For doubts about Kleophon's involvement see Kagan 322 n. 120.

They chose ten other generals: Xenophon does not state clearly whether the previous generals were deposed or simply failed to win reelection, but Plutarch speaks of an expulsion from office (ἀπεχειροτόνησεν, *Lys.* 5.3), as does Nepos (*quibus rebus factum est ut absenti magistratum abrogarent et alium in eius locum substituerent, Alc.* 7). Lys. 21.7 (ἐπειδὴ . . . ἐκείνους . . . ὑμεῖς ἐπαύσατε τῆς ἀρχῆς) also refers to removal from office (compare 7.1). These references to an *apocheirotonia* ought to be accepted in spite of Xenophon's silence, given his attitude toward Alkibiades. On *apocheirotonia* see Aristot. *Ath. Pol.* 43.4, 61.2; Hansen 1975: 41-45. Once each prytany (that is, ten times each year) the assembly passed a vote of confidence in its magistrates. Any magistrate not receiving this vote of approval was considered deposed pending trial. As he had in 415, Alkibiades chose not to risk a trial. He was later exiled (Lys. 14.35).

The election referred to here might have been the normal one for 406/5 (see 1.2 n.); otherwise, the replacement generals were soon reelected. Thrasyboulos' and Theramenes' absence from the new board, combined with Thrasyllos' presence, has led to the belief that the election was a reaction against Alkibiades and that his friends lost their posts (Kagan 326). It is true that Thrasyboulos and Theramenes both had Alkibiadean ties (1.12 nn.). But we should not read too much into their failure to be elected. Theramenes had not been chosen the year before, at the height of enthusiasm for Alkibiades, and Thrasyboulos had now completed his work in Thrace. Alkibiades' friends were by no means shut out in this election: Diomedon, Perikles and Erasinides can be linked to the exiled general, and Leon and Thrasyllos had ties to Diomedon, and Archestratos perhaps to Perikles. The influence of Alkibiades' friends can perhaps also be seen in the fact that Alkibiades was exiled but not condemned to death (J. Hatzfeld, "Alcibiade et les élections des stratèges athéniens en 406," *Revue des études anciennes* 33 [1931] 115).

Diomedon: First attested as a general in 412/1 (Thuc. VIII.19.2, 20.2, 23.1, 24.2, 54.3, 55.1), though Thuc. VIII.73.4, διὰ τὸ τιμᾶσθαι ὑπὸ τοῦ δήμου, may suggest that he had held office earlier. He did not favor the Four Hundred (Thuc. VIII.73.4-5). At 7.16 Euryptolemos, Alkibiades' cousin, claims to be his friend.

Leon: Linked as general with Diomedon in 412/1; both opposed the oligarchy (Thuc. VIII.23.1, 24.2, 54.3, 55.1, 74.4-5). His appearance here and in 6.16 may be a mistake, for the list in Diod.XIII.74.1 lacks Leon and has instead Lysanias, probably a mistake for Lysias, whom Xenophon names in 6.30, 7.2 and Philochoros in *FGrHist* 328 F 142. Alternatively, Leon was on the trireme captured *en route* to get help for Konon at Mytilene. (6.21), and Lysias replaced Archestratos after the latter's death in Mytilene (Lys. 21.8; W. J. McCoy, "The Identity of Leon," *American Journal of Philology* 96 [1975] 193). McCoy argues that this Leon is the Leon of Salamis mentioned at II.3.39.

Perikles: An illegitimate son of the famous Perikles son of Xanthippos of Cholargeus (Plut. *Per.* 24.10, 36.5-6), he may also have served as general in the previous year (4.10 n.). He had intimate connections with his father's ward Alkibiades.

Erasinides: He proposed a decree honoring Phrynichos' assassins (*IG* 1³.102), and may therefore have been a friend of Alkibiades, Phrynichos' enemy.

Archestratos: A friend of Perikles' half-brother, according to Antisthenes at Athen. 5.220d, which may also tie him to Alkibiades. But he may be the Archestratos quoted by Plut. *Alk.* 16.8 as saying that Greece could not endure two Alkibiades. Since he died at Mytilene during this year (Lys. 21.8), he cannot be the Archestratos of II.2.15.

Protomachos: Previously unknown.

Aristogenes: Previously unknown.

17. who was unpopular even in the army: Xenophon has not explained Alkibiades' unpopularity in the fleet, but see § 16 n.

to his forts in the Cherronesos: See also II.1.25 and I.3.8 n.

18. Then: Xenophon clearly puts Konon's arrival after Alkibiades' departure. Diod. XIII.74 says that Alkibiades handed over his forces to Konon, but after his experience in 415 Alkibiades would not have naively awaited his replacement.

Konon, with the twenty ships he had, sailed from Andros: Alkibiades may have left Konon and twenty ships at Andros after the assault described in 4.22, or the Athenians may have sent Konon later, perhaps from Naupaktos, where he had been operating in 414/13 and 411 (4.10 n.). According to Diod. XIII.69.5 Alkibiades left Thrasybouios (a mistake for Thrasyllos?) in command at Andros.

Phanosthenes: He probably came to Athens after the fall of Andros in 411. Thereafter the Athenians honored him for activities connected with the importation of oars (*IG* 1³.182; on the date see B. R. MacDonald, "The Phanosthenes Decree," *Hesperia* 50 [1981] 141-46; the verb διακονεῖν may suggest that Phanosthenes held some official position, but the honors show he was not an Athenian). He has been plausibly identified with the Andrian who served as an Athenian general, according to Sokrates at Plato *Ion* 541d. But since Xenophon does not use the word "general" (*strategos*), I am not confident that Plato meant Phanosthenes had been one of the ten Athenian generals, rather than merely a commander of an Athenian force. For another view see Osborne 3.31-33.

N. D. Buchenauer, "The Athenians and the allies in the Decelean war" (diss. Brown 1980) 97-98, sees Phanosthenes' appointment as a diplomatic gesture aimed at other Andrians who might be sympathetic to Athens. Osborne, on the other hand, stresses a possible "dearth of qualified generals" in Athens.

19. Thourian: Thouriai was founded in Sicily on Perikles' initiative in 443. The Thourians had joined the Athenians during the Sicilian expedition (Thuc. VII.33.6, 35.1, 57.11) but turned against Athens after the expedition's defeat (1.2 n.).

they had pity on their commander Dorieus . . . they released him without ransom: Xenophon later praises the Phleiasians for releasing a man without ransom ("How could anyone deny that men who acted like this are noble and strong?", VII.2.16), so this detail reflects favorably on the Athenians. But it stands out as an exception during the Peloponnesian war (see 1.13, II.1.31-32 and the incidents remembered at II.2.3).

Xenophon does not explain why the Athenians pitied Dorieus, on whom see 1.2 n. Paus. VI.7.5 says they felt sorry for such a great athlete. Perhaps in addition they recognized that as an exile he had little choice but to work for a change of government and a defection from Athens, if he hoped to return home to Rhodes.

by the Athenians: The Athenians claimed jurisdiction over their empire in cases involving major penalties: See *IG* 1³.40 (= Meiggs and Lewis no. 52) lines 71-76; Ps.-Xen. *Ath. Pol.* 14, 16; Antiphon 5.47; Meiggs 224-26.

20. more than one hundred: 134 or 114, by the figures Xenophon gives: one hundred (4.21) + thirty (if Thrasyboulos at § 11 still has the thirty ships Xenophon gave him at 4.9) - fifteen (§ 14) - one (§ 17) + twenty (§ 18 n.; these may be part of the one hundred). Presumably Konon arranged for those triremes left behind to be dried and repaired. For speed, Konon put the best rowers into the seventy he used (see 6.16).

He disembarked at various places and plundered the enemy's territory: Konon made no strategic innovations, but resumed where Alkibiades left off.

21. This section is probably interpolated (1.37 n.).

6.1-15. *Kallikratidas' first acts as admiral*

Xenophon portrays Kallikratidas as an egotistical, impatient commander whose public proclamations do not match his behavior. Kallikratidas serves as a foil for Lysandros, the successful general.

6.1. in which there was an eclipse of the moon one evening: 15 April 406. For Xenophon an eclipse was an omen. Compare II.3.4, where he notes a solar eclipse before tyrannical rule in Thessaly, Sicily and Athens, and IV.3.10, where another solar eclipse precedes news about a naval defeat.

the old temple of Athena in Athens was burned: The foundations surviving east of the Erechtheion must belong to this temple, whose architectural history has been hotly debated (Wycherley 143-45 with references). This passage shows that at least part of the temple was rebuilt following the Persian destruction.

For temple burning as a portent, see 3.1 n. These omens here foreshadow difficult times for the Athenians. Presumably Xenophon has in mind the Arginousai tragedy.

Kallikratidas: A *mothax* (see 5.1 n.), according to Aelianus *VH* 12.43. Diod. XIII.76.2 describes him as young, simple in character, inexperienced in foreign ways and the most just of the Spartiates.

2-3. This brief exchange reveals much about the two Spartans. Lysandros boasts: He had won a battle but does not really control the sea, though his troops might be encouraged to think so. Xenophon believed such self-praise should be tolerated; it is harmless and the desire for praise will lead men to become good (*Ages.* 8.2). In challenging Lysandros, Kallikratidas shows neither tact nor concern for the troops, whom he is willing to put at risk. This attitude returns later (§§ 7, 10), ultimately with disastrous results at the battle of Arginousai (§ 32). Kallikratidas' challenge to move the fleet back to Miletos also hints at his inability to appreciate the Persians' importance, which becomes clearer in §§ 6-8. Thus Kallikratidas fails to show leadership qualities, and the allies' negative reaction in § 4 is predictable. Nevertheless Lysandros responds moderately and shows that he has the right perspective, placing his city above his own love of honor. (Though it appears from § 10 that he returned money to Kyros rather than hand it over to Kallikratidas.)

2.   master of the sea: θαλαττοκράτωρ is a rare word, previously applied only to cities (Hdt. V.83; Thuc. VIII.63.1).
on the left of Samos: That is, between the mainland and the island, with Samos on the right as they sailed south. Plut. *Lys.* 6.2 mistakenly has Kallikratidas challenge Lysandros to sail around Samos, keeping the island on his left as he sailed.
where the Athenian ships were: Xenophon's explanation, not part of Kallikratidas' remark.

4. Lysandros' friends: See 5.10 n.
risked a defeat: Although Lysandros' friends have no rebuttal to Kallikratidas' speech in § 5, their worries have substance, as the sequel shows.
as follows: Xenophon does not follow Thucydides' distinction between *tade* and *tauta* vs. *toiade* and *toiauta* for quotations and paraphrases (see VII.1.30 and VII.3.6 for examples of speeches to which Xenophon applies both pronouns). His practice also differs from Thucydides' regarding style: Xenophon's characters speak more diversely, each in a manner appropriate to his character. Kallikratidas' two speeches (§§ 5 and 8-10), for instance, are both brief, as befits a Spartan. For the most recent discussion of Xenophon's speeches see Gray (79-140), who concludes that Xenophon uses them primarily to bring out the speakers' moral qualities. It is unclear to what extent Xenophon attempts to reproduce what was actually said. Unlike Thucydides, Xenophon makes no claims for authenticity.

5. "I am content . . . : The frequent appearance of the first person pronoun in Kallikratidas' language characterizes him as self-centered. After his earlier exchange with Lysandros, his protest here that he does not care to compete with his predecessor does not ring true. And though he stresses that he is obeying his city's orders, he also refers frankly to his own ambition.
or to sail home and report the situation here: This threat proves effective, but for Xenophon fear and compulsion are not the best ways to secure loyalty. See his careful assessment of Klearchos' leadership, which depended on fear rather than goodwill (*Anab.* II.6.1-15). Xenophon's view that it is better to produce willing allies than to coerce cooperation also surfaces at V.2.18-19, VI.1.7; throughout the *Hieron*; *Kyr.* III.1.28; *Mem.* I.2.10-11, II.6.9.

6. he went to Kyros and asked for pay for the sailors: See § 10 and Plut. *Lys.* 6.1: Lysandros had returned what remained of his Persian money to Kyros.

two days: Not a very long wait. Kallikratidas' impatience contrasts with Lysandros' behavior in 5.6, and it again reveals his failure to put his troops' well-being above his own ego.

7. to attend the court: Literally, "to frequent the gates." Xenophon uses similar phrases elsewhere (*Kyr.* VIII.1.6, 8, 16-20, 6.10, 14) to describe the Persian custom of attendance on rulers. In expecting Kallikratidas to attend his court, Kyros was not requiring anything unusual or dishonorable in Persian eyes.

Saying that the Greeks were in a wretched situation. . . Lakedaimonians: A fine-sounding sentiment, often taken as evidence of Xenophon's anti-Persian panhellenism (as recently by G. Ronnet, "La figure de Callicratidas et la composition des Helléniques," *Revue de philologie* 55 [1981] 112). But Xenophon's characterization of Kallikratidas makes him an unlikely spokesperson for Xenophon's own views. In his monograph on Xenophon's attitude toward the Persians, Hirsch claims that "Panhellenism is not elsewhere [that is, outside the *Agesilaos*] a significant component of Xenophon's thought" (141).

If anyone seriously considered changing Spartan strategy, Xenophon does not say so. Kallikratidas' comment is made in anger, and the topic never recurs.

they flattered the barbarians for the sake of money: Compare Teleutias' words at V.1.17, "for what would be more pleasant than to flatter no one, neither Greek nor barbarian, for the sake of pay." Kallikratidas does not make Teleutias' further point, that it is best to take what you need from your enemies.

if he reached home safely: Kallikratidas' attitude makes his safe return seem doubtful.

8. he sent triremes to Lakedaimon for money: Xenophon does not say whether the request succeeded, though he refers to it again in § 9; it appears from Eteonikos' difficulties in II.1.1-5, however, that Sparta did not send money.

"I, men of Miletos: Kallikratidas' second speech resembles his first. It is short, begins with the first person pronoun and cows the audience (§ 12).

9. the enemy: That is, the Athenians (so too in § 11). Kallikratidas may talk of reconciling the Greeks after he returns home, but he has no hesitation about what his job is now.

10. after giving the remaining money back to Kyros as if it were a

surplus: We now learn that Kallikratidas' ungenerous attitude toward Lysandros cost him (and, more importantly, his men) financially. His failures to deal successfully with Lysandros and Kyros highlight his inability to handle men.
to attend his court: See § 7 n.

12. those who were accused of opposing him: Lysandros' friends; see § 4, and 5.10 n.
five drachmai: On whether *pentedrachmia* refers to a single coin or a combination of coins adding up to five Aiginetan drachmai see W. E. Thompson, "The Chian Coinage in Thucydides and Xenophon," *Numismatic Chronicle* ser. 7 vol. 11 (1971) 323-24, with references.

Since seven of the heavier Aiginetan drachmai equalled ten Attic drachmai (Tod no. 140 lines 21-23), five Aiginetan drachmai per sailor for 28,000 sailors (two hundred on each of 140 triremes) means a total contribution equivalent to 33 1/3 Attic talents.
Methymna, a hostile city: See 2.12 n. Diod. XIII.76.4 places Kallikratidas' capture of Delphinion and Teos, which Xenophon mentions at 5.15 (see n.), before his assault on Methymna.

13. those . . . favored Athens: *Attikismos* and *attikizein* appear first in Thucydides (III.64.5 [the occasion of its invention, according to M. Cogan, "Mytilene, Plataea, and Corcyra: Ideology and Policy in Thucydides, Book Three," *Phoenix* 35 (1981) 16-17], IV.133.1, VIII.38.3, 87.1), where they are not neutral words but are used only by Athens' enemies. In Xenophon, however, they merely describe: "In every city some Lakonized and others Attikized" (VI.3.14). In addition to *attikismos* and *attikizein*, Xenophon uses *argolizein* (IV.8.34, V.2.6), *boiotiazein* (V.4.34), and *lakonismos* anu *lakonizein* (IV.4.15, 8.18, 8.28, V.4.56, VI.3.14, 4.18, VII.1.44, 1.46, 4.34).
by force: Diod. XIII.76.5 says that after he failed in repeated assaults, the city was betrayed to him.

14. he said that while he was in command none of the Greeks would be enslaved, so far as it was in his power: A noble sentiment, but he sells the captured Athenians (§ 15). So much for the sincerity of his plan to reconcile Sparta and Athens.

15-23. *The Battle of Mytilene and the blockade of Konon's fleet*

15. that he would stop him from fornicating with the sea: "The most

startling image in the entire corpus of Xenophon" (Higgins 11), comparing Konon
to an adulterer. Although Xenophon does not quote directly, he uses the Doric
μοιχᾶν rather than the Attic μοιχεύειν; he uses the Attic form at *Mem.* II.1.5.

he saw him putting out to sea: Xenophon is vague about Konon's location.
When last mentioned (5.20), he was plundering unspecified enemy territory.
According to Diod. XIII.77.1-2, Konon had set out to relieve Methymna, but
stopped for the night at one of the Hekatonnesoi islands when he heard Methymna
had fallen.

he set out in pursuit, attempting to cut off the route to Samos:
Xenophon portrays Kallikratidas as the aggressor; he has nothing of Diodoros'
stratagem whereby Konon planned a controlled withdrawal in order to attack the
Peloponnesians once they dispersed in pursuit.

16. Mytilene: The Athenians had easily suppressed its brief revolt in 412 (Thuc.
VIII.22.1-23.3). It had two harbors connected by a strait: The larger north harbor
was outside the walls, the south harbor within (Tuplin 64 n. 99 lists references).

Leon: Leon may be a mistake for Lysias; see 5.16. Apparently another of the
generals, Archestratos, also accompanied Konon to Mytilene, for Lys. 21.8 says he
died there.

sailed along with . . . pursuing: That is, he entered the harbor just behind
the Athenians. Xenophon anticipates here, since the fighting described below took
place outside the harbor.

pursuing with 170 ships: The Peloponnesian total should be 140, as in § 3
and Diod. XIII.76.3; only after capturing thirty (§ 17) did Kallikratidas have 170 (§
26). Since Konon had seventy (5.20), Hatzfeld emended to "pursuing [Konon's]
seventy ships with 140 ships"; alternatively we might read "140" for "170."

17. he was prevented by the citizens . . .: The uncertain text here leaves
Xenophon's meaning in doubt. Delebecque (90) proposes adding "from sailing
through the straits" after "citizens." On this interpretation Konon intended to make
his way from the north harbor through the straits to the south harbor and on to
Samos. But the citizens of Mytilene--who had opposed Athens in the past--
somehow prevented him from getting through, at least at first, and he had to fight at
the rear of the north harbor, somewhat oddly described as "near the harbor."

Tuplin (62-64), who accepts the emendation of "citizens" to "enemies,"
maintains the straits were not navigable. He puts the entire conflict on the south,
where he says Xenophon fails to clarify the distinction between the outer harbor
beyond the walls and the smaller harbor within.

lost thirty ships; the men escaped to the land: Diod. XIII.78.2-4 confirms both the number of ships captured and the sailors' escape, but otherwise his account differs markedly from Xenophon's. In Diod. XIII.77-79.7 Konon rows unhurriedly toward Mytilene, hoping that the pursuing Peloponnesians would become dispersed. They did, and their rowers tired, so that Konon's sudden attack near Mytilene caused great confusion and his left wing routed its opposition. These Athenians pursued too far, however, and found themselves unable to return to the city and forced to land and abandon their thirty ships. The Athenians and Mytilenians (who here show no hostility toward the Athenians) prepared for a siege and attempted to block the harbor entrance, but on the next day Kallikratidas forced his way through. The Athenians then retired "to the harbor in the city" (XIII.79.5) while the Peloponnesians sailed through the barriers and anchored near the city. Diodoros' explanatory note clarifies the topography: "For the entrance over which they had fought has a good harbor, but it is outside the city. For the ancient city is a small island, and the later city is near it on the island of Lesbos; a narrow strait that strengthens the city runs between them" (XIII.79.6). Thus for Diodoros the fleets fought over the north harbor entrance and Konon retired through the straits to the south harbor.

These two accounts complement rather than contradict one another (P. Krentz, "Xenophon and Diodoros on the Battle of Mytilene (406 B.C.)," *Ancient History Bulletin* 2 [1988] 128-30 against, for example, Kagan 335, who discards Diodoros). Xenophon may depend on a Peloponnesian source that gave Konon no credit for a plan, Diodoros on an Athenian source privy to Konon's thinking. Xenophon's interest lies not in the fighting or the topography, but in Konon's clever response to his predicament after Kallikratidas trapped him.

18.   money came to him from Kyros: Plut. *Mor.* 222E says that Kyros sent both money for the troops and a present for Kallikratidas; the admiral accepted the former but declined the personal gift, saying there was no need for a private friendship between Kyros and himself. Xenophon would have admired this sentiment (see 5.6 n.), so his silence is no argument against its truthfulness since the incident would have conflicted with his characterization of Kallikratidas.

19.   to the hold of the ship: Marines normally went on the deck; here they go below to conceal their presence.
side-screens: Normally used to protect rowers from sun, spray and missiles. Fourth-century naval inventories list two kinds: *trichina*, made of hair, and *leuka*, made of linen (some lexicographers, however, define both as made of leather). The difference, if any, between *pararumata* here and *parablemata* in II.1.22 is unclear. Both are Attic terms: The former appears on *IG* 2².1605 lines 40-41 and 1629 line

451, the latter on *IG* 2².1604 line 31.

22. the ship fleeing for the Hellespont escaped: Probably under Erasinides' command, since § 16 reports him with Konon yet he appears at the battle of Arginousai (§ 29). The general Leon may have commanded the captured vessel (4.16 n.).
anchored at the straits: That is, since Konon had taken refuge under the walls in the harbor south of the straits, Diomedon anchored at the north end, since he was away from Konon and open to separate attack.

24-35. *The Battle of Arginousai*

Xenophon's battle narrative relates directly to his version of the "trial" in 7.1-35. Xenophon credits the generals with winning in a desperate situation so they appear all the more wronged when they are summarily condemned and executed for events they could not control. Diodoros' account of the "trial" is preferable to Xenophon's (7.1 n.), and his battle account deserves consideration too.

24. 110 ships: Diod. XIII.97.1 has the Athenians send sixty ships to Samos, where they joined eighty ships gathered "from the other islands," by which he may mean Athenian ships or a combination of Athenian and allied ships rather than eighty from the allies. By Xenophon's count, Konon left thirty-two to fifty-two triremes at Samos (§25 n.), so Diodoros' numbers are not impossible. Plato *Menex.* 243c also has sixty ships in the relief force from Athens. Xenophon has enhanced the picture of activity in Athens itself (see next n. for other exaggerations) but he and Diodoros agree on the new fleet's total size: "more than 150" (§ 25) and "150" (Diod. XIII.97.2).

The Athenians would have needed more than the thirty days of this passage to build even sixty new triremes. According to Meritt's tempting but speculative reconstruction and dating of *IG* 1³.117 (= Meiggs and Lewis no. 91), Alkibiades (his name wholly restored) had arranged in the summer of 407 for the construction of new triremes in Macedon. Perhaps to finance this building program, the Athenians began to melt down the golden Nikai statues and mint gold coins in 407/6 (Schol. Aristoph. *Frogs* 720 = Hellanikos, *FGrHist* 323a F 26; Philochoros, *FGrHist* 328 F 141). W. E. Thompson, "The Golden Nikai and the Coinage of Athens," *Numismatic Chronicle* ser. 7 vol. 10 (1970) 1-6, estimates that they coined gold worth 204 talents.
everyone of military age, both slave and free: Strauss' calculations suggest that in 406 Athens could have filled 110 ships with citizens, not to mention

foreigners and slaves (70-86). Xenophon exaggerates. His presentation of Athenian preparations heightens the sense of despair; thereby the generals' credit for winning the victory will grow.

Slave rowers were not unusual: See Jordan 260-64 against Amit 30-49.

Diod. XIII.97.1 says that the Athenians naturalized immigrants and other foreigners willing to fight for Athens. Justin V.6.5, presumably also following Ephoros, speaks of citizenship granted to foreigners, as well as freedom to slaves. This incident is consistent with Xenophon, though he does not mention it. On this mass enfranchisement see Osborne 3.33-37. Osborne accepts the testimony of Hellanikos (*FGrHist* 323 F 25) that the slaves who fought in the battle of Arginousai were freed and became citizens (συμπολιτεύσασθαι) like the Plataians, saying that to doubt the slaves' naturalization "flies in the teeth of the evidence" (34). Aristoph. *Frogs* 693-94 ("For it is disgraceful for men who have fought one battle by sea/ to become Plataians immediately and masters instead of slaves") supports Hellanikos. But the Ephoran tradition, as cited above, held that only the foreigners became Athenians, not the slaves. The evidence varies. Hellanikos may have depended solely on Aristophanes' rhetorical passage, in which "slaves" (*douloi*) might mean merely "subjects of the Athenian empire."

Many horsemen: Horsemen had previously boarded ships for transport to the Peloponnese, the northern Aegean, Sicily and Asia Minor, but they had not rowed. Their participation now emphasizes the situation's seriousness.

25. whatever ships they happened to have abroad: On Xenophon's figures, there should have been at least thirty-two Athenian triremes already in Ionia (114 or 134 [5.20 n.] - seventy [5.20] - twelve [§ 22]).

26. 120: Kallikratidas had captured forty ships (the initial thirty, § 17 and Diod. XIII.78.4; an additional ten from Diomedon, § 23), bringing his total--unless he had unmentioned losses--to 180. If Kallikratidas left fifty behind with Eteonikos (§ 26), he could have had--had he found crews for them all--130 at Arginousai. Diod. XIII.97.3 gives him 140.

on Lesbos at Cape Malea, [opposite Mytilene]: The text seems corrupt (see also § 27, "opposite Lesbos at Cape Malea opposite Mytilene"), but the remedy is uncertain. Possibilities include (1) deleting "opposite Mytilene" here and "opposite Lesbos at Cape Malea" below, since the Cape Malea described by Strabo XIII.616-17 as the southernmost (more accurately, the southeasternmost) point of the island is not opposite the city; (2) keeping the text here and deleting "at Cape Malea opposite Mytilene" below, on the grounds that Thuc. III.4.5 places Malea north of Mytilene. Gomme (*HCT* 2.258) and Delebecque (94) favor the second possibility, the latter suggesting confusion between Malea and a sanctuary of Apollo Maloeis north of Mytilene and--since the city was on a small island off Lesbos-- "opposite" it. He also notes, however, an important objection to this solution: Kallikratidas could see the Athenian fires at night (§ 28). The well-known Cape Malea was 14.7 km. from Arginousai, or a little more than one hour's rowing.

27. [opposite Lesbos at Cape Malea] opposite Mytilene: See previous n.
the Arginousai: Three small islands near the mainland, 120 *stadia* (21.3 km.) from Mytilene (Str. XIII.2.2 617). The two larger islands lie behind one another, with the third very small island on the north side of the westernmost of these two. Diod. 13.97.3 says they contained a small Aiolic settlement at this time.

28. he attempted . . . to attack unexpectedly: Diod.XIII.97.4 says that the Athenians decided not to fight because of strong winds, but has nothing about this attempted surprise attack by Kallikratidas. It contrasts Kallikratidas with Alkibiades, who used a storm successfully at Kyzikos (1.16).

29-31. § 31 explains the unusual formation described in §§ 29-30. This detailed description is unparalleled in Xenophon's other naval battles. It emphasizes the equal parts played by the generals in an unusual formation that overcame the opposing triremes' speed.
    Diod. XIII.97.6 has Thrasyllos in chief command for the day, which would be at least arguably consistent with the usual Athenian practice (Jordan 117-30).

29.   put out to the open sea with their left: In Diod. XIII.98.3, by contrast, the Athenians stay close enough to shore to put the Arginousai islands in the middle of their line. See n. below.
formed in a single line . . . also in a single line: See § 31 n. for ἐπὶ μιᾶς.
the ten of the division commanders: The *taxiarchoi*, officers responsible for enlisting and commanding hoplites in the ten Athenian *phylai* (tribes) or *taxeis*, also served occasionally in the fleet. Jordan (130-34) plausibly explains their naval activity as required in emergencies when hoplites organized by *taxeis* rowed the ships. Their position in the command structure at Arginousai, where more high-ranking officers than usual were present, is unclear.
behind these: When describing military formations Xenophon uses ἐπί + dative to mean "behind" (II.4.12; *Anab* VI.5.11; *Kyr*.II.2.6, VI.3.24-25, 28-30, VIII.3.13-18). Some scholars, including Kagan (345-46 n. 69), ignore Xenophon's usage and

translate ἐπί as "in addition to" on the grounds that a double line in the center would contradict Xenophon's earlier description of the Samian ten and the taxiarchs' ten as "in a single line." This earlier description may be explained in another way, however. Xenophon gives particular prominence to the Samians, whose commander is the only allied commander named. He wants to make clear that the Samian contingent fought entirely in the front line, in contrast to the Athenians whom he has just described on the left. Xenophon thus describes a double line throughout the Athenian formation. If each Athenian general commanded a contingent of fifteen, the ships in the second center line must have numbered at least ten in order to reach Xenophon's total of more than 150.

"These" refers to the taxiarchs' ten ships and probably also the Samian ten.

admirals: Athenian admirals (*nauarchoi*) also appear at V.1.5-9 and Dem. 18.73. Clearly distinct from generals in Xenophon, they are apparently subordinate officers, perhaps identical with the "commanders of the navy" (ἄρχοντες τοῦ ναυτικοῦ; Jordan 119-30).

31. They were arranged in this way: While Xenophon's story forms an exciting and dramatic prelude to the generals' execution, it lacks clarity as military history. The Athenians' formation protected them from the *diekplous*, but left them vulnerable to the *periplous*--unless we assume that the Athenians spaced their ships more widely than usual or that the overlapping Peloponnesians delivered their attack "in the air" while awaiting orders. Neither solution is in the text. Nor does Xenophon explain how the Athenian center survived intact.

According to Diod.XIII.98.3, Thrasyllos and Perikles led the right wing, where Theramenes was also given a command, though he was not a general. The rest of the generals took positions along the whole line, and they enclosed the Arginousai islands with their formation in order to stretch their line as far as possible. (The Athenians' numerical advantage in Diodoros is only ten ships.)

Some scholars (including Kagan 338-53) try to reconcile the two accounts by imagining double Athenian lines to the north and south of west Arginousai island, with a single line in the center directly west of the island. This attempted reconciliation, however, is true to neither source. Xenophon does not describe a single line in the center, and Diodoros' statement that the Athenians wanted to stretch their line out as far as possible implies that they did not station any ships in front of the islands. We must choose between Xenophon and Diodoros on this crucial point.

Tuplin (58-59) complains that Diodoros explains the Athenian disposition poorly, and that it merely produced "two battles in which the Athenians had no more advantage than they would have done in one." Diodoros might indeed have supplied a lengthier explanation--and of course his source may have done so--but the advantage seems clear: The Athenians forced the Peloponnesians to open four flanks to attack when Kallikratidas split his fleet to fight on either side of the islands. The Athenians still had only two. Their center ships, protected by the islands, could choose the best moment to attack the "interior flanks" of the Peloponnesians (that is, the south wing of the fleet's northern division and the southern division's north wing). Thus Diodoros explains, as Xenophon does not, why the Athenian center survived intact, if that detail be accepted from Xenophon. This version probably goes back to the *Hell. Oxy.* and may be correct, in spite of Diodoros' compression and inconsistency on Perikles' position (compare XIII.98.3 and XIII.99.4). In Xenophon, on the other hand, the generals gain stature by devising a clever defense to overcome their ships' poor quality.

breaking through their line: A ship executing the *diekplous* (literally "sailing through") penetrated the enemy line and turned to ram an enemy ship before it could finish turning to protect itself. Against J. S. Morrison's view that squadrons, rather than individual ships, broke through gaps in the enemy line ("Greek naval tactics in the 5th century BC," *International Journal of Nautical Archaeology* 3 [1974] 23-25), see J. F. Lazenby, "The Diekplous," *Greece & Rome* 34 (1987) 169-77.

for the Athenian ships were slower. . . the Lakedaimonian ships were quicker: This claim is surprising, since the ships left by Konon at Samos should by now have been dried out and repaired, and the new ships should have been fast, while Kallikratidas had had his ships in the water blockading Mytilene (for the effects of roughness and heaviness on speed, see 5.10 n.). Untrained crews might provide a sufficient explanation. Xenophon represents Konon as selecting the best rowers for his seventy ships (6.16), and these men are not present at Arginousai. But the previous actions of the Ionian war show that the Sicilian expedition had not destroyed the superiority of Athens' sailors. At Kynossema the Athenians soundly defeated a larger Peloponnesian force, and Diodoros comments on their greater experience (XIII.39.3) and their pilots' greater skill (XIII.39.5-40.2). Their victorious tactics at Kyzikos required considerable skill again. Neither Lysandros' victory at Notion nor Kallikratidas' at Mytilene, both won against smaller numbers, proved that the Peloponnesians had training to match Athenian rowers. Xenophon may have exaggerated the Peloponnesian triremes' quality in order to make the Athenian victory reflect more favorably on the generals.

in a single line: Or "all in line abreast."

sailing round: For the *periplous*, a flank attack, see Thuc. VII.36.3-4; Plb. I.23.9, 27.11, XVI.4.14. I find unconvincing I. Whitehead's interpretation of the *periplous* as a single-ship manoeuvre equivalent to an *anastrophe*, or "turning back" ("The Periplous," *Greece & Rome* 34 [1987] 178-85). The *anastrophe* normally followed a *diekplous*.

32. Hermon: A Megarian immigrant, who later fought with Lysandros at Aigospotamoi (Demos. 23.212, Paus. X.9.7). Pausanias claims he became a Megarian citizen, but Demosthenes, the earlier source, says the Megarians refused to enfranchise him. He may have been one of Xenophon's sources (see *Oik.* 4.20 for a story reported by an anonymous Megarian who claims to have heard it from Lysandros).

since the Athenian triremes were much more numerous: Earlier Xenophon says Lysandros refused to fight Alkibiades for precisely this reason (5.15), so we have here another contrast between Kallikratidas and Lysandros.

would fare just the same: Because οὐ μή takes the future indicative or the subjunctive, οἰκεῖται must be a contracted future (see Classen-Steup at Thuc. III.58.5) or we must emend.

As noted at § 5, Xenophon's Kallikratidas is an egotistical man; he thinks here of his own reputation rather than the safety of his men and his fleet. Sparta will not, of course, fare just the same after the battle; the Spartans will stretch their law in order to have Lysandros in command once again (II.1.7). Kallikratidas comes off rather better in Diodoros: XIII.97.5 has the Lakedaimonian seer predict that the admiral would die fighting, to which Kallikratidas responds that by dying during the battle he would not harm Sparta's reputation. Diodoros also gives him a short speech to his men, in which he announces the seer's prediction and appoints Klearchos as his successor (XIII.98.1).

33. Kallikratidas fell overboard . . . and disappeared into the sea: According to Diod. XIII.99.5 he died "fighting brilliantly" after being wounded from all sides. On this point Xenophon and Diodoros are not irreconcilable, for Kallikratidas might have fought brilliantly prior to his fall into the sea. Xenophon lets Kallikratidas' disappearance suffice as a comment; he does not give the Spartan an honorable death.

Protomachos and those with him on the right defeated the left: In Diod. XIII.100.6 the Boiotians on the Peloponnesian left wing hold out for some time after the Peloponnesians fled. Busolt (3.2.722 n. 2) argues that Diodoros could not be correct because the Boiotians would have been cut off from Chios. They could have reached Chios by first going further out to sea, however, and if they found themselves outflanked by the Athenians they may have had no choice. Kagan (352 n. 85) defends Xenophon on the weak grounds that if the Lakonians had fled first they would not have lost nine of their ten ships, an argument that depends on the assumption that the Athenians would not have chased the Lakonians while the rest of the battle continued. Xenophon's prejudice against the Thebans might explain his version.

the Peloponnesians fled to Chios, and most of them to Phokaia: Madvig's tempting addition of τινῶν would give "most of the Peloponnesians fled to Chios, and some to Phokaia." Diod. XIII.99.6 says that the Peloponnesians fled to Chios and Kyme, and XIII.100.4 that corpses and debris filled the shore at Kyme and Phokaia. Given Ephoros' predilection for mentioning his hometown even when it did not merit the notice (*FGrHist* 70 F 236), Xenophon is probably right about the flight to Phokaia.

sailed back again to the Arginousai: 7.29 also says the Athenians returned to land before deciding what to do next, which means time elapsed. This delay might have been held against the generals (P. Cloché, "L'Affaire des Arginuses," *Revue historique* 130 [1919] 28); Xenophon might have passed over it out of a desire to present the generals as innocent. Diod. XIII.100.1-3 has the generals confer before returning to land, but it is hard to see how such a conference could have been held. Diodoros probably misunderstood his source.

34. twenty-five ships: So too Diod. XIII.100.3, but in 7.30 Xenophon mentions only twelve. See n.

with their men, except for a few who were carried to land: Twenty-five triremes carried about five thousand men.

the Peloponnesians lost nine . . . and more than sixty allied ships: That is, more than sixty-nine ships; 7.25 says seventy, Diod.XIII.100.3 says seventy-seven.

35. the disabled ships and the men on them: Living men. Diodoros' story differs: In XIII.100.1 (and note 101.2, 6), after pursuing the defeated enemy "adequately (ἐφ' ἱκανόν), the generals discuss picking up the dead (τοὺς τετελευτηκότας) since the Athenians strongly disapproved of allowing dead persons to go unburied. Though corpses do not float on the day of death (Pritchett 4.204-206), the Athenians could have retrieved those caught in the wreckage, and could have recovered additional bodies the next day. Thucydides speaks of corpses recovered after Sybota in 433 (I.50.3, 54.1), Naupaktos in 429 (II.92.4), and Syracuse in 413 (VII.72.1). Sybota provides a particularly striking parallel to Arginousai: The Kerkyrians took up their dead the day after the battle, after the waves had scattered the corpses. Generals had a sacred obligation to bury their dead after naval as well as after land battles.

Xenophon's silence about the corpses suits his overall attempt to show the generals as innocent victims. Xenophon refers to men on the sunken ships (6.35) and to shipwrecked men (7.5, 29), and drives home his point that they were alive by having an anonymous witness claim he talked with men in the water (7.11) and later by having Theramenes say a rescue was possible (II.3.35). So his story defends the generals against the possible charge that they should have tried to save their sailors sooner.

But the wind and a great storm came and prevented them . . . : Here, in his own person, Xenophon states unambiguously that the storm prevented the rescue.

36-38. *Eteonikos' withdrawal from Mytilene. Unification of the Athenian fleet*

Xenophon approved ruses such as the one described here: Compare his account of how Agesilaos altered the negative report of the battle of Knidos (IV.3.13), and note *Mem.* IV.2.17. He recounts another clever device of Eteonikos in II.1.1-5. Both these stories, insignificant for the history of the war, illustrate Xenophon's interest in teaching good leadership.

36.   dispatch-boat: The comic poet Ephippos describes a *keles* as "five thole-pinned," that is with five oars on each side (18a, 19: 17-18 Edmonds [= 5K]). Thucydides mentions this small boat as used by Messenian pirates (IV.9.1).

38. to Methymna: See § 13 for its capture by Kallikratidas. According to Diod. XIII.100.5 (if we accept Palmer's emendation of Τυρραίων to Πυρραίων), Eteonikos withdrew his land troops to Pyrrha. Diodoros is probably correct, since Pyrrha is closer than Methymna both to Mytilene and to Chios, where Eteonikos ultimately rejoined the Peloponnesian fleet (II.1.1).

the wind was calmer: Though it had earlier been favorable for sailing southwest to Chios (§ 37), Konon had to wait before sailing east toward the Arginousai islands.

Samos: From this base, according to Diod. XIII.100.6, they ravaged enemy territory.

7.1-35. *The Arginousai "Trial"*

Xenophon dwells at length on the Arginousai affair, a paradigm for the reversals suffered by individuals and cities that act unjustly. He emphasizes that the Athenians acted contrary to *nomos* (custom or law, §§ 5, 12): Euryptolemos and his supporters are compelled (ἠναγκάσθησαν, § 13) to drop their objections and the presiding committee members are frightened (φοβηθέντες, § 15) into agreeing to the vote. Xenophon thus makes clear that the majority compelled but did not persuade the minority to do as it wished, thereby acting illegally in the sense discussed in *Mem.* I.2.40-46. There Alkibiades leads Perikles to admit that whatever "the stronger" compel "the weaker" to do without persuading them is not *nomos*, whether "the stronger" is a tyrant, a ruling group of oligarchs or the majority in a democracy. When the Athenians suffer catastrophic defeat at Aigospotamoi, they are only the first of many in the *Hellenika* who try but fail to rule by force: the Thirty, Sparta, Jason, Euphron and finally Thebes. Athens' fate provided a lesson left unlearned.

7.1. The Athenians at home deposed these generals except Konon: That is, the assembly deposed the generals by *apocheirotonia* pending trial (see 5.16 n.). As Andrewes points out, "the charge is not stated till 1.7.4, in the assembly. This is quite an extraordinary order of presentation . . . The effect of the abrupt transition is to reinforce the general impression which Xenophon gives, of an unprovoked attack on innocent men" ("The Arginousai Trial," *Phoenix* 28 [1974] 112-13). Andrewes convincingly defends Diodoros' version against Xenophon's (see especially §§ 4, 8 nn.): Xenophon portrays the generals as innocent by maligning their antagonist Theramenes and by concealing the fact that they accused Theramenes first. For another view see M. Sordi, "Teramene e il processo delle Arginuse," *Aevum* 55 (1981) 3-12.

Personal ties may have influenced Xenophon. As G. Nemeth argues, many of the defendants as well as their advocates had connections with Alkibiades ("Der Arginusen-Prozess: Die Geschichte eines politischen Justizmordes," *Klio* 66 [1984] 51-57). But Xenophon's presentation is not only a matter of excusing his friends.
In addition to him they elected: An emergency decision. These three generals presumably had to be elected again at the spring 405 elections.
Philokles: Previously unknown. Since Lysandros later executed him for proposing to chop off the right hands of prisoners (II.1.32-33) and since he rejected Alkibiades' advice at Aigospotamoi (Nep. *Alc.* 8.4), he may have shared Kleophon's anti-Alkibiades and unyieldingly polemical policy. Plutarch calls him a demagogue (*Comp. Lys. and Sulla* 4.8).
Protomachos and Aristogenes did not return to Athens: Diod. XIII.101.5 says they feared the people's anger.

2. When six. . . did sail back: § 30 mentions eight generals at the battle, and § 34 says the eight generals who fought in the battle were condemned, and the six present in Athens were executed. Diod. XIII.101.5-102.1 names eight, but in the

Mem. Xenophon says nine (I.1.18, IV.4.2), and Plato *Apol.* 32b, Ps.-Plato *Axioch.* 368d, and Aristotle *Ath. Pol.* 34.1 have ten. The last group of writers must have been thinking of the standard board of ten generals; when writing the *Memorabilia* Xenophon presumably subtracted Konon but forgot about Archestratos.

Erasinides: Diodoros, who frequently gets names wrong, presumably errs when he names Kalliades instead (XIII.101.5).

Archedemos: "Very capable in speech and action, but poor," according to *Mem.* II.9.4-7. For less favorable comments see Aristoph. *Frogs* 421, 588; Eupolis F 9, 71; Lys. 14.25. Aischin. 3.139 and Plut. *Mor.* 575D say he was pro-Theban. Though his greatest political influence seems to date to the last years of the Peloponnesian war, the Eupolis references suggest some prominence about a decade earlier.

the two-obol fund: The treasurers of Athena paid considerable sums to the *hellenotamiai* "for the two-obol fund" between 410/9 (*IG* 1³.375) and 407/6 (? *IG* 1³.377), including perhaps more than 34 talents in 410/9 (Meiggs and Lewis 259). Kleophon introduced the two-obol fund (Aristot. *Ath. Pol.* 28.3), which has been identified with (1) the theoric fund that enabled citizens to attend dramatic presentations; (2) jury pay; and, most probably, (3) a special relief measure to help the poor survive after the Spartans occupied Dekeleia. For discussions of all these views, see Buchanan 35-48 and W. K. Pritchett, "Loans of Athena in 407 B.C.," *Ancient Society* 8 (1977) 41-45.

charging that he had public money from the Hellespont: Probably an indictment for embezzling sacred funds (Hansen 1975: 85 n. 5). The indictment may have been brought at Erasinides' *euthyna* or official audit. Against P. Cloché's suggestion that the attack on Erasinides was a democratic ploy to spare the other generals ("L'Affaire des Arginuses," *Revue historique* 130 [1919] 41), see Kagan 365-66.

3. Timokrates: Otherwise unknown.

handed over to the people: Timokrates called not for a trial, but for the assembly to determine subsequent procedures. The assembly adjourned before deciding and asked the Council to make a specific recommendation (§ 7).

4. Theramenes: See 1.12, 22.

to undergo the official audit: That is, a *euthyna* before the *thesmothetai* and a jury court. For the interchangeability of *logos* and *euthyna* see Hignett 203.

that they blamed no one else: This phrase, and the letter which Theramenes then introduces as evidence, make sense only as a defense, not an initial prosecution. Diodoros has exactly that: In XIII.100.2 the generals, mistakenly assuming that

Theramenes and Thrasyboulos had accused them, send letters saying they had ordered Theramenes and Thrasyboulos to pick up the corpses. This accusation, Diodoros continues, caused their troubles, since it turned potential supporters into bitter opponents. In II.3.35 Xenophon has Theramenes claim he did not start the accusations, but defended himself when the generals accused him.

a letter: See § 17, where Euryptolemos describes the circumstances for the writing of what must be this letter.

5. for in conformity with the law no opportunity was given them to make a speech: I follow Ostwald's (438) interpretation, implying that a full defense could not be given at an ordinary assembly, rather than the alternative "for the customary time allotment was not given them." See § 3 n.

6. their arguments were persuading the people: That many persons were willing to be sureties supports this assertion to some extent (see next n.). But that the assembly agreed to reconvene and that the Council was to propose how the men should be tried does not suggest the generals were beginning to persuade the people as a whole of their innocence.

7. sureties: Sureties guaranteed the payment of any fine, thus keeping defendants out of prison. Obviously these sureties were not anticipating the death penalty, but it is significant that Xenophon does not say the assembly accepted their offers.

they could not have counted the hands: a clear indication that the assembly voted by a show of hands. For a humorous confirmation of this procedure see Aristoph. *Ekkl.* 263-65, where women who plan to infiltrate the assembly worry that they will forget how to vote properly by raising their hands, since they are accustomed to raising their legs.

8. the Apatouria festival: This Ionian festival of the *phratriai* lasted for at least three days during the month of Pyanepsion (October/November). The *phratriai* were hereditary groups, each with a traditional home at which the men gathered. At the festival male babies were registered, young adult males became official members and wives were introduced.

Also relevant is the story told about the festival's origin, the deception (*apate*) of Melanthos in his single combat against Xanthos. Melanthos saw a figure (later said to be the god Dionysos) behind his opponent. When he objected that it was unfair to fight two against one, Xanthos turned to see who was there--and Melanthos killed him. Xenophon may be playing on this connection to deception as he suggests Theramenes' ploy.

Theramenes' faction: Literally, "those around Theramenes," the commonest Greek phrase for a political group.

pretending to be relatives of those who had died: While Xenophon has Theramenes' faction arrange for spurious mourners, Diod. XIII.101.6 has legitimate mourners appear spontaneously. Other evidence does not lend credibility to Xenophon's version: On Xenophon's own testimony neither the people (§ 35) nor Kritias (II.3.32) held this ploy against Theramenes, and Lysias says nothing about it in a slanderous passage about Theramenes (12.62-78). Since in addition false mourners might have been exposed by real ones, Cloché suggests that Theramenes organized sincere mourners ("L'Affaire des Arginuses," *Revue historique* 130 [1919] 47 n. 2). But it might not have been in Theramenes' interest to arouse volatile emotions further.

Kallixenos: Bicknell (99 n. 33) identifies him as a "satellite of Kleophon" on the grounds that his arrest (§ 35) was "one of the moves against his leader" and that he fled as soon as Kleophon died (§ 35). This view may be correct, but Xenophon implies that the Athenians detained Kallixenos for deceiving the people in the Arginousai affair (where Kleophon is not mentioned) and that he fled not because Kleophon died but because a civil disorder provided a chance to escape. He may have been an Alkmeonid, as was at least one (and perhaps both) of the other fifth-century bearers of his name (Bicknell,"Diomedon Cholargeus?" *Athenaeum* 53 [1975] 175-76). If so, he was related to Euryptolemos (3.12 n.)

Schol. Aristoph. *Frogs* 190, 359 and 538-39, derived from Johannes Tzetzes, blame equally Kallixenos and a Diomedon of Cholargos, otherwise unknown but perhaps related to the general Diomedon, the only other fifth-century Athenian known with that name. Both identifications require relatives acting against one another.

persuaded: Cloché doubts this charge and suggests an oligarchic plot instead ("L'Affaire des Arginuses," *Revue historique* 130 [1919] 49-51). But after his escape Kallixenos returned to Athens with the democrats in 403, not with the oligarchs in 404.

9. that two jars . . . the second jar: In the normal method of voting in the fifth century, each voter placed a pebble in the jar of his choice. This procedure attempted to maintain secrecy, perhaps by having a wicker funnel over the two jars in which the voter could conceal his hand (A. L. Boegehold, "Toward a Study of Athenian Voting Procedure," *Hesperia* 32 [1963] 367-68).

10. the Eleven: The board of jailers and executioners, chosen by lot. Aristot. *Ath. Pol.* 52.1 describes their duties. As Rhodes (580) points out, they presumably

ante-date Kleisthenes' creation of ten tribes, and Aristotle mentions them in connection with Solon in 7.3.
the goddess: Athena.

11. a man came forward: By leaving this speaker anonymous Xenophon shows he disapproves of the man's behavior, just as Herodotos refused to give the name (though he knew it) of the Delphian who inscribed a false dedication (I.51).

12. Saying that Kallixenos had made an illegal proposal: On the *graphe paranomon*, see Hansen (1974). Kallixenos' motion violated the principle that a fair trial should precede a verdict, rather than a particular law (Ostwald 439).
Euryptolemos the son of Peisianax: See 3.12 n., 4.19. According to Ps.-Plato *Axiochos* 368e-369a, an uncle and friend of Alkibiades named Axiochos also defended the generals. What we know about the generals and their defenders suggests that in so far as the trial was politically motivated it was an attack on Alkibiades' friends, rather than a political ploy by partisans of Alkibiades to gain his recall, as maintained by (for example) Roberts (66). Ostwald (435 n. 98) and Kagan (365-67) decline to view the trial in "political" terms.
it would be a terrible thing if someone did not allow the people to do what it   wished: "For the first time in Athenian history the principle of popular sovereignty was asserted to its logical conclusion" (Ostwald 444).

13. Lykiskos: Otherwise unknown.
the mob: ὄχλος is more pejorative than "the majority" (πλῆθος, § 12). The assembly has degenerated.
members of the presiding committee: The *prytaneis*. Since at least the time of Ephialtes the Council of Five Hundred had a standing committee composed of the fifty members from a single tribe serving for one-tenth of the year. The *prytaneis* fixed the agenda for the Council and presided over Council and assembly meetings. From the *prytaneis* a single *epistates* was chosen by lot each day to head the committee.

15. except Sokrates the son of Sophroniskos: The famous philosopher. Henry (194-97) argues persuasively that Xenophon intended the Arginousai affair to reflect well on his teacher Sokrates. After threats cowed Euryptolemos and the other *prytaneis*, Sokrates alone refused to give in. His refusal gave Euryptolemos a chance to propose an alternative trial procedure. The fact that Sokrates ultimately failed to stop the generals' execution does not diminish his courageous stance. We cannot now tell whether Sokrates acted solely out of moral conviction or whether personal

ties to the defendants, who like Sokrates had connections with Alkibiades (5.16, §
12 nn.), also played a significant part.

At *Mem.* I.1.18 and IV.4.2 Xenophon represents Sokrates not only as a
prytanis but also the *epistates* at this meeting. In references to Sokrates as a
prytanis at the trial, neither Plato *Apol.* 32b nor *Gorg.* 473e-474a mentions that he
was *epistates*, though the latter may imply it by saying that Sokrates did not "put
the matter to the vote." The *epistates* could, however, be called simply *prytanis*, as
for example in Thuc. VI.14. Xenophon's testimony in the *Memorabilia* should be
accepted--with the caution that in *Mem.* I.1.18 he has the number of convicted
generals wrong (see § 2 n.).

According to Ps.-Plato *Axiochos* 368d-e, an adjournment followed and only
"on the next day" were the generals condemned. This passage errs in referring to
proedroi, the nine officials who replaced the *prytaneis* as presiding officers of the
assembly in the fourth century, and to ten generals on trial. We can have little
confidence in this source. But Xenophon might have omitted a postponement, if
one did occur, in order to heighten the impression of an impassioned mob hurrying
to a decision. It may be that because Sokrates refused to put the Council's motion
to the vote, the meeting was adjourned until the next day, when a new *epistates* was
in charge (Cawkwell 88-89).

16-33. *Euryptolemos' Speech*

This set speech, the first lengthy one in the *Hellenika*, dominates the trial
scene and emphasizes its function in the *Hellenika* as a whole. It falls into five
parts:

1. Introduction (§ 16). Euryptolemos says he will accuse, defend and advise.

2. Accusation (§§ 17-18). Perikles and Diomedon erred when they persuaded
   the generals not to report immediately that they had entrusted the rescue to
   Theramenes and Thrasyboulos.

3. Advice (§§ 19-29). The Athenians should give each individual at least a
   one-day trial, using either the decree of Kannonos or the law against temple-
   robbers and traitors, and dividing the day into three parts including one-third
   for prosecution and one-third for defense.

4. Defense (§§ 29-32). The generals divided their forces, leaving sufficient
   ships for the rescue. Each group should be held responsible only for the

job assigned to it. The storm, however, prevented both the rescue and the pursuit.

5. Conclusion (§ 33). The Athenians should not behave like losers or forget that some matters are under divine control. It would be fairer to reward than to execute the victorious generals.

Xenophon presents Euryptolemos as a clever but not altogether honest speaker (§§ 16, 30, 32 nn.). Euryptolemos flatters the assembly (§§ 19, 24, 26, 29). He refers repeatedly to justice (§§ 19, 23, 24, 31, 33), piety and the gods (§§ 19, 24, 33), *nomos* (custom or law, §§ 22, 23, 25, 26, 29), and victory (§§ 25, 33). The speech contributes powerfully to Xenophon's impression of injustice hurriedly done. But it avoids the essence of the charge against the generals (that they delayed too long before beginning the rescue operation and that made no effort to recover bodies the next day; see 6.35 n.), and it gives a one-sided view of the legal issues (§ 12 n.).

16. as follows: On *tade* see 6.5 n.
partly to accuse . . . partly to defend . . . partly to recommend: A beginning designed to gain a hostile audience's attention. Euryptolemos does not follow the order proposed here.
my relative: An appeal for sympathy from angry listeners whose relatives died in the battle. In § 21 Euryptolemos claims that he does not value his relative more than the whole city; he implies that others should not overvalue theirs.

17. a letter: See § 4. Thereafter, the generals sent a second letter accusing Theramenes and Thrasyboulos, according to Diod. XIII.101.2. Xenophon's silence about this second letter helps protect the generals.
forty-seven triremes: Euryptolemos repeats this figure, with further details, in § 30. Xenophon himself, however, mentions only forty-six (6.35). Euryptolemos increases the number of rescue ships by one. This minor exaggeration favors the generals.

18. Are they now to share the blame . . . few others?: Euryptolemos uses a rhetorical question to turn from his promised "accusation" to his recommended "just and right" course of action. The question introduces the idea of differences among the generals and even suggests that they have "kindness" (*philanthropia*). Gray (83-91) seizes upon this reference to *philanthropia*, simple human sympathy, as the key to Euryptolemos' entire speech, which she sees as a monument to his personal *philanthropia*. But Xenophon does not portray Euryptolemos entirely positively. I take the speech as designed to drive home injustice as the central point of the Arginousai affair, and secondly to show that even a just man had to twist the truth in arguing before the democratic assembly.

those individuals' . . . those men: The second ἐκείνων must refer to Theramenes and Thrasyboulos. Logically the first should too, but the context requires a reference to Perikles and Diomedon. In speaking a gesture could overcome the difficulty, so the written version has an authentic air.

20. the decree of Kannonos: No specific prosecution under this decree is definitely attested, and its date is unknown. It is best understood as archaizing rather than archaic, passed when the Athenians were recodifying their laws after the oligarchy of the Four Hundred (B. M. Lavelle, "*Adikia*, the Decree of Kannonos, and the Trial of the Generals," *Classica et Mediaevalia* 39 [1988] 19-41). Euryptolemos suggests using this harsh decree in order to gain a trial for the generals, even under circumstances in which guilt seems almost predetermined as the defendants were bound.

executed and thrown into the chasm: Dobree emends to "executed by being thrown" on the basis of schol. Aristoph. *Ekkl.* 1089. Execution by throwing a living person into the *barathron* (to die from the fall, starvation or exposure) had been used earlier, notably in the case of Dareios' heralds in 490 (Hdt. VII.133). The *barathron* has been identified with a human-made chasm, possibly a quarry, northwest of the Hill of the Nymphs (Wycherley 269). By the late fifth century, however, it may have become only a burial place for executed persons (MacDowell 254). Compare Thuc. II.67.4, where Sadokos has some Peloponnesian ambassadors arrested and sent to Athens: "They killed them all and threw them into the chasm (*pharanx*)." MacDowell cautions that the *barathron* ought to be a natural chasm, and that it need not be identical with the *orugma* (pit) mentioned in fourth-century sources (255).

it is disgraceful: Note how Euryptolemos and Kallikratidas differ in their views of what is *aischron* (disgraceful or shameful). Euryptolemos puts the city before the individual; Kallikratidas put himself ahead of his city (6.32 n.). The contrast is not to Kallikratidas' credit.

22. in a jury court: Rather than in the assembly. Perikles instituted pay for democratic jurors in the middle of the fifth century (Aristot. *Ath. Pol.* 27.3-4, *Pol.* 1274a 8-9; Plut. *Per.* 9.3-5), but we do not know when the system began. Ostwald argues that the Athenians divided the archaic *heliaia* into a number of jury courts soon after Ephialtes' reforms in 462/1 (74-77). Sealey, on the other hand, maintains that before the introduction of pay there cannot have been enough willing jurors for more than one court (59-60).

he shall not be buried in Attika: Euryptolemos does not mention the death penalty. It was required by law for temple-robbers (Xen. *Mem.* I.7.22; Isok. 20.6; Lyk. *Leok.* 65), and, scholars generally assume, also for treason cases (for example, Harrison 59). Alternatively, a separate law specified the penalty for temple-robbers, and the court was free to decide the penalty in treason cases.

23. with the day divided into three parts: On the nature of the "divided day" (διαμεμετρημένη ἡμέρα) lexicographers and scholiasts agree with Xenophon (for a list see Rhodes 723) against Aischin. 2.126, which gives the first part of the day to the prosecutor, the second to the defendant and the third to assessing the penalty. Rhodes argues that Aischines must be correct for the procedure of his own day, but that a different version might have obtained earlier.

24. the wrong-doers . . . the innocent: Euryptolemos cleverly suggests a distinction between guilty and not guilty generals; he keeps the idea going with "execute and acquit" in § 26.

25. these victorious men who destroyed seventy ships: Euryptolemos appeals for support by reminding his listeners that the generals won the battle and destroyed seventy enemy ships (in 6.24 Xenophon gives the Peloponnesian losses as more than sixty-nine ships).

26. with a single vote: The position of these words at the end of the sentence emphasizes Euryptolemos' claim that a single vote would be unjust. See Xen. *Mem.* I.1.18 and Plato *Apol.* 32b for the same point.

27. perhaps you will put to death an innocent man, and you will regret it later: As Xenophon says they did (§ 35).

28. Aristarchos: While serving as general under the Four Hundred in 411, Aristarchos had tried to reach an agreement with Sparta, led the building of the fort at Eetioneia and betrayed the border fort at Oinoe to the Thebans (Thuc. VIII.90.1, 92.6, 9, 98; Xen. II.3.46). We know nothing further about his capture and trial except that according to Lykourg. *Leok.* 115, he was executed for defending the oligarch Phrynichos' bones after Phrynichos' assassination.
Oinoe: The deme was next to Eleutherai, and the fort should probably be identified with the remains in northwestern Attika at Myoupolis, which controlled the roads through the Mazi plain, including the main road from Athens and Eleusis past

Eleutherai and into Boiotia through the Kaza pass (Ober 154-55). It was one of only two forts used during the Peloponnesian War primarily for land warfare.

29. Erasinides: Because he had been with Konon at Mytilene (see 6.16 n.), he is an appropriate person to favor freeing Konon as soon as possible.

30. the ten of the division commanders and the ten Samian and the three of the admirals: If pressed, this statement means the Athenian center survived the battle intact (see 6.29).
twelve lost ships: 6.34 and Diod. XIII.100.3 agree that the Athenians lost twenty-five ships. Perhaps thirteen ships had broken apart by the time the generals conferred (triremes appear to have been too light to sink; Morrison and Coates 128). More likely, however, Xenophon intended to portray Euryptolemos as shading the facts to the generals' benefit.

32. one of our generals who survived on a wrecked ship: Diod. XIII.99.3 says that Kallikratidas sank Lysias' ship. Aristot. *Ath. Pol.* 34.1 speaks of several generals rescued from the sea. But the anonymity of this general mentioned by Euryptolemos raises another doubt about his truthfulness. Xenophon's narrative mentions no such incident.
those who did not carry out their instructions: Some editors have objected to these words (and similarly to "the instructions" in § 33), which refer to the other generals, on the grounds that the generals gave rather than received orders. But Euryptolemos is trying to treat the generals on the same level as the captains. He wants to persuade his audience that the captains should be held accountable for their part of the plan, the generals for theirs.

33. It would be more just to reward the victors with garlands: This suggestion recalls Plato *Apol.* 36d-e, where Sokrates says he deserves to be rewarded as a benefactor with maintenance at the prytaneion.

34. Menekles: Otherwise unknown.
lodged an objection under oath: The objection is unclear. Either Menekles swore that he would indict Euryptolemos for an unconstitutional proposal, with the result that Euryptolemos withdrew his motion, or, more likely, Menekles swore that the *prytaneis* had falsified the vote and demanded a recount (Ostwald 441-42 n. 123).
another vote was taken: Apparently to decide whether to approve Kallixenos' motion or to await a court decision on Euryptolemos' proposal.
the six who were present were executed: The Athenians not infrequently

impeached their generals: at least fourteen previously during the Peloponnesian War (Pritchett [2.5-10] lists trials of military leaders). Punishments had included deposition from command, fines, exile and confiscation of property. (Only Alkibiades, who fled rather than stand trial in 415, was condemned to death, and the sentence was not carried out.) Xenophon says the Athenians regretted the Arginousai affair, but in the fourth century they repeatedly followed its precedent. Between 388 and 338, leaders were condemned to death on at least nine occasions. Demosthenes claimed the Athenians put every general on trial for his life two or three times (4.47). The strict control the Athenians exercised over their commanders had one great salutary effect: It kept commanders following the assembly's policies and desires, thereby safeguarding the democracy (Roberts [178-80] makes this point well). Arginousai had its pupil in Chabrias, who remembered Arginousai after routing the Lakedaimonian fleet at Naxos in 376 and halted his pursuit in order to pick up the living and dead sailors (Diod. 15.35.1).

35. This section is the clearest example in the continuation of Xenophon's tendency to narrate a story to its natural conclusion, rather than break it up by summers and winters, as Thucydides did.

Not much later: Diod. XIII.103.1 says "quickly" (ταχύ). It is difficult to be more precise.

the Athenians regretted: Plato *Apol.* 32b and Diod. XIII.103.1 also state that the Athenians regretted their actions.

complaints: In the fourth century a written complaint for sycophancy or "deceiving the people by false promises" could be brought to the *prytaneis*. In the sixth prytany (Aristot. *Ath. Pol.* 43.5) the *proedroi* brought the complaint to the assembly, which heard both sides and voted (Harrison 59-64). This vote perhaps freed any future prosecutor from the penalties for gaining less than one-fifth of the votes (Harrison's suggestion), but a prosecution did not automatically follow. The charge here does not seem quite the same as the fourth-century "deceiving the people by false promises," though it might qualify as sycophancy. The furnishing of sureties also seems foreign to fourth-century procedure. This procedure here may not be the same as that known in the fourth century.

Diod. XIII.103.2 also has Kallixenos charged with deceiving the people.

they were confined by the sureties: Diodoros does not mention sureties: Kallixenos was thrown into the public prison without having a chance to defend himself (XIII.103.2), while the purpose of sureties was to guarantee the court appearance of someone not in prison. Xenophon presumably refers to some sort of private restraint.

Later: Presumably not much later, or the trial would have been held. This means that according to Xenophon the revulsion against Kallixenos occurred shortly before Kleophon's death, some time after the battle of Aigospotamoi (Lys. 13.12).

Kleophon: The only appearance in the *Hellenika* of this prominent politician, whom Xenophon must have disliked. Though he was called a lyre-maker, Kleophon was the son of Kleippides of Acharnai, general in 429/8, and he may have been general himself (schol. Aristoph. *Frogs* 679). He was probably in origin a prosperous manufacturer, though Lys. 19.48 says he died poor. The ostraka against him may demonstrate his prominence as early as 416. Aristophanes found him worth mentioning in the *Thesmophoriazousai* (804-805), presented before the oligarchic revolution in 411. He may have held the office of *poristes*, or provider of funds, when he instituted the *diobelia* (Aristot. *Ath. Pol.* 28.3 with Rhodes 355-56), which appears in the accounts for 410/409 (see § 2 n.). Aristotle pairs him with Theramenes in his list of opposed democratic and aristocratic leaders (*Ath. Pol.* 28.3). How his policies differed from Theramenes' is unclear. Kleophon is said to have opposed making peace with Sparta after Kyzikos (Philochoros, *FGrHist* 328 F 130; Diod. XIII.53.2), after Arginousai (Aristot. *Ath. Pol.* 34.1; schol. Aristoph. *Frogs* 1552), and even after Aigospotamoi (Lys. 13.5-12, 30.10-13; Aischin. 2.76). If *Kleo[phon]* is correctly restored in *IG* 1³.113 lines 32-33, a decree honoring Euagoras of Salamis that (though poorly preserved) may show the Athenians treating the Persian king and Tissaphernes as allies, Kleophon may have favored reaching agreement with the Persians.

According to Lys. 13.12, those who wanted an oligarchy brought Kleophon to trial on the pretext that he failed to spend the night under arms, but really because he had opposed a peace that required the destruction of Athens' long walls. They arranged the jury court and had him executed. See also Lys. 30.12. Xenophon's description of the situation as "civil disorder" (*stasis*) seems a bit exaggerated.

they escaped: Diod. XIII.103.2 has Kallixenos dig his way out of prison and escape to Dekeleia.

when those from Peiraieus returned to the city: In the autumn of 403, when a general amnesty took effect.

died of hunger: According to Suidas, s.v. ἐναύειν, Kallixenos starved when the Athenians refused to share water and fire with him.

II.1.1-5. *Eteonikos' suppression of a conspiracy in Chios*

The way Xenophon handles this incident exemplifies his didactic view of history. Xenophon treats it in detail because it shows how a general ought to handle his troops: Eteonikos acts firmly to eliminate the immediate threat, but also finds the money his men need.

1.3. a man suffering from an eye disease: And therefore defenseless.
he killed him: Xenophon believed a commander should use force when necessary to secure obedience. See *Anab.* I.9.13, II.6.9-10, V.8.

5. in order that the sailors be paid: Xenophon repeatedly stresses the general's obligation to find pay and provisions for his men: See I.5.7, I.6.9, 11, 12, 14; §§ 12, 15, 19; V.1.13; *Anab.* I.2.11, II.6.8, IV.5.7-9; *Hipparch.* 6.2-3; *Kyr.* I.6.9-11; *Mem.* III.1.6, 4.
he gave the signal to embark on the ships: Thereby separating the dissidents into smaller, more easily controlled groups.
exhorted and encouraged: On securing enthusiasm, compare *Kyr.* I.6.13, 19.

> **6-21.** *Lysandros' return as Peloponnesian commander. Kyros'*
> *departure. Operations in Karia and Ionia. The*
> *Peloponnesians move to the Hellespont*

6. the Chians and the other allies assembled at Ephesus: Probably those who gathered now belonged to the political clubs Lysandros had encouraged during his admiralship (Diod. XIII.70.4 and Plut. *Lys.* 5, though Diodoros and Plutarch differ on whether Lysandros' political conniving preceded or followed the battle of Notion). Lysandros secured their support by promising to put them in power.

7. vice-admiral: See I.1.23 n. Diod. XIII.100.8 says that the Spartans sent Lysandros as a private citizen (*idiotes*), but told Arakos to do whatever Lysandros said.
Arakos: Presumably the eponymous ephor of 409/8 (3.10), who remained prominent at Sparta for forty years. The monument at Delphi commemorating the battle of Aigospotamoi included him (Paus. X.9.9). In 398 the Spartans sent him along with two others to inspect matters in Asia Minor and tell Derkylidas to command for another year (III.2.6-8). In 370/69 he served as one of five Lakedaimonian ambassadors to Athens (VI.5.33).
a law forbidding a man to serve as admiral twice: For the date of its institution, see I.5.1 n. Xenophon presents the Spartans as *de facto* breaking the law in order to win the war after Kallikratidas, who boasted about his obedience (I.6.5, 7), had failed. Xenophon omits Athens' rejection of a Spartan offer to evacuate Dekeleia and make peace on the terms that each side retain what it currently possessed (Aristot. *Ath. Pol.* 34.1).
[after twenty-five years of war had gone by]: Probably interpolated

(I.1.37 n.).

8-9. This note on Persian affairs is probably interpolated (I.1.37 n.). It does, however, hint at Kyros' intentions and shed an interesting light on his relationship with Lysandros.

8.   because when they met him they did not push their hands through the long-sleeved garment known as the *kore*, which they do only for the King: On the custom compare *Kyr.* VIII.3.10, where the horsemen stand for a parade with their hands thrust through their sleeves, "just as they still do when the King sees them." By contrast, Xenophon's Kyros keeps his hands outside his sleeves (*Kyr.* VIII.3.14).

9. Hieramenes: Probably the husband of Dareios' sister and the father of Autoboisakes and Mitraios, and most likely the Hieramenes mentioned in Thuc. VIII.58.1 and on the Lykian text of the Xanthos stele (Meiggs and Lewis 282).

10. [when Archytas . . . at Athens,]: Probably interpolated (I.1.37 n.).
Lysandros arrived at Ephesos: With thirty-five ships from the Peloponnese, according to Diod. XIII.104.3. On Lysandros' choice of Ephesos for his base, see I.5.1 n.
with the ships: On Xenophon's count, fewer than 101 total: Eteonikos' fifty (I.6.26) plus the survivors of Arginousai (120 [I.6.26] minus more than sixty-nine [I.6.34]). Xenophon does not say how large a fleet Lysandros now put together; we next hear a specific figure (two hundred) after the battle of Aigospotamoi (2.5).

11.   the money from the King: At I.5.3 Kyros said he had five hundred talents. Andok. 3.29 says that the King gave the Lakedaimonians five thousand talents toward the war; Isok. 8.97 says "more than five thousand" talents.

12. he appointed captains for the triremes: Spartan captains (*trierarchoi*) are known earlier (Thuc. IV.11.4), so--unless the admiral regularly appointed the captains each year--Xenophon means only the newly-built triremes.
were preparing the navy: Accepting Kurz's deletion of πρός. A word or a few words may have dropped out of the text, however: Note the suggestions of Marchant ("were preparing matters for the navy") and Breitenbach ("were preparing an additional thirty ships for the navy"). The Athenians had "more than" 125 + forty = "more than" 165 ships after Arginousai and 180 at Aigospotamoi (§ 20), having left twenty at Samos (Diod. XIII.104.2). Thus they added thirty to thirty-five ships.

13. his father: King Dareios II, who ruled Persia from 423 to 404. For the date of his death see 2.23 n.

Thamneria in Media: Perhaps Abhar (Cook 262).

the Kadousioi . . . had revolted: This revolt, in the impenetrable land southwest of the Caspian Sea, lasted for more than sixty years.

14. all the tribute that was his personally from the cities: That is, Kyros controlled the tribute but not necessarily the cities. Lewis (119) made the attractive suggestion that the "Treaty of Boiotios" (see I.4.2) stipulated that the Greek cities remain autonomous but have financial obligations to the Persians.

after reminding Lysandros of his friendship toward Sparta: Later Kyros successfully called on the Lakedaimonians to repay him for his support against the Athenians (III.1.1).

15. The inhabitants were half-barbarians: That is, of mixed Greek and barbarian race; a justification for their enslavement. Xenophon also notes that Lysandros released the free inhabitants of Lampsakos (§ 19), but he does not include Lysandros' atrocities at Miletos (Diod. XIII.104.5, Plut. *Lys.* 8, Polyain. I.45.1) and Iasos (Diod. XIII.104.7, accepting Palmer's emendation of "Thasos" to "Iasos"). Elsewhere too Xenophon treats Lysandros favorably (§ 28 n.).

16. at Samos: According to Diod. XIII.104.2, the Athenians had 173 ships and left twenty behind when they sailed north.

they chose . . . generals in addition to the ones they had already: Xenophon could mean that the fleet chose three generals besides Konon, Adeimantos, and Philokles (I.7.1), following the precedent of 411 (Thuc. VIII.76.2); or that the assembly elected and dispatched additional generals at the regular election in spring 405. The latter interpretation is more likely, since Lys. 13.10 attests that elections were held in spring 405. See also I.1.2 n.

Tydeus: Probably a commander at Katane in Sicily in 413 (Lys. 20.26). Less certain is the possibility, raised by the existence a Tydeus the son of Lamachos of Oe known from the late fourth century, that his father was the well-known general Lamachos.

Kephisodotos: Previously unknown.

17. from Rhodes along the Ionian coast: Xenophon gives the impression that Lysandros sailed directly to the Hellespont, eluding the Athenians by sailing along the coast while they sailed out at sea (*pelagioi*). Plut. *Lys.* 9.3-4 reports that Lysandros sailed to Aigina and Salamis, met with Agis in Attika, and fled to Asia

when he learned that the Athenians were chasing him (Diod. XIII.104.8 notes this
visit more briefly). Kagan (384-85) maintains that Lysandros wanted to draw the
Athenians away from Samos so he could move safely to the Hellespont. No other
evidence, however, confirms that Lysandros planned the strategy that won the war.
He made no move toward the Hellespont during his earlier period in command.
Agis, who had earlier realized the importance of the grain route for Athens (I.1.35
with n.), probably urged this strategy on Lysandros, if he did not put it into
Lysandros' head for the first time. Xenophon's omission of Lysandros' visit to Agis
credits Lysandros with the strategy that proved triumphant.

to intercept the grain ships: According to Demos. 50.4-6 the grain ships
sailed south during Metageitnion (August/September). This helps date the battle,
since after his victory Lysandros cut off most of the grain headed for Athens (2.1-2).

the cities that had revolted from the Peloponnesians: For Athenian
successes after Kyzikos, see I.1.19-22, 2.15-17, 3.1-22.

18. Thorax: He had earlier commanded hoplites during Kallikratidas' assault on
Mytilene (Diod. XIII.76.6).

19. all the free persons: Presumably including the Athenian garrison left by
Alkibiades and Thrasyllos (Diod. XIII.66.1). In contrast to Kallikratidas, Lysandros
makes no fine-sounding proclamations, and though the comparison with § 15
suggests that Xenophon believed he acted out of similar principles, he may only
have wanted to secure the loyalty of a strategically-located base.

20. 180 ships: Diod. XIII.105.1 and Plut. *Lys.* 9.6 give the same figure
(Demos. 23.212 says that two hundred were captured, clearly a round number). This
very large fleet did not necessarily outnumber Lysandros' ships, for he may already
have had the two hundred he had after the battle (see § 10 n.). Xenophon does not
tell us which side had the numerical advantage, though he does tell us Kyros advised
Lysandros not to fight if outnumbered (§ 14; compare I.5.15). Lysandros' tactics did
not depend on numbers, but on fighting in order against a disordered enemy, as he
had at Notion. Lysandros must have had at least close to 180 ships, or the
Athenians would not have hoped he would fight.

**21. Aigospotamoi, opposite Lampsakos, where the Hellespont is
about fifteen *stadia* wide:** B. S. Strauss, "A note on the topography and
tactics of the battle of Aegospotami," *American Journal of Philology* 108 (1987)
741-45, discusses the topography. Scholars have put Aigospotamoi at the mouth of
the Karakova-dere, southwest of Sütlüce; at the mouth of the Büyük-dere, northeast

of Sütlüce; or somewhere in between. Nowhere along this coast does the Hellespont's width match Xenophon's fifteen *stadia* (2.7 km.; for the *stadion* see I.2.1 n.), but it is closest at Karakova-dere (about 3.3 km.). It is about 4.5 km. at the Büyük-dere, but this site is most nearly "opposite" Lampsakos. Xenophon may simply have erred, since distances across water are less easy to calculate than those on land. But note that the underestimate increases the appearance of stupidity on the Athenian generals' part.

Aigospotamoi was a beach, not a harbor, but it offered the advantages of a close watch on Lysandros and a short distance to be rowed before the anticipated battle.

22-32. *Battle of Aigospotamoi. Execution of Philokles*

§§ 22-24 describe Lysandros' preparations, designed to lull the Athenians into complacency; §§ 25-26 report Alkibiades' unsuccessful attempt to persuade the Athenian generals to relocate; in §§ 27-28 Lysandros launches his unexpected and devastating attack.

In this narrative, Lysandros exhibits several characteristics of Xenophon's ideal commander. In many of his works Xenophon stresses the importance of obedience and discipline (*Anab.* I.5.7-8, 9.30-31; *Hell.* IV.8.19-22; *Kyr.* I.6.13, 20-25, IV.1.3, VIII.1.2-3; *Oik.* 4.19, 21.4-8). Lysandros' tactics illustrate the advice that it is not necessary to fight as soon as possible (*Kyr.* I.6.26), that the human need to eat offers opportunities to find the enemy making mistakes (*Kyr.* I.6.36), and that a general can catch the enemy off guard by inspiring him with overconfidence (*Kyr.* I.6.37). Xenophon required deceptiveness of a good general; a set battle should be fought, he advised, only if necessary (*Kyr.* I.6.41; for the importance of deception in war, see *Ages.* 1.14-17; *Hipparch.* 4.10-12, 17-20, 5.2-3, 5-12, 8.15, 20; *Kyr.* I.6.26-43).

22. the side-screens: See I.6.19 n.

25. From the fort: See I.3.8 n.
the Athenians were anchored at a beach without a city near by, and that they were bringing their provisions from Sestos: On the importance of camping where provisions are available, see *Kyr.* I.23.
fifteen *stadia*: About 2.7 km. (for the *stadion* see I.2.1 n.), but the text is faulty, since Sestos was some twenty km. distant. The erroneous figure may be a copyist's error due to the figure fifteen in § 21 or a corruption from 105 or 115, or perhaps a more serious corruption has altered what was originally a repetition of the point that the enemy fleet (rather than Sestos) was fifteen *stadia* away, as in § 21.

He told the Athenians . . . :   Here Alkibiades merely comments on the unsuitability of the Athenian position--without a harbor and without a source of supplies--and advises the Athenians to move. Since Alkibiades would not have left the security of his fort only to tell the Athenians something they could see for themselves, it is credible that he offered to bring in Thracian land troops from Medokos and Seuthes, as reported--with variations--by Diod. XIII.104.3-4 (probably on Ephoros' authority) and Nepos *Alc.* 8.2-5 (probably on the authority of Theopompos, whom he names at 11.1). Plutarch read Xenophon, Theopompos and Ephoros and tried to combine their accounts in *Alk.* 36.6-37.3 and *Lys.*10.5-7 (for a detailed analysis see C. Zagaria, "Teopompo e la tradizione su Egospotami," *Quaderni di Storia* 6 [1980] 299-319).

On Medokos and Seuthes see *Anab.* VII.2.32. Seuthes' father had been driven from his kingdom, and Seuthes wanted to win it back. Plut. *Alk.* 36.5 says that Alkibiades raised mercenaries and fought the "kingless" Thracians, probably meaning that Alkibiades was helping Seuthes, as Xenophon did later. Thus Alkibiades had kept up the close ties formed as early as 409, when he persuaded many Thracians to campaign with him (Diod. XIII.66.4). Had he fulfilled his promise now, the Athenians might have besieged Lampsakos by land and forced Lysandros to fight.

27. on the fifth day: A striking parallel with Konon, whose two ships escaped the Peloponnesian blockade at Mytilene "on the fifth day" (I.6.20). Other similarities between the two incidents include the use of side-screens and the timing of the action to coincide with the enemies' meal-time. See § 28 n. for a suggestion as to why Xenophon might have created these resemblances. The four-day delay before action is particularly suspect, for it appears in Herodotos (VII.210, for example) as well as elsewhere in the *Hellenika* (III.1.17-19, 3.4), and looks like a storyteller's convention.

28. as fast as possible: B. S. Strauss, "A note on the topography and tactics of the battle of Aegospotami," *American Journal of Philology* 108 (1987) 741-45, emphasizes Lysandros' speed. He estimates that Lysandros could have reached Aigospotamoi in twenty-two minutes if Aigospotamoi was at Büyük-dere (2.8 nautical miles from Lampsakos). G. Wylie's estimate of only ten minutes depends on Xenophon's mistaken figure for the distance at § 21 and is far too low ("What really happened at Aegospotami?" *Acta Classica* 55 [1986] 135).

Estimates of a trireme's top speed vary from seven-eight knots (Casson 279 n. 3) to 11.5 knots (21.3 km. per hour) or even, if it could partially plane along the surface, fifty per cent higher still (V. Foley and W. Soedel, "Ancient Oared Warships," *Scientific American* [April 1981] 154 and Foley, Soedel and J. Doyle,

"A trireme displacement estimate," *International Journal of Nautical Archaeology and Underwater Exploration* 11 [1982] 314-15). In early tests a modern trireme built under the leadership of J. S. Morrison and J. F. Coates reached seven knots. Morrison believes that with more carefully chosen and arranged rowers and lighter oars it can attain at least nine knots ("The British sea trials of the reconstructed trireme, 1-15 August 1987," *Antiquity* 61 [1987] 455-59).

Thorax: See § 18. Diod. XIII.106.4 has Eteonikos commanding the land troops. Eteonikos but not Thorax appeared on the victory monument at Delphi (Paus. X.9.7-10; Meiggs and Lewis no. 95; Bommelaer 14-16), and the Ephesians put up a statue of Eteonikos as well as one of Lysandros (Paus. VI.3.15). Eteonikos' opposition to Xenophon at Byzantion, when Xenophon commanded the remnants of the "Ten Thousand" (*Anab.* VII.1.12, 15, 20), might have caused hostility sufficient to lead Xenophon to suppress Eteonikos' role in this great victory. Thorax, on the other hand, was Lysandros' friend (Plut. *Lys.* 19.7; see 3.7 n.).

Konon's ship and seven others . . . and the Paralos: Other sources give conflicting information on the number of escaped ships: zero (Frontin. II.1.18; one (Polyain. I.45.2); eight with Konon to Cyprus (Plut. *Alk.* 37.4, *Lys.* 11.8; Justin V.6.10); one with Konon to Cyprus, nine to Athens (Diod. XIII.106.6); ten to Cyprus (Paus. III.11.5); twelve, apparently to Athens (Lys. 21.11); a few to Athens (Isok. 18.59-60). *IG* 2^2.1951 may confirm that eight reached Cyprus, but the date and circumstances of this inscription are controversial.

The Paralos, the best known of the twenty to thirty Athenian sacred ships, performed important public business, served as a scout ship and fought in battles. Known as *Paraloi*, its crew members appear in Thucydides as strong supporters of the democracy (VIII.73-74, 86.8-9). See Jordan 172-84.

Lysandros took all the rest: Of the later sources on the battle, Paus. IX.32.9, Plut. *Lys.* 9.6-13.2 and Polyain. I.45.1 all follow Xenophon. We have three other versions of the tactics. Frontin. II.1.18 says that Lysandros challenged the Athenians to battle at the same time each day, so that they relaxed and dispersed when he sailed away. Then one day he turned and attacked. Polyain. VI.27, describing a great naval battle between the Lakedaimonians and the Athenians which is probably Aigospotamoi (though Polyainos names neither Aigospotamoi nor Lysandros), says that the Lakedaimonian sailors embarked one night. The following day their peltasts also embarked, and the Athenians responded by embarking their peltasts. When the Lakedaimonian peltasts disembarked at meal-time, the Athenians did likewise, and the Lakedaimonian sailors successfully attacked the empty Athenian ships. These stories show that various explanations circulated for the sudden Athenian defeat, but neither is credible since the Athenians wanted a battle. They would have embarked fully in the morning and accepted any challenge Lysandros offered.

Diod. XIII.106.1-5, unfortunately much abbreviated but probably from the *Hell. Oxy.* via Ephoros, deserves serious consideration. Nepos *Alc.* 8 and Plut. *Alk.* 36.6-37.5 apparently combine Xenophon with bits from this tradition. Diodoros says that when the enemy refused to fight and the army lacked food, Philokles ordered the captains to follow and led the way with thirty ships. Lysandros heard what was happening through deserters. He attacked and routed Philokles, then caught the other triremes before their crews had finished boarding. Diodoros does not explain Philokles' intentions. In this tradition, Philokles was probably moving the fleet to Sestos for provisions, rather than hoping to lure Lysandros into attacking a part of the fleet which was then to be reinforced by the whole, as C. Ehrhardt argues ("Xenophon and Diodoros on Aegospotami," *Phoenix* 24 [1970] 225-28).

This version is not demonstrably superior to Xenophon's. Thuc. VIII.95.3-7, where Agesandridas' Peloponnesians catch the Athenians scattered in the search for food at Eretria and capture twenty-two of thirty-six Athenian ships, shows that a victory such as Xenophon describes was possible, at least on a smaller scale. Nevertheless Xenophon (or his sources) may have magnified Lysandros' role in the battle. Victory won by deception and discipline required generalship superior to victory won by taking advantage of deserters' information. Lysandros' particular deception is the more impressive as it is practiced on Konon, who had pulled off a similar trick himself. Elsewhere, particularly in his omissions, Xenophon reveals a prejudice in favor of Lysandros. He mentions neither Lysandros' violation of oaths (Diod. X.9.1, Polyain.I.45.3, Plut. *Lys.* 8.4-5) nor his role in the Thirty's election at Athens (Aristot. *Ath. Pol.* 34.3, Diod. 14.3.4-7, Lys. 12.71-76, Plut. *Lys.* 15.6), and he contains no hint of the accusations that Lysandros wanted to change the Spartan constitution so that he could be king (Aristot. *Pol.* 5.1.5, Diod. 14.13.2-6, Nepos *Lys.* 3.1-5, Plut. *Ages.* 20 and *Lys.* 25-26, 30). All this shows that Xenophon favored Lysandros, whose strategic sense (§ 17) and diplomatic skill (I.5.1-7, § 11-14) Xenophon admired. See also § 15 n. For another view, see V. J. Gray, who accuses Ephoros of writing conventionalized battles ("The value of Diodorus Siculus for the years 411-386 BC," *Hermes* 115 [1987] 78-79).

most of the men on land: According to Diod. XIII.106.6 the majority escaped to Sestos. Fourth-century references to survivors (Lys. 21.10, [*P. Ryl.* 3.489] *For Eryximachos* 100-104; Isok. 18.59-60) do not determine who is correct, but see § 22 n.

small forts: The escapees may have stopped at other fortified points on the way even if Sestos was their destination, as Diod. XIII.106.6 says it was.

29. the main sails: Triremes normally left their large sails behind when preparing for a battle; see VI.1.27.

This incident demonstrates Konon's foresight in acting to hamper Lysandros' possible pursuit. Xenophon counted foresight among the necessary qualities for a good general: VI.4.28; *Ages.* 8.5; *Anab.* VII.7.33; *Hipparch.* 4.1, 7.3; *Oik.* 7.36, 38, 9.11; *Kyr.* I.6.8, 21-24, 42.

He himself sailed away with eight ships to Euagoras in Cyprus: Diod. XIII.106.6 says Konon feared the people's anger. On Euagoras, see E. A. Costa, "Evagoras I and the Persians, ca. 411 to 391 B.C.," *Historia* 23 (1974) 40-56. Athens honored him between 411 and 407, perhaps with citizenship, for uncertain reasons possibly connected with negotiations with Tissaphernes (*IG* 1³.113). In 407 he sent Athens a shipment of grain (Andok. 2.20). Diod. XIII.106.1 says that Konon was a personal friend of Euagoras, and Isok. 9.52 says the two immediately discussed "how they were to liberate Athens from her misfortunes." Not until 398, however, did Euagoras negotiate with the Persian King to have Konon put in charge of a fleet.

30. Theopompos the Milesian pirate: According to Paus. X.9.10, Theopompos was from Myndos; the inscription on the victory monument at Delphi lists a Melian Theopompos the son of Lapompos (Meiggs and Lewis no. 95 f). Assuming these references are all to the same Theopompos, we can save Xenophon's credit by supposing that Theopompos received citizenship at Melos, which Lysandros liberated after Aigospotamoi (2.9). The confusion may, however, reflect real uncertainty about the pirate's roots.

on the third day: Noted because Theopompos moved exceptionally quickly. If he left late on the first day, he covered about 390 nautical miles from Aigospotamoi to Gytheion in less than forty-eight hours, an average speed of slightly more than eight knots. Under favorable wind conditions, ancient vessels averaged four-six knots (Casson 281-88).

31. they had already violated custom: Xenophon believed that whatever "the stronger" compels "the weaker" to do without persuasion is force (*bia*), not *nomos* (custom or law; see I.7.1 n.). For years the Athenians had treated their "allies" as subjects. For particular atrocities, see 2.3.

the right hand: Plut. *Lys.* 9.7 says that Philokles had persuaded the assembly to vote that prisoners should have their right thumbs cut off, so they could pull an oar but not carry a spear. Aelianus *VH* 2.9 and Cicero *De Off.* 3.11 refer to a similar decree, limited to thumbs, passed against the Aiginetans. Xenophon may exaggerate here to magnify the horror of the Athenian decision.

Philokles was the Athenian general who had killed them: A merciless act, but all too typical of Athenian behavior during the Peloponnesian war (see 2.13 n.). In Xenophon's eyes, Philokles deserved his fate (though Lysandros' stature would have been enhanced if he had pardoned the Athenian general).

32. they decided to kill all the Athenians among the captives: three thousand, according to Plut. *Lys.* 13.1 and *Alk.* 37.4; about four thousand, according to Paus. IX.32.9, where Lysandros is also said to have refused burial to their corpses. Diod. XIII.106.6-7 mentions only Philokles' execution. B. Strauss defends the historicity of the "mass slaughter" found in Xenophon, Plutarch and Pausanias, but he oversimplifies the evidence ("Aegospotami reexamined," *American Journal of Philology* 104 [1983] 32-34). Xenophon says that the allies voted to execute all the Athenian prisoners, but then describes only Philokles' death. It is not clear that Xenophon agrees with Plutarch and Pausanias.

Against them note manuscript D's interesting variant at the chapter's close: "Philokles said, 'Do as victor what you would have suffered had you lost'; Lysandros immediately cut his throat along with the other generals" (νικήσας ἔφη ποίει ἃ παθεῖν ἔμελλες ἡττηθείς, εὐθὺς τοῦτον ἀπέσφαξε μετὰ τῶν ἄλλων στρατηγῶν). This is not Xenophon, but neither does it come entirely from Plutarch (*Lys.* 13.1), who does not have the conclusion found in D implying that only the generals died. Was this detail taken from a reliable source? We cannot know. If Lysandros released the Athenian captives, no doubt he did so for the same reason Xenophon gives for the later release of other Athenians found outside Athens (2.2): the more people in the city, the sooner provisions would run short. For other arguments against the mass execution's historicity see G. Wylie, "What really happened at Aegospotami?" *Acta Classica* 55 (1986) 138-41.

except for Adeimantos: After returning to Athens, Konon accused Adeimantos of treason (Demos. 19.191). Lys. 14.18 accuses both Adeimantos and Alkibiades. In Plutarch, however, Alkibiades suspects treason by those who rejected his advice (Tydeus, at *Lys.* 10.7; Tydeus, Menandros and Adeimantos at *Alk.* 36.6-37.2). Paus. X.9.11 says the Athenians believed Tydeus and Adeimantos had betrayed them. In fact no general need have committed treason. Any information Lysandros received might have come from deserters, as Diod. XIII.106.2 says. Adeimantos' survival is enough to explain the charges against him. (Konon's decade away from Athens shows he feared he might be held accountable for the defeat.)

2.1-24. Peloponnesian naval operations. Siege of Athens.
Peace negotiations and agreement

2.1. those who had betrayed Byzantion . . . became Athenian

citizens: Xenophon gives five names at I.3.18. At this time the Athenians naturalized foreigners only as a reward for service to Athens. Though the war led to more frequent awards (see I.6.24 § 6 nn.), Xenophon's comment here reminds the reader that recovering Byzantion, and with it the route to grain from the Black Sea, had been a major gain for Athens. Its loss now will be decisive.

2. the sooner they would run short of provision: Isok. 18.61 says that Lysandros announced the death penalty for anyone who brought grain into Athens, but claims some did reach Peiraieus.

Sthenelaos the Lakonian as governor: Plut. *Lys.* 13.5 says that Lysandros now established governors in each hostile and allied city, with ruling committees (dekarchies) of ten men chosen from the political clubs he had previously organized (*Lys.* 5.5). Plutarch has him continue this work after beginning the siege of Athens. Xenophon mentions only the dekarchy at Samos instituted after Athens' surrender (3.7; for later, more general references to the dekarchies, see III.4.2, 7). Diodoros indicates that the ephors sent Lysandros out to change the governments after the war (XIV.10, 13). For a recent discussion, see Hamilton (56-61). Hamilton stresses that the Spartans must have made a formal decision about Athens' former subjects, but notes this decision might have approved measures already taken or at least begun by Lysandros.

    Diod. XIII.106.8 puts the capture of Sestos immediately after the battle, but it probably belongs here because Lysandros would have turned first to the bigger prizes, Byzantion and Kalchedon.

repaired the ships: Compare I.5.10 with n. These passages illustrate Lysandros' understanding of triremes, a sign of his competence.

3. Perhaps Xenophon's most famous sentence, in which he vividly recreates the disastrous news' effect. Justin's rhetorical reworking of the sentence (V.7.4-5) only draws attention to the original's quality. Xenophon's word order mimics geography.

    Xenophon does not flatter the Athenians: They think mostly of themselves. In their variety the examples Xenophon gives of Athenian behavior suggest the Athenians habitually behaved harshly. They had good reason to be afraid. According to Paus. III.8.6, Lysandros and Agis on their own initiative proposed to the allies that they destroy Athens. This proposal was probably made shortly after Lysandros arrived in Attika in 405.

Melians: After the Melians surrendered in the winter of 416/5, the Athenians executed the adult males and sold the children and women (Thuc. V.116.4).

Histiaians: After the Athenians suppressed the Euboian revolt in 446, they expelled the Histiaians and occupied their land (Thuc. I.114.3).

Skionaians: After taking Skione by siege in 421, the Athenians killed the adult males and sold the children and women (Thuc. V.32.1).

Toronaians: After capturing Torone in 422, the Athenians sold the women and children; the male Toronaians, initially sent to Athens, eventually returned home after a prisoner exchange with Olynthos (Thuc. V.3.4).

Aiginetans: In 431 the Athenians had expelled the Aiginetans from their island (Thuc. II.27.1). The Lakedaimonians gave them Thyrea (Thuc. II.27.1), on the border of Argive and Spartan territory, where some lived until the Athenians captured and killed them in 424 (Thuc. IV.57). Others scattered throughout Greece (II.27.2). Lysandros eventually restored to Aigina as many as he could gather (§ 9).

4. to block up the harbors, except for one: Peiraieus had three harbors, Kantharos (the commercial harbor), Zea (the main base for the fleet) and Mounychia. Probably the largest, Kantharos, was to remain open.

in every other way: They also elected new generals, including Nikias' brother Eukrates (Lys. 18.4). For other evidence of Athenian determination, see §§ 6, 11 nn.

5. in other cities of Lesbos and particularly in Mytilene: The Athenians had suppressed Lesbos' revolt in 412 (Thuc. VIII.23.3, 6; 100.2), but Eresos had revolted again (Thuc. VIII.100.3) with unknown results. Kallikratidas had taken Methymna (I.6.12) and Eteonikos may have controlled Pyrrha (I.6.38 n.). Xenophon does not reveal precisely what arrangements Lysandros made, but in 394 the Mytilenians expelled a garrison (Diod. XIV.74.3) and in 390/89 a Lakedaimonian governor controlled the other cities (IV.8.29).

ten triremes: A remarkably small number. Evidently Lysandros expected (and Eteonikos found) little resistance.

6. except for the Samians, who were in possession of the city after slaughtering the aristocrats: For the fall of Samos, after Athens' capitulation, see 3.6-7. Xenophon refers here either to events at Samos in 412, when the commons killed two hundred aristocrats and exiled four hundred others (Thuc. VIII.21; Shipley 125), or (less likely) to a second purge in 405 (Quinn 23). The Athenians granted the Samians autonomy in 412 (Thuc. VIII.21; the grant may have been part of *IG* 1³.96, but if so it is entirely lost). In 405/4, after negotiations initiated by the Samians, the Athenians provided that they be able to acquire Athenian citizenship if they settled in Athens, while remaining autonomous with their own government on Samos. Apparently the Thirty revoked this grant in

404/3; the restored democracy reaffirmed it in 403/2 (*IG* 1³.127).

Xenophon clearly admires the Samians for their loyalty, just as he later and more explicitly praises the Phliasians for their loyalty to Sparta after Sparta's defeat at Leuktra (VII.2.1-3.1). See also 3.6, and the naming of the Samian commander, alone among the allies, at Arginousai (I.6.29).

7. two hundred ships: He arrives, however, with only 150 (§ 9). According to Diod. XIII.106.8 Lysandros began the siege of Samos during this interval, so he probably left forty to fifty ships to carry on the siege. (The numbers can only be approximate: We do not know when Eteonikos took his ten ships towards Thrace, and Diod. XIII.107.2 gives Lysandros more than two hundred ships at Peiraieus).

The Athenians had left twenty ships at Samos (Diod. XIII.104.2; the naturalization decree for the Samians authorizes them to use whatever triremes are there, *IG* 1³.127 lines 25-27).

except for the Argives: Though Athens and Argos were still allied according to the defensive alliance concluded for one hundred years between in 420 (Thuc. V.47; *IG* 1³.83) and renewed for fifty years in 416 (Thuc. V.82.5; *IG* 1³.86), Argos had dropped out of the fighting after almost three hundred Argive hoplites died at Miletos in 412 (Thuc. VIII.25.3, 27.6). For Argives accompanying an Athenian embassy to the Persian king, see I.3.13.

under the command of Pausanias, the other Lakedaimonian king: Since about 506 a law had forbidden the Spartan kings to go out in joint command of the same army (Hdt. V.75.2). In spite of Diod. XIII.107.2 (which speaks of Agis and Pausanias as if they commanded the same forces), then, Agis may have remained at Dekeleia (see 3.3). Alternatively, the campaign's importance overrode the law, as would have happened in 418 had the battle of Mantinea been delayed long enough for Pleistoanax to arrive (Thuc. V.75.1).

8. in the Academy: Northwest of the city, six *stadia* (Cic. *de Fin.* 5.1) or about a Roman mile (Livy 31.24.9) from the Dipylon gate. See Wycherley 219-26, with references.

9. to the Aiginetans, as many of them as he was able to collect: See § 3 n. Lysandros probably installed a governor, for we hear of one at Aigina in 395 (*Hell. Oxy.* I.3).

all the others who had been deprived of their own states: Plut. *Lys.* 14.4 mentions the Melians and Skionaians specifically; the phrase ought to cover the others in § 3 as well as the Poteidaians.

10. In § 3 Xenophon represented the Athenians as fearing they would suffer the same harsh treatment they had given others; here he goes further and has them admitting in their own minds that they acted wrongly. Note the strong language.

11. restoring their rights to those who had been disenfranchised: As Aristophanes had advised earlier in 405 (*Frogs* 686-705). Andok. 1.77-79 quotes Patrokleides' motion, which restored full civic rights to the *atimoi* but did not recall the exiles.
But when food had entirely given out: An exaggeration, since the Athenians held out for more than three months yet, and Xenophon later describes Theramenes as stalling until all the food gave out (§ 16).
Agis: Presumably Pausanias had already withdrawn (Diod.XIII.107.3) and Lysandros had departed for the siege of Samos (Plut. *Lys.* 14.2).

12. for he had, he said, no authority to negotiate: Yet Agis had operated independently while at Dekeleia, negotiating with potential rebels and even the Four Hundred (Thuc. VIII.5.1-3, 70.2-71.1). Had he favored accepting the terms offered, he could have lifted the blockade while the Athenian embassy went to Sparta. His blunt refusal suggests that he still favored destroying Athens (see § 3 n.).

13. in Sellasia, [near Lakonia,]: The qualifying phrase is probably an erroneous interpolation, since Sellasia has been identified with Palaiogoulas hill, about 12 km. north of Sparta and well inside the borders of Lakonia (W. K. Pritchett, "The Polis of Sellasia," *Studies Presented to Sterling Dow* [Durham 1984] 251-54). Perhaps it can mean Sellasia bordered the territory Sparta held directly (Cartledge 188).
at once: Xenophon speaks as if the ephors dismissed the embassy as bluntly as Agis had. The ephors came out to Sellasia, however, an effort that suggests some willingness to negotiate, and in fact they did offer counterproposals: (1) that Athens should dismantle ten *stadia* of the long walls (§ 15; Lys. 13.8), and--less certainly, because the later source is less reliable--(2) that Athens keep the democracy and the islands Lemnos, Imbros and Skyros (Aischin. 2.76). Lysias and Aischines blame Kleophon for Athens' refusal of these terms.

15. Archestratos: Not the Archestratos of I.5.16, who had died, but perhaps the Archestratos who said Greece could not endure two Alkibiades (Plut. *Alk.* 16.8).
ten *stadia*: About 1.8 km. (for the *stadion* see I.2.1 n.).
a decree was passed forbidding any such proposals: See Lys. 13.8,

Aischin. 2.76.

16-17. Lysias comments on Theramenes' negotiations in two hostile passages: 12.68-70 says Theramenes claimed to have discovered something worth a great deal and undertook to make peace without giving hostages, demolishing the walls, or surrendering the ships. He would not reveal his intentions, but told the Athenians to trust him. He then promised to demolish the Peiraieus walls and destroy the existing constitution. 13.9-14 says Theramenes asked to be appointed ambassador with full powers, and promised to see that the Athenians would neither take down their walls nor be weakened in any other way. He claimed he would also gain some other good thing from the Lakedaimonians. He lingered at Sparta in order to make the Athenians desperate enough to accept any terms. The terms he brought called for destroying the long walls and the Peiraieus walls and surrendering the ships. Thus Lysias disagrees with Xenophon about the number of Theramenes' trips, but agrees with Xenophon's view of Theramenes' intentions in stalling the negotiations.

   P. Mich. 5982 contains further conflicting evidence (H. C. Youtie and R. Merkelbach, "Ein Michigan-Papyrus über Theramenes," *Zeitschrift für Papyrologie und Epigraphik* 2 [1968] 161-69). According to this papyrus fragment, Theramenes refused to discuss the peace terms in the assembly on the grounds that no concessions should be granted to the enemy in advance. The Athenians sent him off as ambassador with full powers to make peace. Theramenes immediately sailed to Lysandros at Samos and attempted to reach an agreement. When Lysandros told him, with the Lakedaimonians . . . There the papyrus breaks off. Scholars have evaluated this papyrus variously. M. Treu suggests that it was part of the *Hellenika Oxyrhynchia* ("Einwände gegen die Demokratie in der Literatur des 5./4. Jh.," *Studii Clasice* 12 [1970] 17-31), but the surviving fragments of that work contain no direct speech. A. Henrichs argues that the papyrus was the work of a second-rate historian who copied Lys. 12.69 ("Zur Interpretation der Michigan-Papyrus über Theramenes," *Zeitschrift für Papyrologie und Epigraphik* 3 [1968] 101-108). A. Andrewes accepts Henrichs' arguments and maintains that the papyrus comes from a pro-Theramenean pamphlet ("Lysias and the Theramenes Papyrus," *Zeitschrift für Papyrologie und Epigraphik* 6 [1970] 35-38). G. E. Pesely holds that the papyrus does not show great partisanship for Theramenes, comes from a Hellenistic biographer interested chiefly in rhetoric and is useless for historians ("The Origin and Value of the Theramenes Papyrus," *Ancient History Bulletin* 3 [1989] 29-35). R. Sealey, however, rightly cautions that the author need not have used Lysias ("Pap. Mich. inv. 5982: Theramenes," *Zeitschrift für Papyrologie und Epigraphik* 16 [1975] 279-88). Sealey proposes that Theramenes went on only one mission (as in Lysias), detouring to visit Lysandros *en route* to Sparta. But nothing in the papyrus proves a single trip, and Sealey's hypothesis leaves Xenophon's two distinct missions unexplained.

Theramenes may have had "full powers" on both missions. If so, he probably did believe (as Lysias says) that he could secure better terms than those proposed by the ephors, since he did not need "full powers" to talk to Lysandros about Spartan intentions. For the suggestion that the hostile testimony of Xenophon and Lysias may have Theramenes' goal exactly wrong, see Krentz (36-41). By prolonging negotiations, Theramenes prevented Athens from surrendering. He may have hoped that the sick Persian king would die, initiating a reverse in Persian policy and an opportunity for Athens to make peace with walls intact.

16. more than three months: Kagan (406 n. 119 and 409 n. 128) maintains that "the delay was needed for the difficult negotiations and, perhaps, to allow time for the question to be put to the oracle at Delphi and the response to arrive at Sparta." The sources for this visit to Delphi (schol. Aristeid. 341 and Aelianus *VH* 4.6), however, do not explicitly connect it with Lysandros or place it within the known sequence of events. My own view (see previous n.) is that Lysandros had reasons for wanting a quick agreement, and that Theramenes may have been the one stalling.

17. ambassador with full powers, along with nine others: Xenophon focuses on Theramenes, but the phrase means that the entire embassy, a board of ten members, had full powers (K. J. Dover, "Dekatos Autos," *Journal of Hellenic Studies* 80 [1960] 77; for another view see Jordan 129 n.7). The Athenian assembly could accept or reject an agreement made even by an embassy with "full powers" (Mosley 30-38).

18. Aristoteles: Perhaps the treasurer (*hellenotamias*) from Antiochis (X) in 421/0 (*IG* 1³.285 line 5), who may be the Aristoteles son of Timokrates who held a command in 426/5 (Thuc. III.105.3), and may be the ---eles of Thorai who served as general in 431/0 (? *IG* 1³.366 line 6). These men may, however, be different individuals. The Aristoteles of the present passage is very likely the Aristoteles named by Xenophon's Theramenes as one of the oligarchic generals in charge of building the fort at Eetioneia in 411, through which the oligarchs contemplated betraying the city to the Spartans (3.46). This general probably escaped to Dekeleia along with other oligarchic leaders (Thuc. VIII.98.1). He was a member of the Thirty in 404 (3.2).

19. the Korinthians and Thebans . . . urged their destruction: For other references to Peloponnesian allies wanting to destroy Athens in 404, see III.5.8 and VI.5.35, 46; Andok. 1.142, 3.21; Isok. 14.31, 18.29; Plut. *Lys.* 15.3; Justin V.8.4; Polyain. I.45.5.

20. The Lakedaimonians, however, refused to enslave a Greek city that had done great good at the time of Greece's greatest dangers: Here Xenophon's theme of clemency's value moves to a new order of magnitude. Previous positive examples of this virtue have concerned only individuals (I.3.19, 5.19), as have negative examples of mercilessness (I.2.13, 7.34, II.2.3). The Lakedaimonians, however, now show mercy to an entire city. The importance of forgiving and forgetting on all levels proves to be an important theme of the entire *Hellenika*. At the end of the civil war in Athens, the Athenian democrats have learned the lesson, as they produce and live by an amnesty (II.4.43). A generation later, before the battle of Leuktra, the Athenians offer and achieve peace with Sparta (VI.3). And in Sparta's greatest moment of need after Leuktra, the Athenians overcome their memories of all the harm the Lakedaimonians have done them and, remembering their mercy at the end of the Peloponnesian War (VI.5.47), vote to ally with Sparta. Xenophon's personal experience of exile has probably influenced this presentation, but of course his message is more than simply self-interested.

JustinV.8.4 has another rhetorical expression, that the Spartans refused to tear out the other of the two eyes of Greece. Plut. *Lys.* 15.4 tells a story about a Phokian singing the first chorus from Euripides' *Elektra* at a banquet of the Peloponnesian leaders, which made them feel it would be cruel to destroy a city that had produced such men as Euripides. More prosaically, Polyain. I.45.5 says Lysandros persuaded the Lakedaimonians not to destroy Athens by urging them to use the city as a check to Thebes. Xenophon's Theramenes hints at some such motive when he suggests that the Spartans let the city survive in order to receive help from it (3.41).

they offered to make peace on the following terms: Plut. *Lys.* 14.8 quotes the ephors' proposal (in Doric Greek) as follows: "The Lakedaimonian authorities have decided that you may have peace, if you want it, by taking down the Peiraieus walls and the long walls, by withdrawing from all the cities and having your own land, and by letting the exiles return. With regard to the number of ships, do whatever is decided on the spot." Andok. 3.11-12 cites the inscribed stele for terms including the demolition of the walls, the restriction of the fleet to twelve ships, the abandonment of control over Lemnos, Imbros and Skyros (which were to remain in the possession of "those having" them, originally Athenian settlers), and the restoration of the exiles.

Scholars have debated whether the final peace stipulated that Athens be governed according to the "ancestral constitution" (πάτριος πολιτεία), as Aristot. *Ath. Pol.* 34.3 and Diod. XIV.3.2 maintain. Such a clause would have guaranteed autonomy, like similar clauses in Thuc. V.77.5 and 79.1 (Fuks 61; for another view see Rhodes [427], who believes that "ancestral constitution" meant the dissolution of the democracy). In addition to Xenophon's silence, the main argument against the clause is that it may have been invented to absolve Theramenes of responsibility for the oligarchy of the Thirty (Hignett 285). But Xenophon's silence can be explained (3.2 n.), and the case for bias in Aristotle and Diodoros is not compelling. I accept the clause.

the ships except twelve to be surrendered: So too Andok. 3.12; Diod. XIII.107.4 has ten.

to have the same enemies and friends as the Lakedaimonians and to follow them wherever they might lead on land and sea: De Ste. Croix (343 n. 2) believes that a second treaty, under which the Athenians entered the Peloponnesian league and accepted Sparta's leadership, followed the peace treaty. If so, Xenophon has lumped the two treaties together. It makes little practical difference. As de Ste. Croix says, "the two transactions may have taken place very close together, and their joint provisions will have been regarded as the terms of peace."

This is the first explicit statement of the Peloponnesian league requirement to follow the Spartans wherever they lead. It appears frequently later (IV.6.2, V.3.26 [including the part about enemies and friends], VI.3.7; compare V.2.8 and VII.1.24), and probably goes back to the sixth century (de Ste. Croix 108-112).

22. Although some persons spoke in opposition to him: Lys. 13.13 says some of the generals and division commanders protested to Theramenes about the terms he brought back, and claims they believed they could secure better ones. According to Lysias, Theramenes and others arranged to have Agoratos inform against these opponents and had them imprisoned. Lys. 13.17 specifies that the prosecutions occurred before the assembly discussed the treaty, so that no one would oppose it. Events must have moved quickly.

23. Lysandros sailed into the Peiraieus: Athens surrendered in March 404, as we know from Thucydides' statement that the war lasted "not many days" longer than twenty-seven years (V.26.3, with *HCT* 4.12) and Diodoros' comment that Dareios II died not long after the peace (XIII.108.1), for Artaxerxes was recognized as king by 10 April 404 (Parker and Dubberstein 16, 32). Some scholars see a contradiction with Plutarch's claim that Lysandros entered the Peiraieus on 16 Mounichion, the anniversary of the battle of (Cyprian) Salamis (*Lys.* 15.1), which

normally fell in late April. Perhaps some time elapsed between the acceptance of an
armistice and Lysandros' arrival for the final surrender (J. A. R. Munro, "The End of
the Peloponnesian War," *Classical Quarterly* 31 [1937] 32-38). Alternatively, given
the Athenian calendar's irregularity, 405/404 could have begun as early as 18 June,
which would put 16 Mounichion near the end of March 404 (D. Lotze, "Der
Munichion 404 v. Chr. und das Problem der Schaltfolge im Athenischen Kalender,"
Philologus 111 [1967] 34-46).

they began to raze: In "The Razing of the House," *Transactions of the
American Philological Association* 115 (1985) 97, W. R. Connor comments: "The
event [the razing of Athens' walls] becomes an informal Freedom Festival,
celebrating the liberation of Greece from Athenian rule, much as the razing of the
tyrants' buildings in Syracuse [Plut. *Tim.* 22.1-3] celebrates the end of tyranny."

pipe-girls: The *aulos*, often misleadingly translated "flute," was a reed
instrument. Professional female pipe-players became common in Athens beginning
at the end of the sixth century, and were a regular entertainment at male dinner
parties. It required considerable training to learn to play increasingly complex music
on a difficult instrument, and the pipe-girls were well paid--but as slaves they did not
keep the money themselves. It is unclear how often their services included sex. See
C. Starr, "An evening with the flute-girls," *La parola del passato* 33 (1978) 401-410.

In describing this scene Plut. *Lys.* 15.5 adds that the Peloponnesian allies
garlanded themselves and rejoiced.

thinking that day to be the beginning of freedom for Greece: Recall
what the Spartan ambassador Melesippos said at the beginning of the war: "This day
will be the beginning of great misfortunes for Greece" (Thuc. II.12.3).

Xenophon proceeds to show the emptiness of this belief by referring to
Lykophron (3.4) and Dionysios (3.5) and particularly by telling at length the story
of the Thirty at Athens (3.11-4.43), which includes repeated intervention by the
Spartans.

24. This section is probably interpolated (I.1.37 n.).

3.1-10. *Siege of Samos. Events in Thessaly and Sicily.*
End of the war

3.1-2. Most of § 1 ought to be deleted as an interpolation (I.1.37 n.). I would
delete § 2 as well. It has confused the question of when the Thirty took office. If
retained, it suggests that Lysandros and Agis did not depart before the election (see §
3) and that the election occurred before the end of 405/4, since the archon Pythodoros
was chosen during the oligarchy (§ 1). But if Xenophon first mentions the Thirty in

§ 11, all he tells us is they were elected after the walls were demolished. For discussions of the problem, see Lotze (95-98, advocating April for the election), Rhodes (436-37, end 405/4 or early 404/3), and Krentz (147-50, September).

2.   The people decided: As it does in §11 (Xenophon's own words), the normal democratic formula conceals the fact that the assembly did not agree readily. Lysandros' threats, based on what he claimed was Athens' failure to demolish the walls within the agreed time, left the Athenians little choice (Aristot. *Ath. Pol.* 34.3, Lys. 12.71-76, Diod. XIV.3.5-7, Plut. *Lys.* 15).   Lysias claims that Theramenes favored the constitutional change, while Diodoros says he referred to the "ancestral constitution" clause in the treaty as forbidding Spartan interference in Athenian internal affairs. On this contradiction see J. A. R. Munro, "Theramenes against Lysander," *Classical Quarterly* 32 (1938) 23-24, favoring Diodoros; Rhodes (433-34) supporting Lysias; and W. J. McCoy, "Aristotle's *Athenaion Politeia* and the Establishment of the Thirty Tyrants," *Yale Classical Studies* 23 (1975) 131-45, reconciling the two.   Probably Theramenes first objected to changing the government, on the grounds that the peace treaty guaranteed autonomy (as in Diodoros), but acquiesced after Lysandros' threats, so that Lysias could claim he advocated the constitutional change.

Xenophon's favorable attitude toward Lysandros (see 1.28 n.) may explain why he omitted the Spartan's role in the revolution. As Diod. XIV.3.6 has Theramenes claim, Lysandros violated the peace treaty. Alternatively, or additionally, by omitting events in Athens between the surrender and the election of the Thirty, Xenophon strengthens the link between the Athenian oligarchy and tyrannies elsewhere (Higgins 103). Though he does not use the term "Thirty Tyrants," Xenophon notes the oligarchy's tyrannical features throughout II.3-4 (P. Krentz, "Thibron and the Thirty," *Ancient World* 15 [1987] 75-79).

the ancestral laws: Ostwald (367 n. 119) lists important discussions of the "ancestral constitution." If the motion specified "ancestral" laws--§ 11 and Diod. XIV.4.1 mention laws without the qualification--Lysandros may have permitted this mandate in deference to Theramenes, who had objected that the Thirty's election violated the peace of 404.

according to which they would govern: I take "the Thirty," not "the people," as the subject of πολιτεύσουσι. In Xenophon the active of πολιτεύειν means "to establish a political order," "govern": I.4.13, 5.19, III.1.21, V.2.12; *Anab.* III.2.26. The middle πολιτεύεσθαι means "to live under a social or political order": § 11, 4.22, 43 (twice), V.3.25; *Mem.* II.6.26, IV.3.12; *Kyr.* I.1.1; *Ages.* 1.37. Contemporaries did not accuse the Thirty of usurping power, and other sources say more clearly that they were to govern: Lys. 12.73 refers to the constitution (*politeia*) proposed by Drakontides; Aristot. *Ath. Pol.* 34.3 says the

Athenians voted the oligarchy, as moved by Drakontides of Aphidna; Diod. XIV.3.7 refers to them as managing the city's affairs. Rhodes (434-35) maintains to the contrary that the Athenians elected the Thirty to act as a provisional government only until they completed the new constitution.

Polychares . . . Mnesitheides: Though most likely interpolated, the list appears accurate, so far as our other evidence permits judgment. Against Loeper's hypothesis that the Athenians elected one oligarch from each trittys and that the interpolator listed them in tribal and trittyal order, see D. Whitehead, "The Tribes of the Thirty Tyrants," *Journal of Hellenic Studies* 100 (1980) 208-213.

Of the Thirty, Lys. 12.77 says Theramenes nominated ten, the "ephors" (chosen by Athenian political clubs) nominated ten and the assembly chose ten from those present. Perhaps Lysandros made this concession to Theramenes. I confess to nagging doubts, however, about Lysias' trustworthiness in a context so biased against Theramenes.

3. Lysandros sailed back to Samos: He was at Samos when the Athenian oligarchs summoned him to Athens (Diod. XIV.3.4), probably in September (§ 1 n.), but may have visited the Thraceward region during the summer (Plut. *Lys.* 16.1; A. Andrewes, "Two Notes on Lysander," *Phoenix* 25 [1971] 217-18).

4. near the occurrence of a solar eclipse: 3 September 404.
who wanted to rule all Thessaly: Lykophron hoped, like Jason later (VI.1.8-12), to become ruler (*tagos*) of the Thessalian federation (*koinon*). He did not succeed, however; in 395 he was still fighting Larisa (Diod. XIV.82.5).

5. Beloch included this section among the interpolated Sicilian notices (I.1.37 n.), since the date is incorrect. The Carthaginians defeated Dionysios outside Gela in the summer of 405 (Diod. XIII.109-110; note Timaios' testimony at Diod. XIII.108.4 that the Carthaginians removed the colossal statue of Apollo from Gela on the same day that Alexander the Great later took Tyre--that is, in the month Hekatombaion [July/August; Arr. II.24.6]). But this passage is not attached, like the others, to the interpolated beginnings and endings of years. Xenophon may have made the mistake himself. Note the parallel between Dionysios and the Thirty: The Athenian "tyrants" lose a fight (4.6); Peiraieus revolts (4.10); and the Thirty send cavalry to secure Eleusis (4.8). In Diod. XIII.112-13 the Syracusan horsemen desert Dionysios and flee to Mt. Aitna, whereas in Xenophon Dionysios sends his cavalry to Katana. Diodoros' version does not fit the parallel with the Thirty.

6. every free citizen would leave with a single cloak, but that they

would surrender everything else: These harsh terms recall those the Athenians gave the Poteidaians in 430/29: one garment for the men, two for the women, plus some travel money (Thuc. II.70.3). They were not carried out in this case: Lysandros imposed a dekarchy to control an unreliable population, not to govern four hundred returned exiles.

7. the former citizens: The exiles from Anaia (2.6 n.).
ten rulers: The only dekarchy mentioned by Xenophon, though it was probably not the first one; see 2.2 n. Diod. XIV.3.5 says that Lysandros left Thorax (see 1.18-20, 28 nn.) as governor of Samos. The ephors later executed him for possessing money (Plut. *Lys.* 19.7). Xenophon's silence may be due to Thorax's friendship with Lysandros.

8. the prows of the captured ships: Perhaps Lysandros had burned the ships captured at Aigospotamoi, a hypothesis that might explain how Plutarch could have believed that Lysandros burned the triremes surrendered at Athens (*Lys.* 15.5).
personal gifts: See Plut. *Lys.* 18 for a description of other gifts and honors paid to Lysandros.
470 talents of silver: Lysandros had earlier sent Gylippos home with one thousand (Plut. *Nik.* 28.3) or fifteen hundred talents (Diod. XIII.106.8-10). For discussion see E. David, "The Influx of Money into Sparta at the End of the Fifth Century B.C.," *Scripta Classica Israelica* 5 (1979-80) 30-45.
the tribute which Kyros had assigned to him for the war: See 1.14.

9. All these things he handed over to the Lakedaimonians: This forceful statement may be a defense of Lysandros against suspicions that, like Gylippos and Thorax, he had kept some money for himself.

Sparta refused to share the booty with its allies (III.5.12; Justin V.10.12-13), except that the Thebans took a tenth of the booty at Dekeleia to give to Apollo (an act that angered the Lakedaimonians, according to III.5.5).
[The war lasted twenty-eight years and six months . . . what has been described.]: Interpolated (I.1.37 n.). The figure for the war's duration is wrong. Thucydides says the war lasted a few days more than twenty-seven years (V.26.3), and even if we add six months for the time elapsed between Athens' surrender and Lysandros' return to Sparta, the text here has an extra year. The mistake is probably a deduction from the fact that twenty-nine ephors served during the war if Eudikos took office just before Lysandros returned home.
Ainesias . . . Eudios: Like the list of the Thirty in § 2, this list of ephors is accurate as best we can tell.

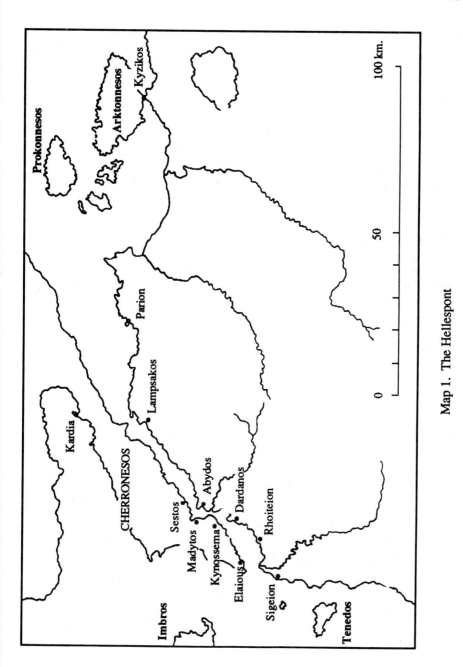

Map 1. The Hellespont

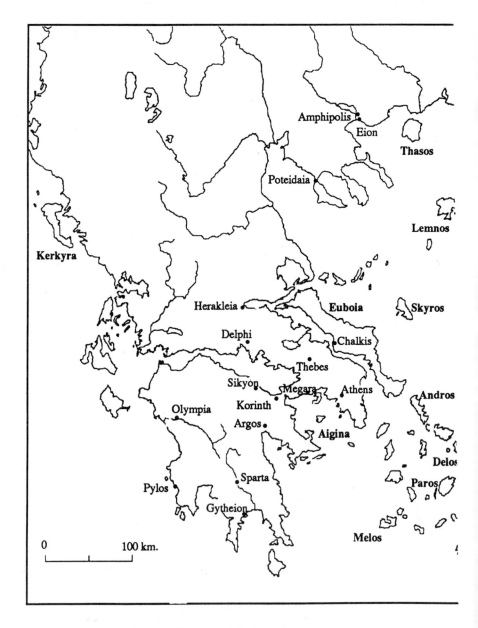

Map 2. Greece and the Aegean

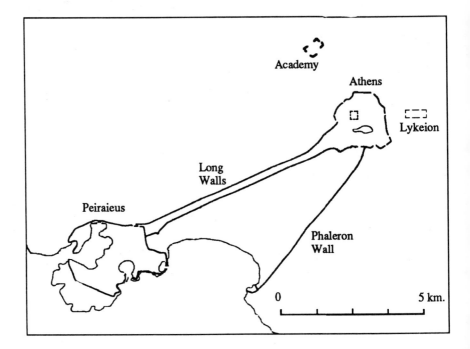

Map 3. Athens, Peiraieus and the Long Walls

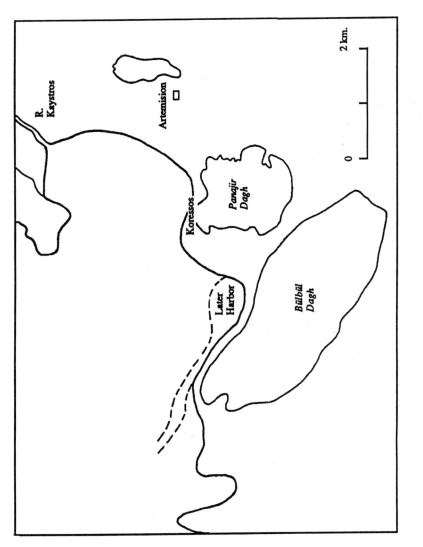

Map 4. Ephesos

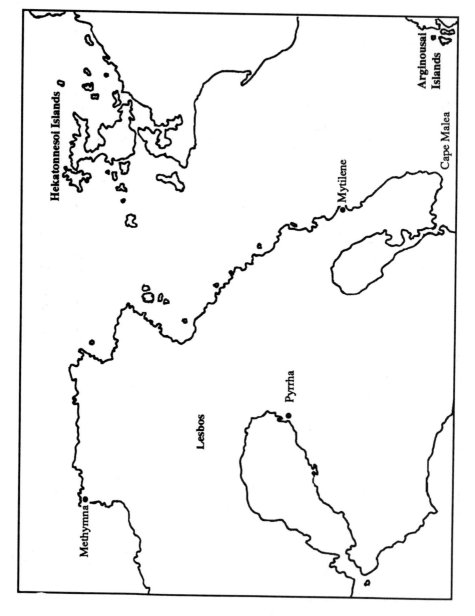

Map 5. Lesbos and the Arginousai Islands

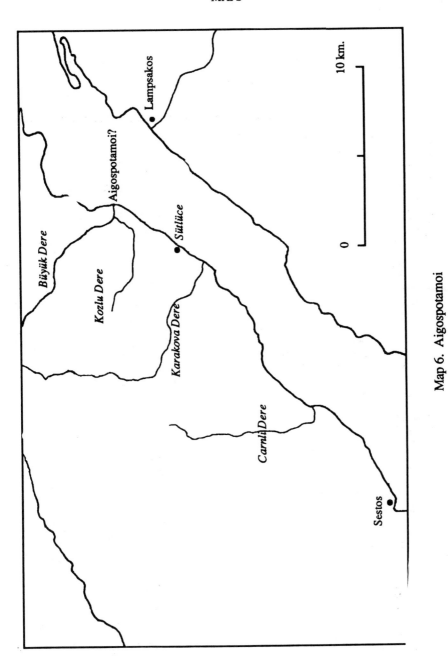

Map 6. Aigospotamoi

INDEX

Page numbers in plain type refer to the introduction and commentary; in *italic* type to the text; in **bold** type to the maps.